D0607516

# Louis Osteen's Charleston Cuisine

# Louis Osteen's CHARLESTON CUISINE

## Recipes from a Lowcountry Chef

— by —

LOUIS OSTEEN

ALGONQUIN BOOKS OF CHAPEL HILL 1999

Published by
ALGONQUIN BOOKS OF CHAPEL HILL
Post Office Box 2225
Chapel Hill, North Carolina 27515-2225

a division of
Workman Publishing
708 Broadway
New York, New York 10003


Printed in the United States of America.
Published simultaneously in Canada by Thomas Allen & Son Limited.
Design by Anne Winslow.
Illustrations by Sue Meyer.

Library of Congress Cataloging-in-Publication Data

Osteen, Louis.
Louis Osteen's Charleston cuisine / by Louis Osteen.
p. cm.
Includes index.
ISBN 1-56512-087-6 (hc.)
1. Cookery, American—Southern style. 2. Cookery—
South Carolina—Charleston. I. Title.
TX715.2.S68088 1999
641.5'09757'915—dc21 99-32156
CIP

10 9 8 7 6 5 4 3 2 1
First Edition

I dedicate this book to the inspiring women in my life,
who have made it endlessly exciting and fulfilling:

Marlene

Charlotte, Heather, and Lara

Abbie (and her brother Nate)

Martha Barbara

# Acknowledgments

As far back as I can remember, I always had a peculiar interest in the stove and food. I think it was a combination of fate and good luck that landed me in the kitchen, the place that I have happily lived since the mid-seventies.

A good many of my recipes have evolved from memories of family meals. Some are interpretations of very old, yet still popular, regional favorites; others have their roots in classical foods of Europe. Many of the recipes have been influenced by people with whom I shared the stove.

Marion Sullivan, the project consultant, made the work easier with her idea of order and sense of integrity. Her plan to incorporate Johnson & Wales University students in the test kitchen made for recipes that are well tested by cooks of varying proficiency. Patricia Agnew, the test kitchen director, handled the team of student volunteers with skill and finesse and is responsible for the recipes' accuracy. I'd like to thank that eager test-kitchen team: Will Cabaniss, Brad Crawford, James Gardner, Keith Godlewski, Graham Mitchell, and David Tetzloff. Shelly Cooper, the pastry chef and baker at Louis's, was responsible for refining all of the dessert recipes. Without her help, both this book and Louis's would be poorer.

I would like to thank Marion Young, my agent, for beating the bushes until she placed the book, and beating me until I finished it. I am also indebted to Shannon Ravenel at Algonquin, who placed her faith in the book and exhibited much-needed patience in waiting for its completion. My editor at Algonquin, Kathy Pories, is due much gratitude for making the prose shine. Bret Lott and Jonathan Green both gave the book their wholehearted support.

My deep appreciation is extended to François Delcros, who gave me my first job in the kitchen, a stern yet compassionate French chef who shared the culinary secrets of his country, and became a great friend as well. François, I hope you are sitting happily on the beach in Perpignan reading this testimonial to you.

Much thanks and appreciation go to my excellent business partners, Scotty Trotter and Katy Close.

Finally, and most importantly, I am very lucky to be able to thank Marlene Osteen, my wife and partner, and the person who has contributed the most to this undertaking. Her support, suggestions, and singular focus have made this book become a reality. For that, and lots more, I thank her.

Without the support of all these people, plus many, many more, this book could not have been written.

Charleston, South Carolina
March 1, 1999, the first anniversary of
Louis's Restaurant & Bar

## SUMMER/Cooking Outside 231

The first time I cooked for Louis Osteen and his wife, Marlene, I got worked up. I wanted to impress him, wanted him to think that I could cook, and cook well.

I'd been a fry cook in college, working the line at a chain restaurant and turning out baskets of onion rings, omelettes, or a steak now and again. Mostly, though, I'd grilled lots of hamburgers.

Now, here was my chance. This was Louis Osteen. Louis Osteen, whose restaurant had been named by *Esquire* as one of the best in the country, the same restaurant where my wife and I had enjoyed the best meals of our lives. This was Louis Osteen, who'd been featured in *GQ*, and who'd won an Ivy Award. This was the man who cooked for Prince Charles when he visited Charleston.

Prince Charles!

So I got worked up.

It was herbed pork risotto I was intent on making (risotto is notorious, of course, for not turning out just right), and I was going to grill spicy shrimp out on the barbecue, and roast vegetables, too.

I was cooking for Louis Osteen. How could I have known the man who cooked for a prince was a regular guy?

When he and Marlene got to the house, Louis promptly cracked open a beer and said, "What's for supper?"

I told him, and he smiled. "Sounds terrific," he said, and took a sip of the beer. "It's so nice to be cooked for, I'd be happy with a hot dog, but anything you make will be great. I know it. We're just glad to be here."

Louis Osteen loves his friends as much as he loves food. All of which is why, it seems to me, this book exists: as a gift, from Louis, of food, for friends.

He's a big man, which speaks well, to my way of thinking, of the quality of his skills. In his restaurant, he's always attired in his chef's smock with his name stitched on the left pocket and those ubiquitous black-and-white checkered pants. If he's not in the kitchen taking care of your food, he's out on the floor taking care of you, moving from table to table, guest to guest, handshake to handshake. He's the man humbly accepting praise after praise after praise, though he has ulterior motives for being out here: he wants to know if you're enjoying the crabcakes, what might be made to taste even better, is your glass full, and is the Buttermilk Tart with Fresh Raspberries sweet enough?

Louis will be the first to tell you he had no idea that food would be his passion, his palette, his heart. Instead, he grew up believing he would work in the theater business, just as his father did.

In Anderson, South Carolina, a small town with only a few stoplights, Louis spent boyhood weekends and summers running the popcorn popper at the Center Theater. While the likes of Lash LaRue, Roy Rogers, Smiley Burnette, and Pat Butram played out their cowboy lives for the kids in the darkened auditorium, Louis began his love affair with food out in the lobby. When he realized that the second batch of popcorn always tasted better, he began to throw away the first. He made certain every batch after that was popped and popped well.

Louis started in on that career in theater, owning and operating a series of movie houses through his young adulthood, but as is often the way, he found that something else was to be his passion and his vocation. For Louis, it wasn't about the movies, but about making those popcorn batches the best they could be. It wasn't until he was thirty-three that he took his first job in the world of food—peeling potatoes, slicing carrots and onions, and hauling garbage out to the dumpsters behind one of Atlanta's most important restaurants of the time, Le Versailles, under the exacting eye of chef François Delcros.

From there, it took a fateful trip to the Lowcountry for Louis to come fully into his own. It was here—up in Murrells Inlet, just south of Myrtle Beach—that his friend and sometimes partner Warren Johnston had settled and invited Louis and Marlene to spend some time relaxing by the water.

They must have walked down narrow Charleston sidestreets. Or stood on a warm barrier island beach and seen the way live oak branches lean out over sand; the way palmetto trees stand tall in a blue summer sky, fronds sharing in the midday breeze; the way the shoreline is dotted at low tide with treasure: conch shells, driftwood, sand dollars. They must have watched the sunset shift light down on the world, the marsh illuminated, the world gone wild with color, the island across the water lit up as well, the trees there an old and heavy and reverent green. All around him, Louis must have seen the Lowcountry bounty: shrimp brought in by the bushel from Shem Creek in Mount Pleasant, Wadmalaw Sweet Vidalias harvested out on the island and piled high at market, young oysters gathered on the corkscrew creeks off the Ashepoo and Edisto and Combahee rivers.

That was 1979. They've never looked back.

Within weeks they had opened up a restaurant at Pawleys Island, a retreat of summer cottages, where the exacting elegance and simplicity Louis had learned from Delcros were brought to bear on the Lowcountry's bounty. And within weeks, Louis and Marlene began to cultivate a crowd of eager yet discriminating diners who swore allegiance to his new restaurant. People drove up from Charleston—and down from Charlotte, and over from Atlanta—for dinner at Pawleys Island Inn. Customers began to call up not only to make reservations for tables, but also to get dibs on the dishes, often ordering crème brûlée hours ahead.

Then, in 1989, to the disappointment of Pawleys Islanders (but to the glee of Charlestonians who'd been making the pilgrimage to Pawleys), Louis and Marlene opened up Louis's Charleston Grill, and the *Atlanta Journal-Constitution* declared that he was "the man who helped lead the revival of Southern cuisine."

*Revival.* It's a word that resonates here in the South, a word that holds a deeper meaning than simply starting over. It captures the joy of life Louis helped rediscover in the indigenous bounty of the Lowcountry. What some regarded as Southern clichés began to be made over by Louis into elegant Lowcountry favorites: Preserved Duck with Fried Grits (Grits? As serious food?); Catfish Filets with Roasted Tomatoes, Saffron, and Black Olives (Catfish with saffron?); Fried Green Tomatoes with Black-Eyed Pea Vinaigrette

(Fried green tomatoes we can laugh about, but it's the vinaigrette that turns the world on its ear).

Now, a few years and a host of prestigious culinary awards later, Louis has settled into Charleston as serenely and securely as if he'd always been here. His newest restaurant, the pièce de résistance of his culinary career (if I may borrow one of those stuffy French phrases), is Louis's Restaurant & Bar, a coolly elegant place that continues to trumpet the cause of Southern cuisine.

Yet here is Louis in that smock, those pants, smiling and talking, moving from table to table, guest to guest, handshake to handshake, wanting to know, "How's that Pawleys Island Pie?"

Good food for good friends. That's the gift of *Louis Osteen's Charleston Cuisine,* recipes that bring you the Lowcountry, straight from Louis's heart.

Bret Lott
March, 1999

# Louis Osteen's Charleston Cuisine

# THE BASICS

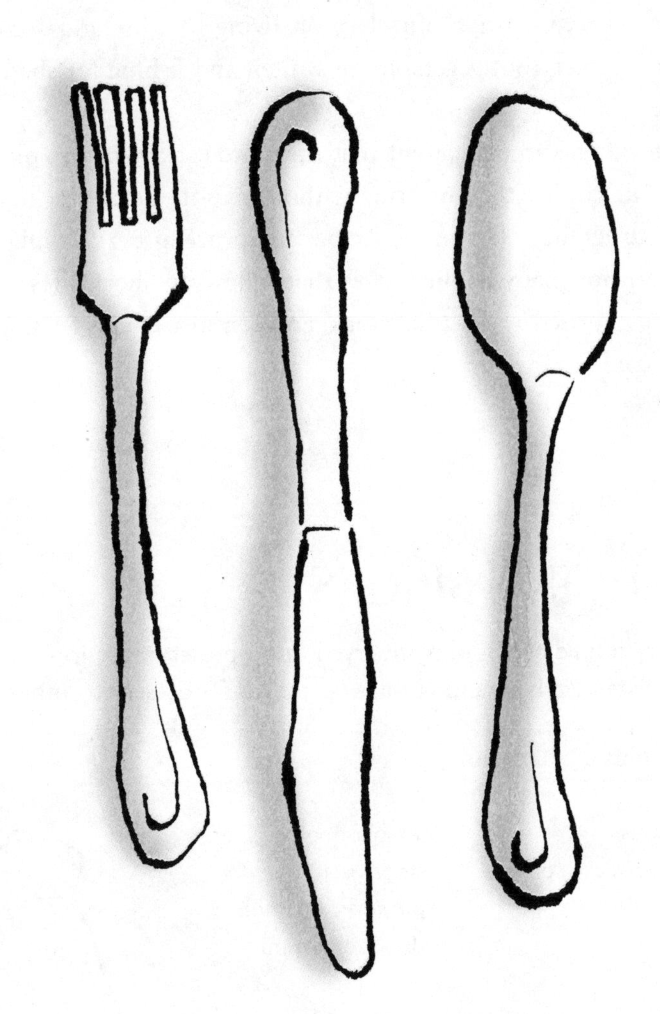

# The Basics of Good Food

As I began organizing my recipes for a cookbook, it seemed natural to group them according to the seasons. The economy of the Lowcountry was largely agrarian until recently, so we've traditionally eaten in time with the seasons. As you will see from the menus and recipes that follow, we pride ourselves on living off the land—enjoying tomatoes in summer, root vegetables in winter, and fishing for shad roe in early spring.

Yet it quickly became apparent that there are certain basics, or fundamentals, of our cuisine that are truly without season. I have included this chapter to instruct the reader in the recipes and procedures that will provide the foundation for many of the dishes that follow. In short, these are the recipes that comprise my essential stock, and I suspect that of many other Lowcountry cooks as well.

## Spices

### PRESERVING SPICES

A necessary ingredient in our preserved duck, preserving spices are useful for flavoring pâtés, terrines, and sausages as well as for preserving other meats.

Makes 1 cup plus 2 tablespoons.

36 bay leaves
2 tablespoons each of:
ground cloves
mace
dried thyme
nutmeg
paprika

1 tablespoon each of:
dried basil
ground cinnamon
dried marjoram
dried sage
dried savory
black peppercorns

In a blender, grind all the ingredients until well combined. If you are using a food processor instead, the metal blade must be sharp to work well. Process the bay leaves, basil, marjoram, sage, and savory for 1 minute. Substitute ground black pepper for the black peppercorns. Add the remaining ingredients 1 at a time, processing for about 45 seconds after each addition. Stored in a tightly covered container in a cool place, the preserving spices will keep for 2 months.

# PÂTÉ SPICES

This quicker, simpler version of preserving spices is a great blend for seasoning pâtés and other richly flavored homemade meats and sausages.

Makes ¾ cup.

- 4 tablespoons coarsely ground white pepper
- 4 tablespoons coarsely ground black pepper
- 2 tablespoons coriander seed
- 2 tablespoons ground ginger
- 1 tablespoon ground cloves
- 1½ teaspoons nutmeg

In a spice grinder or blender, grind all the ingredients until the coriander is the texture of the other spices. Stored in a tightly covered container in a cool place, the pâté spices will keep for 2 months.

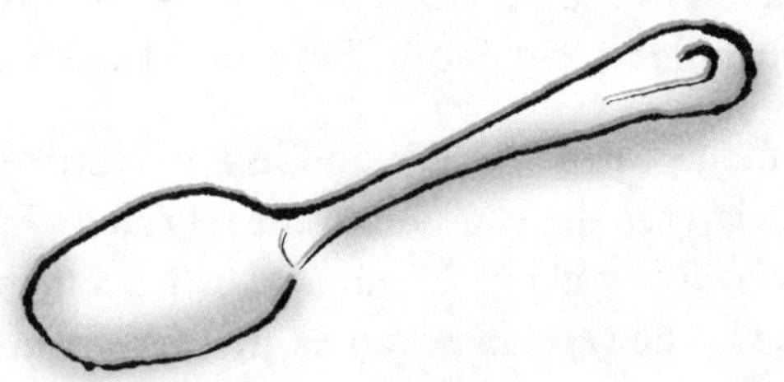

## Stocks

While homemade stocks are certainly the best kind to use, all of the stocks in this book can be substituted with the high-quality stocks (actually stock bases) found in specialty food shops. There is also acceptable canned chicken stock to be had in the grocery store—I prefer Swanson's—but canned beef stock is always too strong and too salty. Bouillon cubes won't work either. They are too salty as well and some have been known to contain MSG.

# BEEF STOCK

In hearty, robust dishes such as John Henry's Texas Schoolhouse Chili (see page 127), this stock can be substituted for veal stock. In some instances, however, a dish is more delicate and chicken stock would be a better substitution for veal stock.

Makes 4 cups.

- 5 pounds beef bones, all or mostly knuckles, split by the butcher to expose the marrow (if using frozen bones, be sure they are fully thawed)
- Peanut oil
- ¾ pound yellow onions, peeled and sliced
- 2 cups peeled and sliced carrots
- 2 cups sliced celery
- 1 leek, white part only, washed thoroughly and roughly chopped
- 14 cups water
- 5 tablespoons tomato paste
- 2 bay leaves
- 1 sprig fresh thyme
- 5 sprigs fresh parsley
- 1 tablespoon black peppercorns

1. Preheat the oven to 375°F.

2. Rub the bones with a small amount of peanut oil and place them in a single layer in roasting pans or on heavy-duty baking sheets. Roast the bones in the preheated oven, turning occasionally, for 45 minutes or until they are nicely browned but not scorched. (This step gives the stock most of its final color, so don't be timid.) Remove the bones to a large nonreactive stockpot.

3. Toss the onions, carrots, celery, and leek in a little peanut oil and place them in a single layer in the pans. Roast the vegetables in the preheated oven, turning occasionally, for about 25 minutes or until they are nicely browned but not scorched. The vegetables can easily overbrown and burn, thus imparting a bitter taste to the finished stock, so be careful.

4. Scrape the vegetables into the stockpot with the bones. Scrape any brown bits that remain in the pans into the pot. A cup of hot water will help loosen and dissolve them. These are bits of flavor and color, so it is well worth the extra effort to get them into your stock. Add the 14 cups of water to the stockpot, using more if needed to cover the bones and vegetables. Bring the mixture to a boil, then quickly reduce the heat until the mixture settles down to a moderately fast simmer. Simmer for 45 minutes, carefully skimming off any fat or impurities that come up in a foam.

5. Add the tomato paste, bay leaves, thyme, parsley, and peppercorns. Stir well and continue to simmer, partially covered, for 4½ hours, adding hot water as necessary to keep the bones and vegetables covered.

6. Strain the stock through a colander, pressing the solids to release all of the juices. Strain the stock through a medium-fine sieve and let it rest for ½ hour. Spoon off any fat that rises to the surface. Strain the stock again through a very fine mesh sieve, known as a *chinois,* or a colander lined with several layers of dampened cheesecloth. Measure the stock. If there are more than 4 cups, briskly simmer until it is reduced to 4 cups.

7. Cool the stock to room temperature, cover, and refrigerate overnight. The stock must be cooled before it is covered or it could spoil. The next day, spoon off any fat that has risen to the top. Tightly covered, the stock will keep in the refrigerator for 4 days. Beef stock also freezes well. It is convenient to freeze it in 1-cup increments.

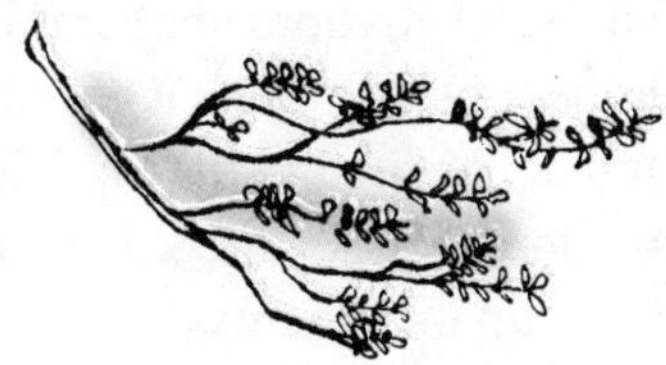

# CHICKEN STOCK

Chicken stock is one of the most important elements in good cooking. Most soups that we make use it as a base, and we also use it instead of water to make flavorful sauces. Be sure to cook the stock long enough to extract all the available flavor and slowly enough not to make it bitter, and be sure to reduce it to the prescribed amount so that your efforts will produce a very flavorful stock. You'll be surprised by the additional flavor and body that the veal bones add.

Makes 6 cups.

3 pounds chicken necks, backs, and wings
1 pound split and blanched veal bones (if no veal bones are available, increase the amount of chicken to 4 pounds)
¾ pound yellow onions, peeled and thinly sliced
2 cups peeled and thinly sliced carrots
2 cups thinly sliced celery
6 cups water
1 bay leaf
1 small sprig fresh thyme or ⅛ teaspoon dried thyme
3 sprigs fresh parsley
2 cloves garlic, unpeeled
12 black peppercorns
1 teaspoon salt

1. Place the chicken, veal bones, onions, carrots, celery, and water in a large nonreactive stockpot. Bring the mixture to a boil, then quickly reduce the heat until the mixture settles down to a fast simmer. Simmer for 45 minutes, carefully skimming off any fat or impurities that come up in a foam.

2. Add the bay leaf, thyme, parsley, garlic, and peppercorns. Continue to simmer for 3 hours, adding hot water as necessary to keep the bones and vegetables covered.

3. Strain the stock through a colander, pressing the solids to release all of the juices. Let the stock rest for 10 minutes, then spoon off any fat that has risen to the surface. Strain the stock again through a fine mesh sieve, known as a *chinois*, or a colander lined with several layers of dampened cheesecloth. Measure the stock. If there are more than 6 cups, briskly simmer until it is reduced to 6 cups. Add the salt.

4. Cool the stock to room temperature, cover, and refrigerate overnight. The stock must be cooled before it is covered or it could spoil. The next day, spoon off any fat that has risen to the top. Tightly covered, the stock will keep in the refrigerator for 4 days. Chicken stock also freezes well. It is convenient to freeze it in 1-cup increments.

**TO BLANCH VEAL BONES:** Have the butcher split the bones to expose the marrow. Put them in a saucepan, cover with cold water, and bring to a boil. Reduce the heat and simmer for 15 minutes. Remove the bones and rinse with cold water.

# DUCK STOCK

A somewhat arduous and long process, but worth the effort if you want to achieve the full flavor of the recipes that use this stock.

Makes 2 cups.

- 1½ pounds duck bones, broken in half with the back of a chef's knife or cleaver
- Peanut oil
- ¼ pound yellow onions, peeled and thinly sliced
- ½ cup peeled and thinly sliced carrots
- ½ cup thinly sliced celery

- 1 teaspoon salt
- 4 cups water
- 1 crushed bay leaf
- 1 small sprig fresh thyme
- 2 sprigs fresh parsley
- 1 clove garlic, unpeeled
- 6 black peppercorns

1. Preheat the oven to 375°F.

2. Toss the bones with a small amount of peanut oil, place in a single layer on a heavy-duty baking sheet, and roast in the preheated oven for 30 minutes, turning occasionally.

3. Toss the onions, carrots, and celery with a small amount of peanut oil and add to the bones. Continue to roast for about 25 minutes or until the vegetables are nicely browned but not scorched.

4. Scrape the bones and vegetables into a large nonreactive stockpot. Scrape any browned bits that remain on the baking sheet into the pot. A cup of hot water will help loosen and dissolve them. Add the salt and 4 cups of water to the stockpot, using more if needed to cover the bones and vegetables. Bring the mixture to a boil, then quickly reduce the heat until the mixture settles down to a fast simmer. Simmer for 45 minutes, carefully skimming off any fat or impurities that come up in a foam.

5. Add the bay leaf, thyme, parsley, garlic, and peppercorns. Continue to simmer for 3 hours, adding hot water as necessary to keep the bones and vegetables covered.

6. Strain the stock through a colander, pressing the solids to release all of the juices. Let the stock rest for 10 minutes, then spoon off any fat that has risen to the surface. Strain the stock again through a fine mesh sieve, known as a *chinois,* or a colander lined with several layers of dampened cheesecloth. Measure the stock. If there are more than 2 cups, briskly simmer until it is reduced to 2 cups.

7. Cool the stock to room temperature, cover, and refrigerate overnight. The stock must be cooled before it is covered or it could spoil. The next day, spoon off any fat that has risen to the top. Tightly covered, the stock will keep in the refrigerator for 4 days. Duck stock also freezes well. It is convenient to freeze it in 1-cup increments.

# FISH STOCK

To make a simple all-purpose fish stock, you should use fresh, white fish such as grouper, flounder, or sole. You can use the skeletons, heads, or a combination of both when preparing the stock.

Makes 2½ cups.

2½ pounds fish bones and/or heads
Peanut oil
¾ pound yellow onions, peeled and sliced
⅓ cup dry white wine or ¼ cup dry vermouth
3 sprigs fresh parsley
2 sprigs fresh thyme or ¼ teaspoon dried thyme
12 black peppercorns
4 cups water
Scant ½ teaspoon salt

1. Preheat the oven to 350°F.

2. Wash the bones well under cold running water, then soak them in cold water for 30 minutes in the refrigerator to be sure that all the blood is out. Drain the bones. If you are using fish heads, remove any trace of viscera, pull out the gills, remove the eyes, and follow the same procedure for washing and soaking.

3. Brush a shallow nonreactive baking pan such as a broiler pan with peanut oil. Layer the bottom of the pan with half of the onions. Top the onions with the fish bones and/or heads. Pour the wine over them. Scatter the parsley, thyme, peppercorns, and remaining onions over them. Cover the pan tightly with aluminum foil and bake in the preheated oven for 20 to 30 minutes or until all of the bones are opaque.

4. Transfer the mixture to a large nonreactive stockpot. Add the water. Bring the mixture to a simmer and cook for 45 minutes, carefully skimming off any fat or impurities that come up as a foam.

5. Rinse a large tea towel with cold water, wring it out, and line a colander with it. Put the colander over a large pot or bowl and pour the stock into it. Let the stock drip through the towel, then squeeze the towel to release all of the juices from the solids. Measure the stock. If there are more than 2½ cups, briskly simmer until it is reduced to 2½ cups. Add the salt.

6. Cool the stock to room temperature, cover, and refrigerate overnight. The stock must be cooled before it is covered or it could spoil. The next day, spoon off any fat that has risen to the top. Tightly covered, the stock will keep in the refrigerator for 2 days. Fish stock also freezes well. It is convenient to freeze it in 1-cup increments.

# BROWN VEAL STOCK

Brown veal stock has an obvious place in veal dishes, but it also can be used to enhance the flavor of some chicken and fish dishes, as you will see in my recipes.

Makes 4 cups.

5 pounds veal bones, all or mostly knuckles, split by the butcher to expose the marrow (if using frozen bones, be sure they are fully thawed)
Peanut oil
¾ pound yellow onions, peeled and sliced
2 cups peeled and sliced carrots
2 cups sliced celery
1 leek, white part only, washed thoroughly and roughly chopped
14 cups water
5 tablespoons tomato paste
2 bay leaves
1 sprig fresh thyme
5 sprigs fresh parsley
1 tablespoon black peppercorns

1. Preheat the oven to 375°F.

2. Rub the bones with a small amount of peanut oil and place them in a single layer in roasting pans or on heavy-duty baking sheets. Roast the bones in the preheated oven, turning occasionally, for 45 minutes or until they are nicely browned but not scorched. (This step gives the stock most of its final color, so don't be timid.) Remove the bones to a large nonreactive stockpot.

3. Toss the onions, carrots, celery, and leek in a little peanut oil and place them in a single layer in the pans. Roast the vegetables in the preheated oven, turning occasionally, for about 25 minutes or until they are nicely browned but not scorched. The vegetables can easily overbrown and burn, thus imparting a bitter taste to the finished stock, so be careful.

4. Scrape the vegetables into the stockpot with the bones. Scrape any brown bits that remain in the pans into the pot. A cup of hot water will help loosen and dissolve them. These are bits of flavor and color, so it is well worth the extra effort to get them into your stock. Add the 14 cups of water to the stockpot, using more if needed to cover the bones and vegetables. Bring the mixture to a boil, then quickly reduce the heat until the mixture settles down to a moderately fast simmer. Simmer for 45 minutes, carefully skimming off any fat or impurities that come up in a foam.

5. Add the tomato paste, bay leaves, thyme, parsley, and peppercorns. Stir well and continue to simmer, partially covered, for 4½ hours, adding hot water as necessary to keep the bones and vegetables covered.

6. Strain the stock through a colander, pressing the solids to release all of the juices. Strain the stock through a medium-fine sieve and let it rest for ½ hour. Spoon off any fat that rises to the surface. Strain the stock again through a very fine mesh sieve, known as a *chinois,* or a colander lined with several layers of dampened cheesecloth. Measure the stock. If there are more than 4 cups, briskly simmer until it is reduced to 4 cups.

7. Cool the stock to room temperature, cover, and refrigerate overnight. The stock must be cooled before it is covered or it could spoil. The next day, spoon off any fat that has risen to the top. Tightly covered, the stock will keep in the refrigerator for 4 days. Veal stock also freezes well. It is convenient to freeze it in 1-cup increments.

NOTE: Veal demi-glace is highly reduced, thus highly concentrated, veal stock. It is very easy to prepare once the basic veal stock is made. Briskly simmer 4 cups of veal stock in a heavy-bottomed nonreactive saucepan until it reduces to 1 cup. Demi-glace freezes well and is a good flavor enricher for all sorts of sauces and soups.

# BASIC VINAIGRETTE

As its name suggests, this salad dressing is good on just about anything.

Makes 1½ cups.

1 tablespoon finely minced onion
1 tablespoon Dijon mustard (I use Grey Poupon)
1 large egg yolk
⅓ cup red wine vinegar
1 tablespoon fresh lemon juice
½ cup peanut oil
½ cup extra virgin olive oil
Salt and freshly ground black pepper to taste

1. Put the onion, mustard, egg yolk, vinegar, and lemon juice in a small non-reactive bowl, a blender, or a food processor. Whisk or process these ingredients until well combined.

2. Slowly whisk in the peanut oil and olive oil or very slowly pour them into the blender or food processor, teaspoon by teaspoon. Be careful not to add them too quickly or you will break the emulsion.

3. Add salt and pepper to taste. Tightly covered, the dressing will keep in the refrigerator for a week. If it separates, whisk to bring it back together.

# BALSAMIC VINAIGRETTE

Balsamic vinaigrette is a little milder than most. Its natural sweetness is a welcome flavor addition to assertive greens.

Makes ¾ cup.

¼ cup balsamic vinegar
½ cup plus 1 tablespoon extra virgin olive oil
Salt and freshly ground black pepper to taste

Whisk the vinegar and oil together, adding the oil slowly, or put the vinegar in a blender and very slowly pour the oil into the blender, teaspoon by teaspoon. Add salt and pepper to taste. Tightly covered, the dressing will keep in the refrigerator for a week. This dressing is not an emulsion, so it will separate. Whisk to bring it back together.

# BLACK-EYED PEA VINAIGRETTE

This is an interesting dressing that we use for seasonal greens. In the summer, we often add a couple slices of fried green tomatoes (see page 214) to the plate.

Makes 4 cups.

- 2 cups (about 12 ounces) dried black-eyed peas, soaked in water overnight and drained
- 1 red bell pepper, cored, seeded, and finely diced
- 1 yellow bell pepper, cored, seeded, and finely diced
- 1 red onion, peeled and finely diced
- 2 tablespoons finely chopped fresh basil
- 2 tablespoons finely chopped fresh oregano
- 1 tablespoon finely chopped fresh thyme
- 1 tablespoon finely chopped fresh chives
- ¼ cup red wine vinegar
- ¼ cup balsamic vinegar
- ½ cup extra virgin olive oil
- Salt and freshly ground black pepper to taste

1. In a large pot over high heat, add the drained black-eyed peas and enough fresh water to cover. Bring the peas to a simmer, reduce the heat to medium, and cook for about 45 minutes or until tender. Drain, transfer to a large serving bowl, and set aside to cool.

2. Add the red and yellow peppers, onion, basil, oregano, thyme, and chives to the cooled peas, cover, and reserve at room temperature.

3. Whisk the vinegars and olive oil together, adding the oil slowly, or put the vinegars in a blender and slowly pour the oil into the blender, teaspoon by teaspoon. Add salt and pepper to taste. This vinaigrette is not an emulsion, so it will separate if not used immediately. Whisk to bring it back together. Toss the vinaigrette with the black-eyed pea mixture. Tightly covered, the black-eyed pea vinaigrette will keep in the refrigerator for a week. Serve over seasonal greens.

# CITRUS VINAIGRETTE

A handy, versatile dressing that can spice up a mundane salad. We've used it with a crab-and-avocado composed salad, with watermelon and watercress, and even to dress spinach leaves.

Makes 2⅔ cups.

- Juice of 2 lemons
- Juice of 1 orange
- 1½ teaspoons fresh lime juice
- 1 tablespoon white wine vinegar
- ¼ teaspoon honey
- 1½ teaspoons Dijon mustard (I use Grey Poupon)
- 1 cup walnut oil
- ¾ cup extra virgin olive oil
- Salt and freshly ground black pepper to taste

1. Measure the citrus juices. The total must equal 1 cup. Use more fruit if necessary.

2. Put the citrus juices, white wine vinegar, honey, and mustard in a small nonreactive bowl, a blender, or a food processor. Whisk or process these ingredients until well combined.

3. Slowly whisk in the oils or very slowly pour them into the blender or food processor, teaspoon by teaspoon. Be careful not to add them too quickly or you will break the emulsion.

4. Add salt and pepper to taste. Tightly covered, the dressing will keep in the refrigerator for a week. If it separates, whisk to bring it back together.

# TOASTED CUMIN VINAIGRETTE

This is a fine topping for grilled fish with a high fat content, such as bluefish or mackerel. While it's not particularly Lowcountry in flavor, the vinaigrette makes a fresh grilled fillet sing.

Makes 1¼ cups.

- 2 tablespoons plus 1½ teaspoons ground cumin
- ½ teaspoon minced garlic
- 1½ teaspoons finely chopped shallots
- ¼ cup champagne vinegar
- 1½ teaspoons Dijon mustard (I use Grey Poupon)
- 1 cup extra virgin olive oil
- ⅛ teaspoon salt
- ⅛ teaspoon freshly ground black pepper

1. Roast the cumin in a dry sauté pan over medium heat for 5 to 6 minutes or until the color darkens a few shades around the edges. Stir or shake the pan for 5 to 7 seconds, then pour the cumin into a cool mixing bowl, which will instantly stop it from cooking further.

2. Put the cumin, garlic, shallots, vinegar, and mustard in a small nonreactive bowl, a blender, or a food processor. Whisk or process these ingredients until well combined.

3. Slowly whisk in the olive oil or very slowly pour it into the blender or food processor, teaspoon by teaspoon. Be careful not to add the oil too quickly or you will break the emulsion.

4. Add the salt and pepper. Tightly covered, the dressing will keep in the refrigerator for a week. If it separates, whisk to bring it back together.

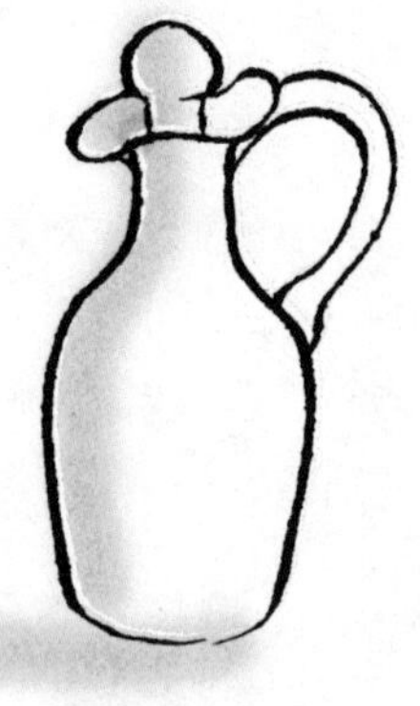

# Sauces, Gravies, and Other Condiments

The difference between a sauce and a gravy does not have to do with sophistication. Indeed, many Southerners are as proud of their pan gravies as any 3-star French chef is of his sauces. The difference between them is small: gravy is made from pan drippings and juices; sauces are made independently (mayonnaise, hollandaise, and Tabasco, for example, are all sauces).

## GARLIC AND HERB MAYONNAISE

This magic potion has its roots in Provençal France. We have found that it is good with just about everything except dessert. It's great as a utility dip—try it with crispy French fries or fried oysters—and it's a unique substitute for mayo on a sandwich.

Makes 1½ cups.

- 1 cup extra virgin olive oil or ½ cup olive oil and ½ cup safflower oil
- 2 large egg yolks, chilled
- 1 teaspoon dry mustard (I use Colman's English mustard)
- 1 teaspoon salt
- Tiny pinch of cayenne pepper
- Juice of 1 lemon
- 4 large cloves garlic, peeled and minced, then mashed to a paste
- ¼ cup chopped fresh herbs of your choice, such as chives, parsley, tarragon, or basil

1. Pour the oil into a pitcher with a good pouring spout.

2. In a medium bowl, combine the egg yolks with the mustard, salt, and cayenne. Beat the mixture until smooth with a wire whisk.

3. Add half of the olive oil, *one droplet at a time,* whisking continuously until the oil is well incorporated before adding another droplet.

4. Whisk a small amount of the lemon juice into the mixture. Alternate adding the lemon juice and remaining olive oil until both are used up, ending with the oil. Whisk in the garlic paste and fresh herbs. Add more salt and cayenne to taste. Tightly covered, the mayonnaise will keep in the refrigerator for 4 days.

# RED-EYE GRAVY

Red-eye gravy is a quick pan gravy that probably originated around the campfire (or at least it seems to have in my mind). After frying up slices of country ham in a black iron skillet, a cup of coffee was tossed in with the rendered fat and boiled up until it was reduced. This gravy was then poured over the ham slices. We have taken the original version and used the principle of this time-honored accompaniment to make a splendid gravy. It's wonderful with preserved duck (see page 52).

Makes 1 cup.

- 2 teaspoons rendered duck fat (see page 42)
- 1 cup coffee
- 1 cup duck stock (see page 6)

1. Heat the duck fat in a small heavy-bottomed skillet over medium-high heat.
2. Pour in the coffee and duck stock. Increase the heat to high and cook for about 8 minutes or until the gravy is slightly thickened and the bubbles that appear on the surface are large; the volume will have reduced by approximately half. Serve immediately.

# HORSERADISH CREAM SAUCE

We use this sauce for Spicy Fried Oysters (see page 60), but it also works as an accompaniment for oysters on the half shell or Southern Fried Catfish (see page 64), as an alternative to the garlic and herb mayonnaise. To use with spicy fried oysters, wash, rinse, dry, and warm the empty oyster shells. Place 1 tablespoon of hot Horseradish Cream Sauce in each half shell and add 1 or 2 hot Spicy Fried Oysters, depending on their size. Sprinkle with grated fresh horseradish and serve very quickly.

Makes 2 cups.

4 tablespoons unsalted butter
4 tablespoons all-purpose flour
¼ cup thinly sliced shallots
2 cups whole milk
½ cup heavy cream
¾ teaspoon salt
1 teaspoon freshly ground black pepper
1 teaspoon fresh lemon juice
2 tablespoons prepared horseradish
2 tablespoons grated fresh horseradish (or more if you want a hotter sauce)

1. Heat the butter in a heavy-bottomed nonreactive saucepan over medium heat. When hot, add the flour, whisking to combine without lumps. Cook for 5 minutes, whisking to prevent browning.

2. Add the sliced shallots and stir well to combine. Cook for 1 minute. Add the milk and cream, whisking to avoid lumps. Bring the mixture to a slow simmer and cook for 15 minutes, whisking occasionally and reducing the heat if necessary. Add the salt and pepper.

3. Put the lemon juice, prepared horseradish, and fresh horseradish in a bowl large enough to hold the sauce. Strain the shallot mixture over them and stir to combine. Discard the shallots. Use the sauce immediately, keep it warm in a double boiler, or let it cool to room temperature and pour it into a refrigerator container. Tightly covered, the sauce will keep in the refrigerator for 3 days.

# WINTER TOMATO SAUCE

We make this rich sauce in wintertime when fresh tomatoes are not available, adding winter vegetables to increase the intensity of the flavors. It's a perfect topping for pasta of all shapes, as well as a great foil for your favorite meatballs.

Makes 8 cups.

Four 28-ounce cans imported whole plum tomatoes or high-quality regular tomatoes
⅓ cup extra virgin olive oil
¾ cup finely diced red onion
¾ cup finely diced celery
¾ cup peeled and finely diced carrots
¼ cup minced garlic
¼ cup very finely chopped prosciutto (about 1 ounce)
½ cup chopped fresh parsley
¼ cup coarsely chopped fresh basil or 2 tablespoons dried basil
¾ cup dry red table wine
1½ cups chicken stock (see page 5)
¼ teaspoon freshly ground black pepper
Salt to taste (optional)

1. Drain the tomatoes in a colander, reserving the juice. Carefully open the tomatoes with your fingers. Run cold water over them to remove the seeds. Drain well. Remove the stem end of the tomatoes and discard. Roughly chop the tomatoes and reserve.

2. Heat the olive oil in a heavy-bottomed pan over medium-high heat until hot but not smoking. Add the onion, celery, carrots, garlic, prosciutto, and parsley and sauté for 15 to 20 minutes or until very well cooked, stirring occasionally.

3. Add the reserved tomatoes, reserved tomato juice, basil, and wine and bring the mixture to a simmer over medium heat. Simmer, stirring occasionally, for 20 to 25 minutes. The sauce will have thickened but will still be juicy.

4. Heat the chicken stock and add it to the tomato sauce. Stir well and add the pepper. You may add salt to taste, but the salt in the canned tomatoes usually suffices. Cook over medium heat for about 20 minutes, stirring occasionally. The sauce should be thick enough to cling to pasta but still chunky and juicy, not homogenized. Use immediately or cool to room temperature, cover, and refrigerate for up to 10 days. The sauce may also be frozen.

# CARAMELIZED RED ONION SAUCE

Another great use of onions, this sauce will work with pork or beef extremely well. I like to spoon about 2 to 3 tablespoons of it over a serving of sliced meat.

Makes 3½ cups.

- 2 tablespoons unsalted butter
- 16 cups julienned red onions (about 4 pounds)
- 2 tablespoons sugar
- 6 ounces dark beer (I use Beck's)
- 2 tablespoons balsamic vinegar
- 2 cups chicken stock (see page 5) or duck stock (see page 6)
- 2½ teaspoons chopped fresh thyme
- Salt and freshly ground black pepper to taste

1. Heat the butter in a large heavy-bottomed nonreactive saucepan over medium-high heat. Add the onions and cook for 30 minutes or until they begin to caramelize, stirring occasionally. Add the sugar, stir well to combine, and cook for 3 minutes.

2. Deglaze the pan with the beer and vinegar, scraping the bottom to loosen any browned bits. Cook, stirring occasionally, for about 8 minutes or until the liquid has reduced by half. Add the stock and stir well to combine. Bring the mixture to a boil and cook for 20 minutes or until the liquid has again reduced by half, stirring occasionally. Stir in the thyme.

3. Remove the saucepan from the heat. Season to taste with salt and pepper. When the mixture is cool enough to handle, puree it, by batches if necessary. Be careful not to overprocess the sauce. It should be the consistency of loose applesauce. Adjust the consistency, returning it to the heat if it needs thickening or adding more stock to thin it. Tightly covered, the sauce will keep in the refrigerator for a week.

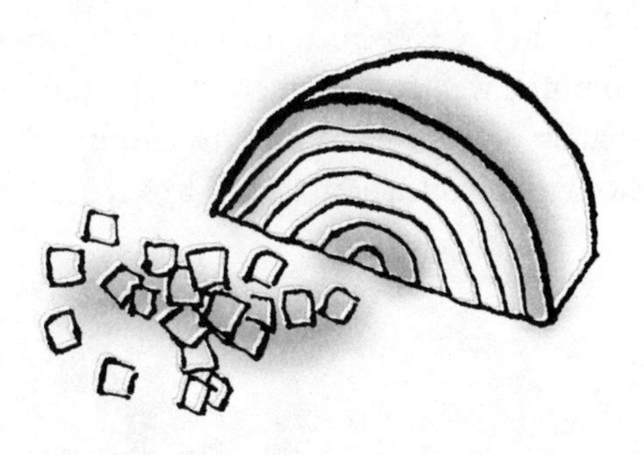

# WADMALAW SWEETS MARMALADE

This rather simple onion sauce surprises many people because of its rich smoothness, a quality not usually associated with onions. We use it often at Louis's to accompany veal, pork, lamb, and even panfried flounder. But as is often the case, the kitchen crew discovered that it tastes best on top of a big bowl of mashed potatoes.

Makes 3 cups.

12 cups finely sliced Wadmalaw Sweets or other sweet onions such as Vidalia or Maui (about 3 pounds)
1½ cups chicken stock (see page 5)
2 cups heavy cream
¼ teaspoon salt
¼ teaspoon freshly ground black pepper
¼ cup red wine vinegar

1. Bring the onions and chicken stock to a simmer in a heavy-bottomed saucepan over medium-high heat. Reduce the heat to low, cover, and let the mixture gently simmer for 1 hour, stirring occasionally.

2. Meanwhile, put the cream in a small heavy-bottomed saucepan and bring it to a simmer over medium heat. Reduce the heat to low and simmer for 30 minutes or until the cream reduces by half.

3. Uncover the onions, add the salt and pepper, and increase the heat to medium. Cook the onions, stirring occasionally, for about 10 minutes or until the liquid begins to get syrupy. The onions should be very slightly browned. Stir in the reduced cream and let the mixture simmer for about 20 minutes or until it is a little thicker than heavy cream.

4. Add the vinegar to provide a counterpoint to the rich sweetness. Stir to combine well and simmer for 1 to 2 minutes to meld the flavors. Use immediately or cool to room temperature. Tightly covered, the marmalade will keep in the refrigerator for 2 to 3 days.

# CABERNET SAUCE

This sauce makes a good accompaniment for red meats like beef and lamb. If you sauté the meat in a skillet, pour off the cooking oil and scrape up the brown bits of flavor. They'll give the sauce an even greater depth of taste.

Makes about ½ cup, which is enough for 4 steaks.

1½ cups Cabernet Sauvignon wine
1 cup red wine vinegar
½ cup sliced shallots
2 tablespoons unsalted butter
½ teaspoon freshly ground black pepper

1. Combine the wine, vinegar, and shallots in a small heavy-bottomed non-reactive saucepan. Bring the mixture to a low boil over medium-high heat and continue to boil for 7 to 8 minutes or until it is reduced to 4 tablespoons.

2. Remove the mixture from the heat and strain. Whisk in the butter and pepper. Reserve the sauce until ready to use. Tightly covered, the sauce will keep in the refrigerator for a week.

# PEAR AND WALNUT CONSERVE

I serve this conserve with game, pork, and all the meats that tend to like sweet things with them. It provides a delicate, fresh taste.

Makes 7 cups.

- 2 tablespoons fresh lemon juice
- 5 cups water
- 10 very firm Bosc pears
- One 750-ml bottle dry white wine
- 3 cups sugar
- 2 teaspoons pure vanilla extract
- 2 bay leaves
- 2 sprigs fresh thyme or a small pinch of dried thyme
- 2 cups large walnut pieces, toasted and cooled
- ¼ cup chopped fresh chives
- 1 teaspoon freshly cracked black pepper
- 1 teaspoon curry powder
- 1 teaspoon peeled and minced fresh ginger
- 2 tablespoons apple cider vinegar

Candy thermometer
Baking parchment paper

1. Mix the lemon juice and 2 cups of the water in a nonreactive pan or bowl. Peel the pears and reserve the peelings. Cut the pears in half and scoop out the seeds with a spoon or melon baller. Quarter the pears and toss them in the acidulated water to keep them from turning brown.

2. Combine the wine, sugar, vanilla, bay leaves, thyme, pear peelings, and remaining 3 cups of water in a nonreactive saucepan. Stirring gently to dissolve the sugar, heat the mixture over medium heat until it comes to a boil. Boil the mixture until it reaches 225°F on the candy thermometer. This will be your poaching liquid.

3. Remove the pears from the acidulated water and place them in a heavy-bottomed saucepan just large enough to hold all of them. Pour the poaching liquid over the pears, being sure to cover them completely. Don't worry if the pears have browned; they will miraculously return to their light color when poached. Lay a piece of parchment paper on top to ensure that the pears stay under the poaching liquid.

4. Bring the poaching liquid to a simmer. Cook the pears over medium heat for 5 to 10 minutes or just until they can be easily pierced with a knife. Remove the pan from the heat and cool the pears in the liquid until they reach room temperature.

5. Remove the pears from the liquid, place them in a covered container, and refrigerate. Strain the liquid back into the saucepan and return it to the stove. Gently boil the strained liquid over medium-high heat for about 30 minutes or until it has reduced to 1 cup.

6. Add the walnut pieces to the saucepan and continue to cook for 5 minutes.

7. Combine the poaching liquid, chives, pepper, curry powder, ginger, and vinegar in a large bowl. Finely chop the pears and add. Toss everything gently to combine. Cool to room temperature, cover, and refrigerate overnight to allow the flavors to meld. Tightly covered, the conserve will keep in the refrigerator for 2 weeks.

# CHILI PASTE WITH GARLIC

This homemade chili paste brings a little something extra to a recipe.

Makes about ½ cup.

- 2 tablespoons extra virgin olive oil
- 2 tablespoons minced garlic
- 2 tablespoons red pepper flakes
- 2 tablespoons red wine

Place all of the ingredients in a food processor and grind them to a paste. Tightly covered, the chili paste will keep in the refrigerator for at least a month.

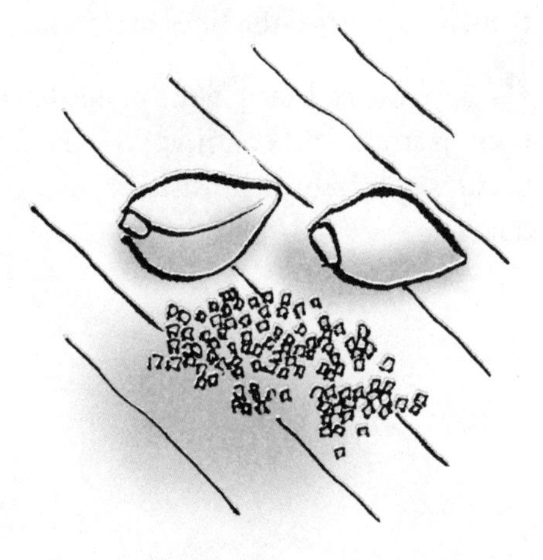

# FLATBREAD

When Louis's Charleston Grill opened in 1989, we put a big bowl of Pâté of the South (see page 109) out at the bar for our customers to snack on. Right beside it we had a big platter of lavosh, or Armenian flatbread. When we moved the restaurant to its present location, our pastry chef Deanie Cooper decided to make her own flatbread. It has become almost as popular as the pâté.

Makes 12 large pieces.

- 4 cups bread flour
- ¼ cup sesame seeds
- 2 tablespoons kosher salt
- 1 tablespoon ground black pepper
- 1½ cups warm water

1. Preheat the oven to 400°F.

2. Combine the flour, sesame seeds, salt, and pepper in the bowl of an electric mixer. Using the flat beater attachment with the mixer on medium speed, slowly add the water and mix the dough for about 5 minutes or until it comes together and forms a ball.

3. Turn the dough out onto a floured surface and cut it into 12 equal pieces. Roll the pieces out in circles as thinly as possible; the shape isn't important, but the thinness is. Place the circles on ungreased baking sheets and prick them all over with the tines of a fork.

4. Bake the flatbread in the preheated oven for 2 to 3 minutes, turn the sheets back to front, and continue to bake for another 2 to 3 minutes or until the bread is golden brown, blistered, and crispy. Cool and store in a covered container.

# CORNBREAD

■ You'll find this cornbread extremely delicious. If you don't own a cast-iron skillet, go down to the hardware store and get one. I cut the hot cornbread into wedges, slice them in half so there's a top and a bottom, slather the inside of each half with lots of butter, layer paper-thin slices of sweet onion over the bottom half, and replace the top. I then have food for which there is no equal on earth.

Makes 8 to 10 pieces.

2 cups stone-ground white cornmeal
½ teaspoon baking powder
½ teaspoon baking soda
1 teaspoon salt
1½ cups buttermilk
1 large egg, lightly beaten
¾ cup unsalted butter, melted

10" well-seasoned black cast-iron skillet

1. Place the skillet in the oven and preheat the oven to 450°F.

2. In a medium bowl, combine the cornmeal, baking powder, baking soda, and salt, mixing well.

3. In a small bowl, combine the buttermilk, egg, and ½ cup of the butter. Pour the mixture into the dry ingredients, stirring *just* to combine.

4. Working quickly and carefully, remove the hot skillet from the oven. Pour the remaining butter into the skillet and swirl it around to coat the skillet. Add the cornbread batter and bake in the preheated oven for 25 minutes or until it is firm and golden brown on top. Serve immediately.

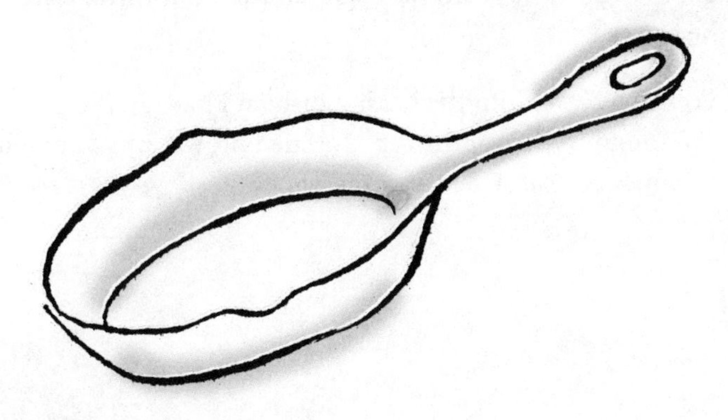

# SPOON BREAD

I think of spoon bread as a truly Southern concoction and have been in many strong discussions on that point. In any event, it's certainly welcome at my Southern table, and all who sit there love it.

Serves 8 people.

- 1⅔ cups whole milk
- 1 cup heavy cream
- ⅓ cup buttermilk
- 1 tablespoon plus 1 teaspoon unsalted butter
- 1 cup stone-ground white cornmeal
- ⅓ cup grated fresh Parmesan cheese
- 1⅓ teaspoons baking powder
- ⅔ teaspoon baking soda
- 4 large eggs, separated
- 1 tablespoon plus 1 teaspoon chopped fresh chives
- 2 teaspoons sugar
- ⅔ teaspoon salt

10" × 12" × 2" baking dish, buttered

1. Preheat the oven to 350°F.

2. Combine the milk, cream, buttermilk, and butter in a heavy-bottomed saucepan over medium-high heat and scald the mixture until it is just about to boil. Remove from the heat and set aside.

3. In a large bowl, combine the cornmeal and Parmesan cheese. Pour the scalded mixture over them and mix until smooth. Let the mixture cool about 30 minutes or until lukewarm. When the mixture has cooled, mix in the baking powder and baking soda. Lightly beat the egg yolks and mix them in. Fold in the chives.

4. Beat the egg whites with the sugar and salt until stiff. Carefully fold them into the batter.

5. Pour the batter into the baking dish and bake in the preheated oven for about 30 minutes or until the top is golden brown and a knife inserted in the middle comes out clean. Serve immediately.

# BUTTERMILK BISCUITS

Buttermilk biscuits have always been the staple breakfast bread of the South. I remember my grandmother, up early on her farm, gently kneading the lard into the flour. Next buttermilk, a by-product of milk fresh from her cow, was added, the dough was patted down, and individual biscuit-size pieces were pulled from the dough and gently shaped by hand into rounds, rather than rolled and cut with a round cutter.

Since I can remember, cooks have always relied on self-rising Southern (soft wheat) flour, which produces delicious biscuits. Be sure to measure correctly and use a light hand when incorporating the buttermilk.

Makes fifteen 2" biscuits.

- 3 cups self-rising soft wheat flour, such as White Lily
- 10 tablespoons unsalted butter, cut into ½" pieces and chilled
- 1¼ cups buttermilk
- 6 tablespoons unsalted butter, melted for brushing the tops

1. Preheat the oven to 425°F.

2. Place the flour and chilled butter in a medium mixing bowl. Work the butter into the flour with a pastry cutter, a fork, or your fingertips until the butter pieces are a little larger than an English pea, but not larger than a lima bean. If you are using your fingers, work quickly so that the heat of your hands won't melt the butter.

3. Pour in all of the buttermilk and, using light pressure, fold the mixture a few times with a plastic spatula until it just holds together. Do not overmix. In order to make light biscuits, it is important to work the dough as little as possible.

4. Turn the dough out onto a floured board and knead it quickly and gently 6 to 10 times or until it just begins to be almost homogenized. There will be large pieces of butter throughout. Sprinkle a little flour under the dough so that it won't stick to the board and lightly dust the top of the dough so that it won't stick to the rolling pin. Roll the dough out to about ½" thickness.

5. Cut the dough into 2" rounds, place on an ungreased baking sheet, and bake in the preheated oven for about 15 minutes. I like the biscuits to be crispy and brown on the top and bottom, but not dry in the middle. Remove the baking sheet from the oven and brush the tops of the biscuits with the melted butter. Serve right away.

6. Now comes the important part: deciding how many biscuits you want to eat. When they are served, take that many. Then, instead of using a knife to cut them, use your fingers to separate the tops from the bottoms. Butter the centers lavishly and replace the tops. Another taste treat, a Southern tradition that has all but become history, is to mix together equal parts sorghum and butter with a fork and spread on your hot biscuits. If you can't find sorghum, use regular molasses. The results won't be quite as exquisite, but you'll get the idea.

## Pastry Doughs

# BEST PIE DOUGH

This way of making pie dough might seem lengthy at first, but once you've done it a couple of times it's a cinch. My recipe is really pie dough with a nod to puff pastry, which explains the rather large bits of butter. The resulting pie crust is very tender and flaky and is well worth the investment of a little time.

Makes two 12" tart crusts or two 10" deep-dish pie crusts.

- 24 tablespoons unsalted butter, chilled
- 4 cups all-purpose soft wheat flour, such as White Lily
- 1 tablespoon sugar
- 1 teaspoon salt
- ⅔ cup ice water
- 1 large egg, lightly beaten with 1 tablespoon water and a pinch of salt

Two 12" tart pans or two 10" Pyrex deep-dish pie pans

1. Cut the butter into ½" pieces and refrigerate.
2. Place the flour, sugar, and salt in a large bowl and mix well.
3. Incorporate the chilled butter into the flour by rubbing the flour with the butter, using your fingertips. If you use your palms, the heat from your hands tends to melt the butter. Do not overwork the mixture, or the butter will lose the desired texture and size to achieve a properly flaky crust. The mixture should look dry and crumbly when finished.

4. Pour the ice water into the mixture and use a spatula to quickly incorporate it. The dough should not be wet looking. It will be lumpy.

5. In order to achieve the desired layers, handle the dough almost like puff pastry: Keeping it in the bowl, gather the dough together and fold it in half toward you. Pat it down and turn it a half turn. Repeat this step for 5 more half turns, gathering in the loose butter and flour as you go. Don't worry if you don't get all of it. Again, the less you handle the dough, the better.

6. Turn the dough out onto a floured board and start to shape it into a round with your hands, actually turning it on the board as you do so. When it is a roughly round shape, cut the dough in half. You should be able to see multiple layers. Gently pat the halves into disks about 1½" thick. It is okay, even desirable, to have splotches of butter in the finished dough. Wrap the dough in plastic wrap and refrigerate it for at least an hour or overnight. The dough will keep for 2 to 3 days in the refrigerator. It will keep for a month in the freezer if sealed in an airtight bag. Always thaw frozen dough in the refrigerator.

7. To bake, lightly grease and flour the pans.

8. Remove half the dough from the refrigerator. On a lightly floured, smooth surface, roll out the disk away from you in a single long stroke (using short back-and-forth strokes would develop the gluten and make the dough tough). Turn the dough 90° and roll out again, keeping the shape as round as possible. Continue rolling out the dough until you have a circle about 2" larger than the pan. Trim the edges of the circle, reserving any scraps of dough to patch holes or cracks.

9. Fold the circle in half and then in half again. You will have a triangular piece of dough. Place the point of the fold in the center of the pan. Unfold the dough and let it fall loosely into the pan. Rest the dough on the top edge of the pan and gently press it into the sides. Fold the overhanging dough onto itself to form a double-layered edge. It will extend higher than the edge of the pan. Gently press the dough onto the pan edge to help hold it up.

10. Cover the crust with plastic wrap and refrigerate for at least an hour or overnight. This allows the gluten in the dough to relax and helps keep the crust from shrinking during baking.

11. If you are making 2 pie crusts, repeat steps 7 through 10 using the second half of the dough.

12. When ready to bake, preheat the oven to 375°F.

13. Line the bottom and sides of the crust with aluminum foil, lightly pressing it against the crust. Fill the pan to the top with dried beans, rice, or the aluminum pellets made for this purpose. Place the pan on a baking sheet and bake the crust in the preheated oven for 25 to 30 minutes or until it has baked enough to be dry and firmly set. If the dough is still wet and raw looking, return it to the oven and continue to bake it for another 10 to 15 minutes with the foil still over it. It is very important that the bottom be completely baked, because it won't bake anymore once it is filled. You can always cover the edges with foil if they start to brown too much.

14. When the crust is dry and firmly set, take it out of the oven and remove the foil and weights. Prick the bottom of the crust with the tines of a fork. Brush the crust with the egg wash. Return the crust to the oven and continue to bake it for about 10 minutes or until it is baked through and light brown in color. Remove the crust from the oven and let it sit on a cooling rack while you prepare the filling.

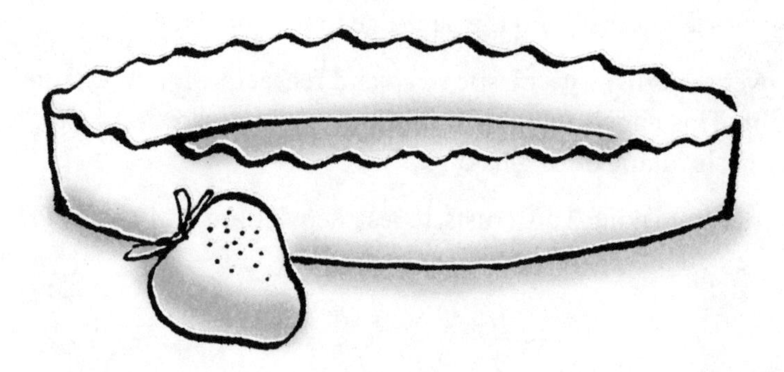

# SUGAR DOUGH

Sugar dough is often specified for dessert tarts and is also good cut into shapes for cookies. You can make this recipe by hand if you have a strong arm and a practiced hand, but the dough is somewhat fragile to roll and shape. Be sure to chill it well and roll quickly. If it cracks when you are rolling it or placing it in the pan, simply pinch it back together with your fingers.

This recipe makes a little more dough than you need to make a single crust. Roll out the scraps, cut with cookie cutters, sprinkle with sugar, and you will have a few nice sugar cookies.

Makes one 12" tart crust or one 10" deep-dish pie crust.

16 tablespoons unsalted butter, at room temperature
1¾ cups cake flour
1¾ cups all-purpose flour
¼ teaspoon salt
6 tablespoons sugar
2 large egg yolks
1 tablespoon heavy cream
1 large egg, lightly beaten with 1 tablespoon water and a pinch of salt

12" tart pan or 10" Pyrex deep-dish pie pan

1. Cut the butter into 16 pieces and put them into the bowl of an electric mixer. Add the cake flour, all-purpose flour, salt, and sugar and, using the flat beater attachment, mix on low speed until the ingredients are thoroughly combined.

2. Add the egg yolks and cream and continue to mix, scraping down the sides of the bowl as necessary, until the dough pulls away from the sides.

3. Gently pat the dough into a disk and wrap it in plastic wrap. Refrigerate it for at least 3 hours or overnight. The dough will keep for 5 days in the refrigerator. It will keep for a month in the freezer if sealed in an airtight bag. Always thaw frozen dough in the refrigerator.

4. To bake, lightly grease and flour the pan.

5. Remove the dough from the refrigerator. On a lightly floured, smooth surface, roll out the disk away from you in a single long stroke (using short back-and-forth strokes would develop the gluten and make the dough

tough). Turn the dough 90° and roll out again, keeping the shape as round as possible. Continue rolling out the dough until you have a circle about 2" larger than the pan. Trim the edges of the circle, reserving any scraps of dough to patch holes or cracks.

6. Fold the circle in half and then in half again. You will have a triangular piece of dough. Place the point of the fold in the center of the pan. Unfold the dough and let it fall loosely into the pan. Rest the dough on the top edge of the pan and gently press it into the sides. Fold the overhanging dough onto itself to form a double-layered edge. It will extend higher than the edge of the pan. Gently press the dough onto the pan edge to help hold it up.

7. Cover the crust with plastic wrap and refrigerate for at least an hour or overnight. This allows the gluten in the dough to relax and helps keep the crust from shrinking during baking.

8. When ready to bake, preheat the oven to 375°F.

9. Line the bottom and sides of the crust with aluminum foil, lightly pressing it against the crust. Fill the pan to the top with dried beans, rice, or the aluminum pellets made for this purpose. Place the pan on a baking sheet and bake the crust in the preheated oven for 25 to 30 minutes or until it has baked enough to be dry and firmly set. If the dough is still wet and raw looking, return it to the oven and continue to bake it for another 10 to 15 minutes with the foil still over it. It is very important that the bottom be completely baked, because it won't bake anymore once it is filled. You can always cover the edges with foil if they start to brown too much.

10. When the crust is dry and firmly set, take it out of the oven and remove the foil and weights. Prick the bottom of the crust with the tines of a fork. Brush the crust with the egg wash. Return the crust to the oven and continue to bake it for about 10 minutes or until it is baked through and light brown in color. Remove the crust from the oven and let it sit on a cooling rack while you prepare the filling.

# CRÈME FRAÎCHE

Not as sweet as the more frequently used whipped cream, this is a light and creamy alternative with an almost nutlike flavor. It's perfect for fruit desserts.

Makes 2 cups.

2 cups heavy cream
½ cup buttermilk

1. Mix the cream and buttermilk together in a sterile glass jar, cover, and leave out overnight at room temperature to thicken.

2. The next day, cut a piece of cheesecloth large enough to *double*-line a large mesh sieve. Rinse the cheesecloth with cold water and wring it out. Line the sieve and set it over a bowl.

3. Pour the crème fraîche into the sieve and cover the sieve and bowl lightly with plastic wrap. Place them in the refrigerator overnight. The crème fraîche should thicken even more, draining off excess liquid into the bowl. Tightly covered, crème fraîche will keep in the refrigerator for a week.

# CRÈME ANGLAISE

Crème anglaise is the culinary name for what Southerners know as boiled custard. One of my earliest food memories is of Jell-O topped with boiled custard. I have never tasted any crème anglaise that could outdo that memory. This recipe can be made by hand using a whisk, depending on how strong your arm is, and how practiced your hand.

Makes 5 cups.

3½ cups whole milk
8 large egg yolks
1 cup sugar
½ cup heavy cream, chilled
2 tablespoons pure vanilla extract

1. Bring the milk to a low boil in a heavy-bottomed saucepan over medium heat.

2. Meanwhile, put the egg yolks into the bowl of an electric mixer. With the whisk attachment, slowly beat the sugar into the yolks until the mixture lightens in color.

3. Prepare an ice bath by fitting an empty 2-quart bowl into a large bowl of ice.

4. Remove the milk from the heat. Take 2 cups of the hot milk and slowly pour it into the bowl of the electric mixer, continuing to use the whisk attachment to combine it with the yolks and sugar. Slowly pour the mixture into the saucepan with the remaining hot milk, now whisking by hand.

5. Return the saucepan to the stove. Stirring constantly with a wooden spoon or rubber spatula, gently cook the mixture over low heat for 5 to 10 minutes or until it is thick enough to coat the back of a spoon. You now have custard. Immediately remove the saucepan from the heat. Stir in the chilled cream and, using a fine mesh sieve, strain the custard into the 2-quart bowl in the ice bath to avoid further cooking. Stir in the vanilla extract.

6. Chill the custard in a covered container. Tightly covered, it will keep in the refrigerator for 3 days.

# ESPRESSO CRÈME ANGLAISE

This intensely flavored coffee custard has a special affinity for chocolate desserts. We offer it at the restaurant every night and have regular patrons who expect it.

Makes 5 cups.

¾ cup crushed espresso beans (crush with a coffee grinder, nut grinder, or mortar and pestle)
3½ cups whole milk, chilled
8 large egg yolks
1 cup sugar
½ cup heavy cream, chilled
2 tablespoons pure vanilla extract
1 tablespoon Kahlúa or Tia Maria liqueur

1. In a medium bowl, combine the espresso beans with the chilled milk. Cover and refrigerate overnight.

2. The next day, heat the espresso beans and milk over medium heat.

3. Strain the hot milk into a heavy-bottomed saucepan and discard the espresso beans. Bring the milk to a low boil over medium heat.

4. Meanwhile, put the egg yolks into the bowl of an electric mixer. With the whisk attachment, slowly beat the sugar into the yolks until the mixture lightens in color.

5. Prepare an ice bath by fitting an empty 2-quart bowl into a large bowl of ice.

6. Remove the milk from the heat. Take 2 cups of the hot milk and slowly pour it into the bowl of the electric mixer, continuing to use the whisk attachment to combine it with the yolks and sugar. Slowly pour the mixture into the saucepan with the remaining hot milk, now whisking by hand.

7. Return the saucepan to the stove. Stirring constantly with a wooden spoon or rubber spatula, gently cook the mixture over low heat for 5 to 10 minutes or until it is thick enough to coat the back of a spoon. You now have custard. Immediately remove the saucepan from the heat. Stir in the chilled cream and, using a fine mesh sieve, strain the custard into the 2-quart bowl in the ice bath to avoid further cooking. Stir in the vanilla extract and liqueur.

8. Chill the custard in a covered container. Tightly covered, it will keep in the refrigerator for 3 days.

# HAZELNUT CRÈME ANGLAISE

Frangelico liqueur is fragrant with the smell of hazelnuts. It doesn't take much of it to add flavor. This custard is great with chocolate ice cream or cake.

Makes 5 cups.

- 1 cup hazelnuts
- 3½ cups whole milk, chilled
- 8 large egg yolks
- 1 cup sugar
- ½ cup heavy cream, chilled
- 2 tablespoons pure vanilla extract
- 1 tablespoon Frangelico liqueur

1. Preheat the oven to 325°F.

2. Spread the hazelnuts on a baking sheet and toast them in the preheated oven for about 6 minutes or until very lightly browned. Remove them from the oven and cool to room temperature. Rub the hazelnuts in a clean terry cloth kitchen

towel, working in batches if necessary, until the skin flakes off. (Very tiny pieces of skin sometimes stick to the nuts, but you can ignore them.) Crush the nuts.

3. In a medium bowl, combine the hazelnuts with the chilled milk. Cover and refrigerate overnight.

4. The next day, heat the hazelnuts and milk over medium heat.

5. Strain the hot milk into a heavy-bottomed saucepan and discard the nuts. Bring the milk to a low boil over medium heat.

6. Meanwhile, put the egg yolks into the bowl of an electric mixer. With the whisk attachment, slowly beat the sugar into the yolks until the mixture lightens in color.

7. Prepare an ice bath by fitting an empty 2-quart bowl into a large bowl of ice.

8. Remove the milk from the heat. Take 2 cups of the hot milk and slowly pour it into the bowl of the electric mixer, continuing to use the whisk attachment to combine it with the yolks and sugar. Slowly pour the mixture into the saucepan with the remaining hot milk, now whisking by hand.

9. Return the saucepan to the stove. Stirring constantly with a wooden spoon or rubber spatula, gently cook the mixture over low heat for 5 to 10 minutes or until it is thick enough to coat the back of a spoon. You now have custard. Immediately remove the saucepan from the heat. Stir in the chilled cream and, using a fine mesh sieve, strain the custard into the 2-quart bowl in the ice bath to avoid further cooking. Stir in the vanilla extract and liqueur.

10. Chill the custard in a covered container. Tightly covered, it will keep in the refrigerator for 3 days.

# VANILLA ICE CREAM

My family often teases me about my lack of adventure because I prefer vanilla ice cream over the more esoteric flavors, but it continues to be my favorite.

Makes 1½ quarts.

4 cups heavy cream
1 cup whole milk
2 vanilla beans, split lengthwise
6 large egg yolks
3 cups sugar
5 tablespoons dark rum (I use Myers's)

1. Combine the cream and milk in a heavy-bottomed saucepan over medium heat. With the side of a spoon, scrape the seeds out of the vanilla bean pods and add both the seeds and the pods to the saucepan. Stir to combine the ingredients and bring the mixture to a low boil.

2. Meanwhile, put the egg yolks into the bowl of an electric mixer. With the whisk attachment, slowly beat the sugar into the yolks until the mixture lightens in color.

3. Prepare an ice bath by fitting an empty 3-quart bowl into a large bowl of ice.

4. Remove the cream and milk from the heat. Take 2 cups of the hot mixture and slowly pour it into the bowl of the electric mixer, continuing to use the whisk attachment to combine it with the yolks and sugar. Slowly pour the mixture into the saucepan with the remaining hot cream and milk, now whisking by hand.

5. Return the saucepan to the stove. Stirring constantly with a wooden spoon or rubber spatula, gently cook the mixture over low heat for 5 to 10 minutes or until it is thick enough to coat the back of a spoon. You now have custard. Immediately strain the custard into the 3-quart bowl in the ice bath to avoid further cooking. Stir in the rum.

6. Chill the custard overnight in a covered container. When ready to churn, pour the chilled custard into a prepared ice cream maker and proceed according to the manufacturer's instructions.

# CARAMEL SAUCE

This is an all-purpose caramel sauce that works well with ice cream and a lot of pastries. You'll find that if you keep it in the refrigerator or freezer, it will quickly disappear. One word of caution: To make a caramel sauce, you need to use a heavy-bottomed saucepan that is deep enough to hold the cream that bubbles up when it is added to the hot sugar. Estimate 4 times the height of the ingredients to be safe.

Makes 2½ cups.

2¼ cups sugar
½ cup cold water
1½ cups heavy cream
4 tablespoons unsalted butter, cut into 4 pieces and chilled

1. Put the sugar and cold water in a heavy-bottomed saucepan over medium-high heat and bring to a boil, stirring only until the sugar dissolves. If there are any sugar crystals on the side of the pan, brush them down with a clean pastry brush that has been dipped in water. Watching carefully, let the sugar continue to boil until it is a deep golden caramel color. This should take about 20 to 25 minutes.

2. While the sugar is cooking, heat the cream. When the sugar reaches the caramel color, pour the cream in all at once. The mixture will bubble violently, but if you have used the right size pot it won't overflow. Quickly stir the cream into the caramel, which will tighten up. As you stir the caramel over the heat, it will loosen again and absorb the cream.

3. Once the cream has been absorbed into the caramel, take the pan off the heat and add the butter. The caramel will cool as it absorbs the butter. You may use the sauce right away or cool it to room temperature, cover, and refrigerate. Tightly covered, it will keep for at least a week in the refrigerator. The sauce also freezes well.

# WARM FUDGE SAUCE

This is basically another version of ganache, the pastry chef's workhorse. You can alter the texture by adding more or less cream. By changing the type of chocolate, you can also alter the flavor, and if you'd like to change the flavoring element, that's okay too. The sauce is terrific over any ice cream, and especially exotic over shortcake.

Makes 1 cup.

½ cup heavy cream
8 ounces bittersweet chocolate, chopped into small pieces
2 teaspoons pure vanilla extract

1. Bring the cream to a boil in a small heavy-bottomed saucepan over medium heat.

2. Put the chocolate pieces in the top of a double boiler. Pour the hot cream over the chocolate and stir over barely simmering water until the chocolate melts. Stir in the vanilla.

3. Serve the sauce hot or cool it to room temperature and refrigerate. Tightly covered, it will keep in the refrigerator for a week, and it also freezes well. To reheat, place the container in hot water and stir occasionally until the sauce reaches the desired temperature.

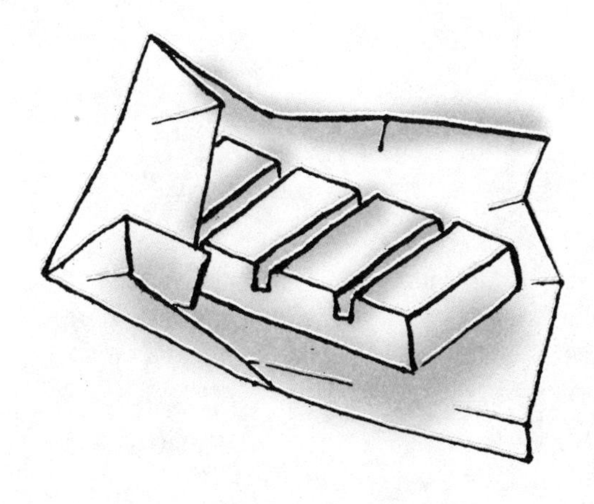

# KAHLÚA FUDGE SAUCE

The addition of Kahlúa to traditional fudge sauce provides a touch of smoothness and another flavor dimension—that of rich coffee. This can be used as you would any fudge sauce; it is especially good over ice cream or a big piece of Toasted Corn Cake (see page 228).

Makes 2½ cups.

1 cup whole milk
1 cup heavy cream
½ cup sugar
1 tablespoon unsalted butter
12 ounces semisweet chocolate, chopped into small pieces
6 tablespoons Kahlúa liqueur

1. Combine the milk, cream, and sugar in a heavy-bottomed saucepan and bring to a boil over medium heat, stirring well to dissolve the sugar.

2. Put the butter and chocolate in the top of a double boiler. Pour the hot mixture over them and stir over barely simmering water until the chocolate melts. Stir in the liqueur.

3. Serve the sauce hot or cool it to room temperature and refrigerate. Tightly covered, it will keep in the refrigerator for a week, and it also freezes well. To reheat, place the container in hot water and stir occasionally until the sauce reaches the desired temperature.

# STREAK O'LEAN

Streak o'lean is a kind of salt-pork fat through which a streak of lean meat runs. Traditionally, streak o'lean has been the cooking medium of choice in the South. It is considered the BMW of fatback. If you'd like to try rendering its fat, here's how to do it. And if you find that you like streak o'lean, make twice as much as you need, because you'll end up eating half of the crisp meat.

Makes about 6 tablespoons of rendered fat.

¼ pound streak o'lean

1. Cut the streak o'lean into ¼"-thick slices.
2. Place the slices in an unheated 10" black cast-iron skillet and cook them over very low heat for about 20 minutes. Turn them over and cook for 20 to 25 minutes to make sure both sides are equally brown. The fat should be rendering, or melting away, from the lean part, so that you can separate the lean meat from the fat. Drain off the fat and reserve for other uses.
3. Raise the heat to medium and sauté the meat until it is golden brown and slightly crisp, stirring occasionally to keep it from sticking to the bottom of the skillet. Remove the meat and place it on a paper towel, which will absorb any remaining fat. Tightly covered, both the fat and the meat can be kept in the refrigerator for several days.

# RENDERED DUCK FAT

Duck is one of the unsung heroes of the restaurant business. It is readily available and relatively inexpensive, and every last piece can be utilized with style. A whole duck offers 2 fine breasts for a simple yet elegant sauté and the legs will produce nice confit for fried grits (see page 52) or a green lentil salad (page 55). The stripped carcasses can be used to make stock (page 6) that can be refined into either a sauce or soup. Finally, scraps of fat and skin can be rendered for preserved duck (page 52) and then used to make cracklings or a topping for a salad.

Makes 2 cups.

3 domestic ducks (4½ to 5 pounds each)

1. Preheat the oven to 275°F.

2. Remove the skin and fat of the 3 ducks and reserve it, except for the fat deposits just under the tails, which should be discarded. Rinse and coarsely dice the reserved skin and fat.

3. In a heavy ovenproof saucepan, cover the skin and fat with ½ cup of cold water. Bring the mixture to a simmer, then put the pan in the preheated oven. Cook the skin and fat for about 2 hours or until the water has evaporated and all of the fat has melted. Be sure to keep an eye on it and turn down the heat if you see any sign of the fat coloring. The fat should not be allowed to turn an amber color.

4. Pour the fat into a heatproof container, reserving the pieces of skin. Let the fat cool to room temperature, then cover it and refrigerate. Tightly covered, it will keep in the refrigerator for a month.

5. Raise the oven temperature to 325°F. Return the saucepan with the reserved pieces of skin to the oven and bake them until they are crisp. These crispy bits of skin are now "cracklings." Place them on a paper towel to drain and discard any fat remaining in the pan.

# CLEANING SOFT-SHELL CRABS

Soft-shell crabs are easy to clean, although some people are reluctant to be involved in their demise. (I know this to be true because I once demonstrated the process on television and the station received lots and lots of objections from viewers.) It is vital to know when the crabs died, however, lest you risk food poisoning. Fortunately, soft-shell crabs are often available frozen in fish markets, already dressed.

To clean your own crabs, there are 3 easy steps:

1. Lift a pointed end of the crab's shell and, with shears, carefully cut off the breathers—soft little cartilaginous fingers that act as lungs—as close to their bases as possible. Discard the breathers and repeat with the other side of the shell.

2. Again using shears, cut through the front of the shell just behind the eyes and discard the eyes.

3. Turn the crab over and lift the flap that covers part of its underside, trim the flap off with shears, and discard it. Rinse the crab under running water and proceed with your recipe.

# QUICK PEELED TOMATOES

The easiest way to peel a tomato is to drop it into a pot of boiling water. Remove the tomato after about 10 seconds and refresh it under cold water until it is cool enough to handle (about 10 seconds). The skin should peel off easily.

If you have a large number of tomatoes, put them in the boiling water a few at a time. They may take longer than 10 seconds to be ready to peel, but even those few additional seconds make the labor savings worthwhile. The riper the tomato, the shorter the time needed in the boiling water. Conversely, firm tomatoes can take up to 30 seconds. It is easy to tell by their looks when the tomatoes are ready, as the skin begins to look looser.

# Four Suggested Fall Menus

Baked Mussels with Almonds /49
Panned Quail with Pan Gravy /68
Potato and Mushroom Gratin /83
Spoon Bread /26
Gingered Pear Tarte Tatin /90

Grilled Pears with Spinach and Clemson Blue Cheese
in a Warm Onion Dressing /58
Preserved Duck with Fried Grits /52
Southern Fried Catfish with Garlic and Herb Mayonnaise /64
Cornbread /25
Pecan Pie with Rum Cream /93

Caesar Salad with Spicy Fried Oysters /60
Oven-Roasted Veal Chop /72
Beer-Braised Onions /82
Warm Chocolate Soufflé Cake with a Molten Center /94

Country Ham and White Bean Soup with Mustard Greens /63
Quick BBQ Pork Sandwich with Sweet and Sour Onions
and Cucumbers /76
Stewed Apples /79
Old-Fashioned Banana Pudding /88

## Fall in the Lowcountry

In the temperate climate of the Lowcountry, seasonal changes are subtle. At September's start, it's still hot here, but as the days shorten and the light becomes more muted, we know that cooler air is on the way and the hunting season is commencing. Even as early as September 5, when the dove season officially opens, we are thinking about changing what is on our dinner table. By then deer season has opened on private lands as well, and sometime around Thanksgiving, local hunters will be bagging waterfowl, geese, quail, and rabbit.

When we lived in Pawleys Island, many of the local hunters would share their catch with us. One especially generous hunter was Chip Lachicotte, whose family was among the island's earliest settlers. Chip was an avid and proficient hunter and he regularly shared his catch of mallard and teal with us. I cooked them up so rare that we subsequently named a dish Bloody Duck. It was a simple preparation, but no less wonderful for its simplicity. The ducks were seasoned merely with salt and pepper, seared quickly in a hot black cast-iron skillet, and cooked just until the texture had changed, with the meat still very red. Sometimes I would prepare a rich red wine gravy as an accompaniment (like a Cabernet sauce). The flavor of the duck was rich, intense, and simply wonderful, and not much else was needed on the plate, although we did sometimes serve it with the local greens that were still growing in late fall.

Sadly for visitors and Lowcountry residents who were not hunters, until recently South Carolina restaurants were not allowed to cook wild game. I found out the hard way about the state wildlife department's stance on game in restaurants when I was arrested at the Pawleys Island Inn for serving a domesticated deer I had purchased from a Midwestern producer. The gaming commission eventually released me and in 1998 the state legalized the sale of wild game. Thankfully, squab has always been readily available, and South Carolina has the country's largest producer, the Palmetto Pigeon Plant. And like the wild teal and mallard, the rich meat of the squab does not need much tending.

Fall, of course, has always been the time for the first harvesting of oysters. Actually, now that oyster farming has been instituted here and elsewhere, oysters are available year-round. I prefer the wild oysters that are grown in beds in our sounds and estuaries; they're best when the water temperature is at its coolest and the oyster at its most saline. In early fall, I often batter and fry them and serve them either on top of a spicy salad or in a basket with a hefty serving of horseradish sauce.

When the days get shorter and the dinner table is set sooner, simple one-pot meals seem more in order. Quick to assemble and often made with heartier ingredients, they sate the appetite for full-flavored foods and get us through the night. Families are more likely to gather over a stew or soup pot or even someone's favorite meat loaf. Frequently there's game or sausage, and most likely rice and gravy.

No less at the core of Southern cooking are vegetables and fruits. The recipes for autumn reflect not only my Southern and childhood eating traditions, but also the growing season in the Lowcountry when summer has given way to cabbages, greens, apples, pears, and nuts.

# BAKED MUSSELS WITH ALMONDS

A derivation of a classic French appetizer, this dish will make an icy crisp sauvignon blanc taste like gold.

Serves 4 to 6 people.

**FOR THE MUSSELS:**

- 4 pounds live mussels in their shells, preferably cultivated
- 1 cup dry white wine
- 1 cup water
- 1 sprig fresh thyme
- 3 bay leaves

**FOR THE ALMOND BUTTER:**

- 1 pound unsalted butter, at room temperature
- ¼ cup minced garlic
- 3 tablespoons fresh lemon juice
- 3 tablespoons dry white vermouth
- 1 tablespoon Tabasco sauce
- ½ teaspoon salt
- ¼ teaspoon freshly ground black pepper
- ¾ cup chopped fresh Italian parsley
- ⅔ cup sliced blanched almonds, toasted

1. Wash the mussels well, pulling off any beards that are attached.

2. Combine the wine, water, thyme, and bay leaves in a heavy-bottomed Dutch oven. Bring the mixture to a hard boil over medium heat and add the mussels. Cover the pot and steam the mussels for 2 to 4 minutes, gently stirring once or twice. Keep a sharp eye on the mussels and remove them as they open. This will keep them juicy and prevent them from becoming tough. (They should be easy to remove from their shells when they are cooked.) When all the mussels are cooked, strain the broth and reserve it to use for a soup base. Discard any unopened mussels.

3. When the mussels are cool enough to handle, remove them carefully from their shells. With a paring knife, scrape away the muscle that attaches them to the shell and keep one side of each mussel's shell for serving. For the prettiest presentation, use the same side of the shell for all of the mussels—either all right sides or all left sides. You can tell if the shells match when you hold them in the same position. (This reads trickier than it is in real life.)

4. Cut the butter into 12 pieces, put them in the bowl of a food processor, and process until smooth. Scrape down the bowl and add the garlic, lemon juice, vermouth, Tabasco, salt, pepper, and parsley. Process about 30 seconds to combine, stopping to scrape down the bowl again if necessary.

5. Add the almonds. Pulse 2 or 3 times to coarsely break them up. Be careful not to grind them too finely. Remove the almond butter to a bowl and reserve, at room temperature if possible. If you need to make it ahead of time, refrigerate it but bring it back to room temperature before using.

6. Preheat the oven to 450°F.

7. Place the mussels in the reserved shells. Cover each mussel with about 1 teaspoon of almond butter, filling any empty space in the shell. Put the mussels on a baking sheet or, better yet, put them in a nice baker that can go directly from the oven to the table. If you are assembling the mussels in advance and must refrigerate them before baking, put them on a plate in the refrigerator and transfer them to the baking sheet just before the actual cooking. This way the mussels will not go into the oven on a cold baking sheet, which will slow the cooking process.

8. Bake the mussels on the top rack of the preheated oven for 8 to 10 minutes, checking every few minutes. When the mussels are ready, the butter will have melted and the almonds will be slightly browned.

9. Remove the mussels from the baking sheet and place them decoratively on a serving platter or serve them in the baker in which they were cooked. A good reason to use an oven-to-table baker is that none of the wonderful buttery, garlicky juices are lost: this is the stuff for which French bread was designed.

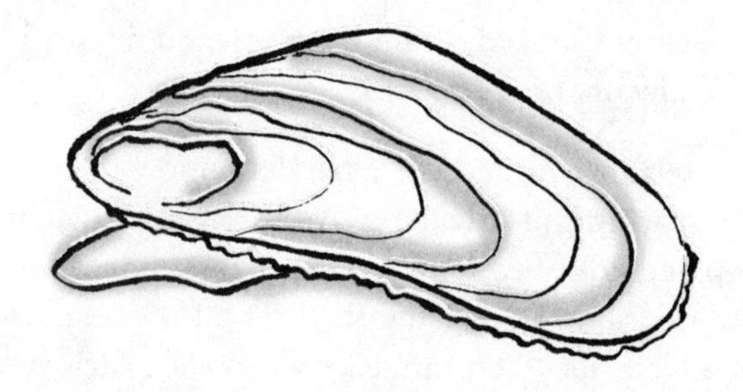

# BARBECUED PORK RILLETTES

The cooking preparation known as rillettes began in France before the days of refrigeration as a method for preserving meat, usually pork. Traditionally the pork was slowly cooked in seasoned fat and then mashed along with some of the fat into a paste. The blend was then packed into small pots, covered with a thin layer of fat, and stored for several weeks to fully develop its flavors.

A time-honored appetizer in France, pork rillettes are great cocktail fare as well. Along with our Pâté of the South (page 109), they had a special place at Louis's original bar. Rich and spicy, they stand up to all drinks and at the same time add a little fuel to the belly, lessening the possibility that the next drink will sneak up on you. We used to vary the preparation occasionally by adding barbecue sauce, which is how this recipe came about. Both versions were received with equal gusto.

Serves 20 people as an hors d'oeuvre.

- 5 pounds pork shoulder, cut into 2" cubes
- 3 tablespoons minced garlic
- 2 tablespoons salt
- 4 tablespoons freshly ground black pepper
- 4 cups water
- 2 cups Chad's Homemade BBQ Sauce (see page 265)

1. Combine the pork, garlic, salt, pepper, and water in a large heavy-bottomed saucepan and bring to a simmer over medium heat. Skim off any impurities as they come to the top, trying not to remove any of the fat.

2. Adjust the heat to maintain a brisk simmer for approximately 2 hours. Stir occasionally so that the pork doesn't brown on the bottom. As the pork starts to come apart, use a fork to help break it into shreds. As the water begins to evaporate, it will separate from the liquid fat and you will see steam rising from the pot. When the pork juices and other liquid have evaporated, remove the pork and rendered fat to a bowl.

3. Shred the pork, breaking the meat into very small pieces. The meat should be slightly oversalted and very spicy. Add the barbecue sauce and mix well. Let the mixture cool to room temperature, cover, and refrigerate overnight.

4. The next day, place the pork on a baking sheet with sides. With 2 forks, gradually mix all of the ingredients together, using long pulling motions. When you finish, the pork should be bound by its own fat. The mixture should be a little coarse and very spicy.

5. Place the rillettes in a crock and refrigerate for at least 4 hours or overnight. Remove from the refrigerator at least 1 hour before serving. Serve with toasted French bread rounds. Barbecued pork rillettes will keep for several weeks in a crock in the refrigerator if you cover them completely with a layer of fat.

# PRESERVED DUCK WITH FRIED GRITS

Preserved duck is one of my favorite foods. Best made in bulk, it is versatile, stores well, and improves with age. I introduced this combination on my menu in 1981. It's a hit with visitors from other parts of the country who are getting their first taste of grits. It's hard to imagine a better introduction to one of our region's most cherished staples than these fried grits—crispy on the outside and creamy and succulent on the inside.

Serves 8 people.

**FOR THE DUCK:**

- 1 tablespoon Preserving Spices (see page 2)
- 1½ tablespoons salt
- 1½ teaspoons minced garlic
- 1½ teaspoons finely crushed juniper berries
- 2 duck leg quarters from a 4½ to 5-pound domestic duck (save the breasts for other purposes)
- 2 cups rendered duck fat (see page 42) or peanut oil

**FOR THE GRITS:**

- 4 cups whole milk
- 1 teaspoon salt
- ½ teaspoon freshly ground black pepper
- 1 cup uncooked quick grits *(not instant)*
- ½ cup heavy cream
- 6 large egg yolks
- 3 large eggs, lightly beaten

2 tablespoons water
1 tablespoon peanut oil
½ cup all-purpose flour
¾ cup dried bread crumbs, preferably homemade from French bread (if using store-bought crumbs, be sure they are unflavored)

9" × 13" × 2" Pyrex dish or baking sheet with sides at least 1" high, buttered

**TO ASSEMBLE:**

¼ cup peanut oil
Reserved duck fat or peanut oil from the preserved duck
2 cups shredded preserved duck
1 cup chicken stock (see page 5)

10" heavy-bottomed cast-iron skillet

1. Combine the preserving spices, salt, garlic, and juniper berries in a bowl. Sprinkle the duck leg quarters with 1 tablespoon of this mixture and place them in a single layer in a nonreactive pan. Cover the pan with plastic wrap and refrigerate overnight.

2. The next day, wipe the duck leg quarters with a damp paper towel to remove most of the preserving mixture. Place them in a heavy saucepan or Dutch oven and cover completely with the duck fat or peanut oil. Warm the duck fat slightly if necessary to be able to pour it.

3. Bring the fat to a simmer over medium heat. Quickly reduce the heat until the fat barely shimmers with a faint simmer. This gentle cooking is necessary for the duck to be completely cooked but still succulent. Watch the pan carefully to be sure that the duck doesn't cook too fast.

4. After 1 hour, pierce a leg quarter with a skewer or fork. If it has finished cooking, the juices should run clear and the leg should feel soft and tender when slightly squeezed. If it is not finished cooking, continue to simmer for another 15 minutes and check again. When done, remove the leg quarters carefully and let them cool on a plate. Reserve the fat or oil.

5. Although the duck can be used at this point, extra aging adds an enormous amount of flavor. To age, place the cooled leg quarters in a small bowl and strain the cooled fat or oil over them to cover completely. (If you are using duck fat and you don't have enough, use peanut oil mixed with the fat as needed to cover.) Cover the bowl tightly with plastic wrap and refrigerate. The duck will keep for up to a month.

6. When it is time to eat the duck, remove it from the fat. Reserve the fat. Discard the skin and pull off the meat in not-too-small shreds, discarding any tendon. You should end up with about 2 cups of shredded duck meat.

7. To prepare the grits, bring the milk to a simmer in a heavy-bottomed saucepan over medium heat, being careful not to scorch the bottom. Add the salt and pepper, then add the grits. Stir constantly until the grits begin to thicken. Reduce the heat to low and cook for 5 minutes, stirring occasionally and watching carefully. Remove the grits from the heat and let them cool slightly in the saucepan for about 15 minutes.

8. In a small bowl, mix the cream and egg yolks together. Add them to the cooked grits, whipping thoroughly and quickly to prevent lumps. Cook over medium heat for 3 to 4 minutes or until the mixture bubbles vigorously. Remove the saucepan from the heat and let the grits cool for about 30 minutes.

9. Pour the grits into the prepared pan; they should be ¾" high and fairly stiff. Put the pan in the refrigerator to cool. Once cold, cover with plastic wrap and refrigerate for 2 hours or until firm.

10. Using a knife or cookie cutter, make cakes by cutting the cold grits into the shape you choose. At the restaurant, I make rectangles by making 4 cuts on the 13" side and 3 cuts on the 9" side. These rectangles may then be cut diagonally into triangles.

11. In a small bowl, mix the 3 eggs, water, and peanut oil. Dip the cakes into the flour, then into the egg mixture, and finally into the dried bread crumbs. Place them on a pan and refrigerate for 1 hour to let the breading dry.

12. To assemble, preheat the oven to 150°F.

13. Heat the skillet over medium-high heat until hot but not smoking. Add the ¼ cup of peanut oil. Let the oil heat for 1 minute, then begin adding the cakes. Cook them for about 1 minute on each side or until they are golden brown, carefully turning with a spatula. As they are finished, place them on a baking sheet lined with paper towels and keep them warm in the preheated oven.

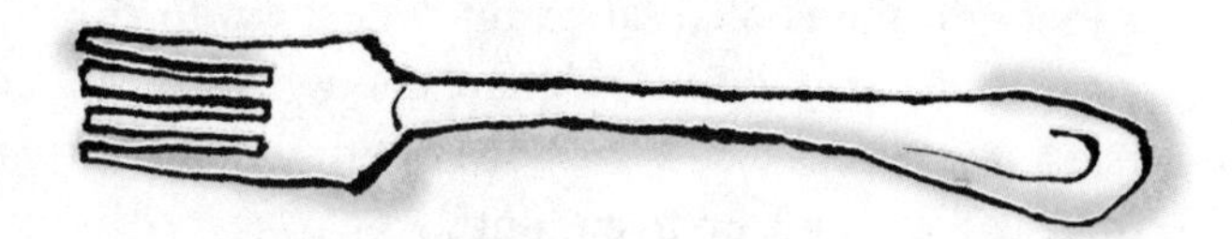

14. Wipe the skillet with a paper towel and return it to the stove. Add 2 tablespoons of the reserved duck fat or peanut oil. When very hot but not smoking, add the shredded duck and sauté for 3 minutes over medium-high heat. The finished duck should be hot, a little crispy, but not tough. Remove the meat to a warm plate. Add the chicken stock to the skillet and boil rapidly for about 1 minute or until the bubbles grow larger, indicating that the stock has thickened appropriately. Transfer to a sauceboat.

15. Place 1 or 2 hot grit cakes on each serving plate, top with ¼ cup of the preserved duck, and pass the sauce separately.

# WARM PRESERVED DUCK AND LENTIL SALAD

This is an unusual and hearty fall dish. It has many fall flavors and is a very satisfying lunch, or even a light supper. Served with a bottle of Beaujolais or a light Pinot Noir, it will put you at peace with most things.

Serves 8 people.

½ cup sherry wine vinegar
⅓ cup walnut oil
¼ cup plus 1 tablespoon peanut oil
Salt and freshly ground black pepper to taste
1 large ripe regular tomato or 3 ripe plum tomatoes
2 tablespoons extra virgin olive oil
4 cups water
1 tablespoon salt
½ cup peeled and finely diced carrots
⅓ cup baby green beans, trimmed at both ends and cut into thirds
⅓ cup peeled and finely diced turnips
1 cup Green Lentils (see page 84)
1½ cups shredded preserved duck plus the reserved fat (see steps 1–6 on pages 53–54)
¼ cup radicchio, cut into ½" strips
½ cup Kentucky Bibb or baby romaine lettuce, cut into ½" strips
¼ cup finely diced white mushroom caps
¼ cup finely chopped fresh chives
8 large Boston lettuce leaves, gently washed and dried
1 tablespoon chopped fresh parsley

1. Whisk the vinegar, walnut oil, and ¼ cup of the peanut oil together, adding the oils slowly, or put the vinegar in a blender and very slowly pour the oils into the blender, teaspoon by teaspoon. Add salt and pepper to taste. This dressing is not an emulsion, so it will separate. Whisk to bring it back together when ready to use.

2. Bring a saucepan of water to a boil. Drop in the tomato and leave it for about 10 seconds. Remove the tomato from the saucepan and drop it in ice water to cool. Drain and peel off the skin. Remove the core and seeds and dice the tomato's meat into ½" pieces. Toss the diced tomato with the olive oil and season with pepper to taste. Reserve at room temperature until ready to use.

3. Bring the 4 cups of water and 1 tablespoon of salt to a boil in a nonreactive saucepan and drop in the carrots. Gently boil them for 3 to 4 minutes or until just tender. Drain and rinse with cold water to avoid further cooking. Repeat with the green beans and then the turnips. The green beans should take 4 to 5 minutes, the turnips 3 to 4 minutes.

4. In a heavy-bottomed sauté pan, heat the remaining tablespoon of peanut oil until hot but not smoking. Add the carrots, green beans, and turnips. When they are warm, add the lentils. Toss everything together to mix well. Season with salt and pepper to taste.

5. Meanwhile, heat 2 tablespoons of the reserved duck fat in a heavy-bottomed sauté pan over medium-high heat. Add the preserved duck and sauté, stirring so that it does not stick to the pan. When the duck is warm and crisp, remove it from the pan and reserve.

6. Add the radicchio, Bibb lettuce, mushrooms, and chives to the pan of vegetables, again tossing lightly to mix. Heat only long enough to warm everything through. Toss with 3 tablespoons of the dressing, tasting as you go for salt and pepper.

7. Place a leaf of Boston lettuce on each of 8 serving plates. Divide the warm vegetable mixture equally among the plates, placing it on top of the lettuce leaf. Top with the warm preserved duck. Add the chopped parsley to the reserved tomato mixture and spoon it over the salads. Serve immediately.

# PRESERVED DUCK, BROCCOLI RABE, AND WARM POTATO SALAD

Bitter broccoli rabe may be somewhat of an acquired taste for many folks, but even those who don't normally eat it will probably find that they enjoy it this way, with the bitterness offset by the rich duck and creamy potatoes. This salad may be served at room temperature if you need to prepare it in advance. You can cook the broccoli rabe and potatoes up to 2 hours ahead, but crisp the duck and mix it all together just before serving the salad.

Serves 6 to 8 people.

- 7 tablespoons walnut oil
- 1 pound broccoli rabe, with the large stems discarded and the rest chopped into 1" pieces (see note if broccoli rabe is not available)
- 4 cups new red potatoes, peeled, cut into ½"-thick slices, cooked in salted water until just barely tender, and drained well
- 2 cups shredded preserved duck plus the reserved fat (see steps 1–6 on pages 53–54)
- ¼ cup water
- 3 tablespoons apple cider vinegar
- ¼ cup chopped fresh Italian parsley
- Salt and freshly ground black pepper to taste

1. In a heavy skillet, heat 4 tablespoons of the walnut oil over medium-high heat and sauté the broccoli rabe for 3 to 5 minutes or until it begins to wilt. Add the potatoes and toss to heat through.
2. Heat 3 tablespoons of the reserved duck fat in a heavy-bottomed sauté pan over medium-high heat. Add the preserved duck and sauté, stirring so that it does not stick to the pan. When the duck is warm and crisp, add it to the pan of broccoli rabe and potatoes.
3. Deglaze the sauté pan used for the duck with the ¼ cup of water. Add the vinegar and remaining 3 tablespoons of walnut oil. Whisk to mix into a dressing.
4. Pour the dressing over the broccoli rabe, potatoes, and duck. Add the parsley and toss to mix. Add salt and pepper to taste. Divide among warm bowls or place on a heated platter. Serve immediately.

NOTE: If broccoli rabe is not available, you may use regular broccoli. Cut the florets into quarters and steam, covered, for 1 minute over ¾ cup of boiling water. Then proceed to step 1.

# GRILLED PEARS WITH SPINACH AND CLEMSON BLUE CHEESE IN A WARM ONION DRESSING

■ This is our most popular fall salad. We have been using Clemson blue cheese since 1980. I attended Clemson years ago and have a soft spot for their cheese, which is very good. It is now more widely distributed, but back then the only way to buy it was at the retail counter of the college dairy center.

Serves 4 people.

**FOR THE DRESSING:**

3 cups Wadmalaw Sweets or other sweet onions, such as Vidalia or Maui (about ¾ pound), peeled and cut into ½"-thick slices
1 cup peanut oil
½ cup red wine vinegar
1½ teaspoons cracked black pepper
¾ teaspoon kosher salt
1¾ tablespoons Dijon mustard (I use Grey Poupon)
1 tablespoon plus 1½ teaspoons chopped fresh chives
½ cup extra virgin olive oil

**FOR THE SALAD:**

2 firm pears of your choice, halved and cored
2 tablespoons vegetable oil
Salt and freshly ground black pepper to taste
1 bunch spinach, washed, dried, and leaves torn into bite-size pieces
½ cup crumbled Clemson or other crumbly blue cheese

1. To prepare the dressing, preheat the oven to 450°F.

2. Toss the sliced onions with 2 tablespoons of the peanut oil, place them on a baking sheet, and roast them in the preheated oven for 6 to 8 minutes or until they soften slightly.

3. Prepare a medium-high grill. Grill the onions for 4 minutes on each side. They should be soft but not charred, which would make them bitter.

4. Put the vinegar, pepper, salt, mustard, and chives in a food processor. Add the grilled onions and process until the onions are finely chopped but not pureed. If there are 2 or 3 large pieces of onion left, it is preferable to remove them rather than overprocess the mixture and end up with a puree.

5. Transfer the mixture to a bowl. Slowly whisk in the olive oil and remaining peanut oil, teaspoon by teaspoon. Be careful not to add them too quickly, which could break the emulsion. Tightly covered, the dressing will keep in the refrigerator for a week. If it separates, whisk to bring it back together.

6. To cook the pears, heat the grill to medium or preheat the oven to 350°F.

7. Rub the pears with the vegetable oil and sprinkle with salt and pepper. Grill the pears for 8 to 10 minutes on each side or roast them on a lightly greased baking sheet in the preheated oven for 30 to 35 minutes. When the pears are done, they will be soft with a little firmness in the center. Set aside until cool enough to handle. Slice each pear half into 3 or 4 slices.

8. Toss the pear slices with the spinach in a large bowl. Season with salt and pepper to taste. Add enough of the dressing to moisten the spinach and pears (there will be dressing left over). Toss to combine. Place the salad on a serving platter, sprinkle with the crumbled blue cheese, and serve immediately.

# CAESAR SALAD WITH SPICY FRIED OYSTERS

This salad was on the menu at Louis's Charleston Grill from opening day to closing day and was the most popular of all the salads offered. At the new Louis's, we offer it as a special and it always gets rave reviews. It is fairly easy to do, but it does require last-minute preparation, as the oysters must be fried and served immediately. The Spicy Fried Oysters by themselves make a great appetizer with Horseradish Cream Sauce (see page 17).

Parmesan shards are very thin triangular slices carefully shaved from a large wedge of Parmesan cheese. Their size and shape give a sense of drama to the salad's presentation. If this is not practical for you, grated fresh Parmesan works as well tastewise, but be sure to use a fine Parmigiano-Reggiano.

Makes 4 entrée salads or 6 first-course salads.

**FOR THE DRESSING:**

1 tablespoon finely minced onion
1 tablespoon Dijon mustard (I use Grey Poupon)
1 large egg yolk
⅓ cup red wine vinegar
1 tablespoon fresh lemon juice
2 tablespoons minced garlic
3 anchovy fillets, crushed
½ cup peanut oil
½ cup extra virgin olive oil
¼ teaspoon salt
¼ teaspoon freshly ground black pepper

**FOR THE OYSTERS:**

⅓ cup salt
2 tablespoons cayenne pepper
1 tablespoon plus 1 teaspoon gumbo filé powder (available in grocery stores)
1 tablespoon onion powder
1 tablespoon garlic powder
1 tablespoon ground white pepper
1 tablespoon paprika
1 tablespoon freshly ground black pepper
2 cups all-purpose flour
6 cups peanut oil
½ gallon select shucked oysters (about 40 oysters)

**FOR THE CROUTONS:**

1-pound loaf French bread
½ cup extra virgin olive oil
Salt and freshly ground black pepper to taste

**TO ASSEMBLE:**

8 cups (about ¾ pound) romaine lettuce, washed, dried, and cut into ½"-thick slices
¾ cup dressing
24 croutons
The fried oysters
4 tablespoons fresh Parmesan cheese shards

1. To prepare the dressing, put the onion, mustard, egg yolk, vinegar, lemon juice, garlic, and anchovies in a nonreactive bowl, a blender, or a food processor. Whisk or process these ingredients together.

2. Slowly whisk in the peanut oil and olive oil or very slowly pour them into the blender or food processor, teaspoon by teaspoon. Be careful not to add them too quickly, which could break the emulsion. Add the salt and pepper. Tightly covered, the dressing will keep in the refrigerator for a week. If it separates, whisk to bring it back together.

3. To make the croutons, preheat the oven to 350°F.

4. Cut the French bread into ½" pieces, leaving the crust on. Toss the bread with the olive oil, salt, and pepper.

5. Place the croutons on a baking sheet and bake in the preheated oven for about 20 minutes or until they are browned and crisp. Toss them once or twice while baking so that they brown evenly. Remove from the oven and reserve.

6. To prepare the oysters, combine the salt, cayenne pepper, gumbo filé powder, onion powder, garlic powder, white pepper, paprika, and black pepper. Stir to mix well. Add 2 tablespoons of this spice mixture to the 2 cups of flour. Stir to mix well. Stored in a tightly covered container in a cool place, the remaining spice mixture will keep for 2 months. If you fry oysters often, having the spice mixture already made will be handy.

7. Heat the peanut oil in a heavy skillet that is large enough for the oil to be 1½" deep but not more than halfway up the sides. The temperature of the oil should be 350°F on a frying thermometer.

8. Working with a dozen oysters at a time, sprinkle them with ½ teaspoon of the spice mixture and toss to coat evenly. Then toss the oysters quickly in the spice-flour mixture, coating them well but shaking to remove any excess flour. Do not leave the oysters sitting in the flour or they will get soggy.

9. Drop the oysters gently into the hot oil. Do not crowd the skillet by adding too many at once. The oysters should not touch each other. If you put in too many, the temperature of the oil will drop and the finished oysters may be greasy. Move them around with a slotted spoon so that they don't stick to the skillet or each other. Fry the oysters for 45 to 60 seconds. When they are done, they should be golden brown. It is important not to overcook them, because they will lose their delectable juices. If you suddenly hear popping and sputtering from the skillet, remove the oysters immediately; that's a sign that they're beginning to overcook. Otherwise, remove the oysters with a slotted spoon when they are golden brown and place them on a paper towel to drain, changing the towel if it begins to get saturated with oil.

10. To assemble individual salads, divide the lettuce among 4 to 6 plates, depending on whether the salad is an entrée or a first course. Add the dressing. Sprinkle the croutons, oysters, and Parmesan cheese over the lettuce. Serve immediately.

NOTE: Oysters actually need no cooking to be eaten, as on the half shell. When frying, they are ready when they float to the top; however, most people like to cook them a little longer so that they get extra crispy and more golden brown.

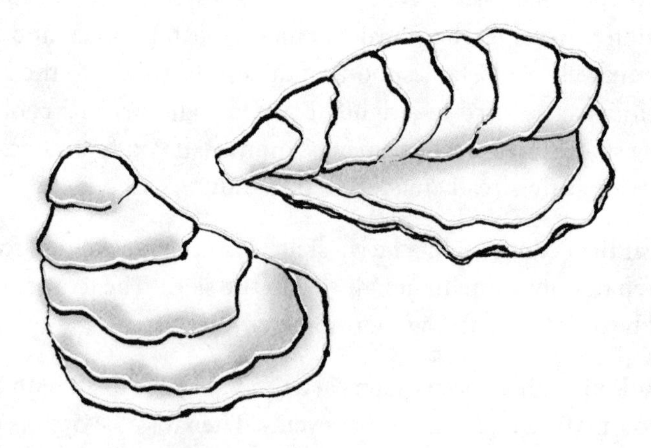

# COUNTRY HAM AND WHITE BEAN SOUP WITH MUSTARD GREENS

This is our restaurant's favorite soup for cold weather. It's a rather simple soup, but it's extremely satisfying. We make a number of variations through the year by changing the country ham to pancetta or sometimes prosciutto, and the greens might include spinach or arugula. Be sure to try the soup at least once with a hot skillet of cornbread. Cornbread is part of the soul of the South.

Serves 4 to 6 people.

- ½ pound dried Great Northern beans
- 2 tablespoons extra virgin olive oil
- ½ pound country ham, trimmed of all fat and julienned into ¼" × 1" pieces
- 1 cup finely diced yellow onion
- 2 teaspoons minced garlic
- 6 sprigs fresh thyme
- 4 cups chicken stock (see page 5)
- 8 ounces mustard greens, rinsed and stemmed
- Salt and freshly ground black pepper to taste

1. Pick through the beans for stones and imperfections. Rinse well in cold water. Cover with water and soak overnight. When ready to cook the beans, drain them and rinse again with cold water. Set in a colander to drain.

2. Heat the olive oil in a heavy-bottomed soup pot over medium-high heat. Add the ham, onion, garlic, and thyme. Stir well to combine and sauté for 6 to 8 minutes or until the onion is translucent but not brown. Add the beans and chicken stock and simmer for about 1 hour or until the beans are tender but not mushy. Add the mustard greens and simmer for 8 to 10 minutes or until they are tender and wilted. Season with salt and pepper to taste, keeping in mind that the country ham has already added salt to the soup.

# SOUTHERN FRIED CATFISH

As a bottom-feeder, line-caught catfish have frequently been shunned by many people, but now that most catfish are farm raised, attitudes have changed. An additional advantage of today's aquaculture is the availability of fresh catfish throughout all the seasons. We feature this dish on the menu several times a year, especially in the summer as part of Louis's Fish Fry Platter. It's a good fish and it's a good value. Serve the fried catfish with creamy grits (see page 71) or garlic and herb mayonnaise (see page 15).

Serves 4 people.

1 cup buttermilk
⅔ cup beer (do not use dark beer)
Eight 4-ounce catfish fillets or four 8-ounce fillets split down the middle
1 cup yellow cornmeal
1 cup all-purpose flour
½ cup rice flour
1 tablespoon paprika
2 tablespoons salt
2 tablespoons freshly ground black pepper
Peanut oil for deep frying

1. Combine the buttermilk and beer in a nonreactive bowl. Add the catfish fillets and refrigerate for 2 hours, but no longer.

2. Combine the cornmeal, all-purpose flour, rice flour, paprika, salt, and pepper in a small bowl and mix well.

3. Drain the fillets and toss them lightly in the breading mixture to coat them. Place the breaded fillets in a single layer on a baking sheet lined with wax paper. Don't let the fillets touch. Refrigerate for 30 minutes.

4. Preheat the oven to 200°F.

5. Pour enough peanut oil into a heavy skillet so that it is 2" deep. Heat the oil to 355°F on a frying thermometer. Carefully drop in the fillets 2 at a time. Fry them for about 2½ minutes on each side or until they are just golden brown.

6. Remove the fillets with a slotted spoon and place them on a paper towel to drain. Transfer the fillets to a platter and keep them warm in the preheated oven until they are all fried. Work quickly so that they do not get overdone. Serve immediately.

# PEPPER-SEARED TUNA WITH GREENS AND BEANS

This is a great recipe to enjoy with a bottle of red wine. Because the tuna takes on a meaty texture when seared in this manner, it can be paired with a fairly meaty Cabernet or Cabernet-Merlot blend. Dan Kennerty, a local farmer, brings us very young mustard greens that are much less assertive than the ones usually available in stores. Any will work well, but the young ones are quite a delicacy.

Serves 4 people.

**FOR THE GREENS AND BEANS:**

- ½ cup dried cannellini beans
- 2½ cups chicken stock (see page 5)
- ¼ cup roughly chopped yellow onion
- 2 sprigs fresh thyme
- 1 bay leaf
- ½ cup julienned yellow onion
- ½ cup white wine
- 1 teaspoon saffron
- ⅓ cup julienned apple-smoked bacon
- 6 cups young, tender mustard greens, washed and stemmed
- 2 tablespoons sesame oil
- Salt and freshly ground black pepper to taste

**FOR THE TUNA:**

- Four 6-ounce tuna fillets, grade-A or sushi grade
- 2 tablespoons, more or less, freshly ground coarse black pepper (do *not* use cracked pepper)
- 1 tablespoon peanut oil
- ½ teaspoon salt

1. Pick through the beans for stones and imperfections. Rinse well in cold water. Cover with water and soak overnight.

2. When ready to cook the beans, drain them and rinse with cold water. Place the beans in a nonreactive pot. Add the chicken stock, chopped onion, thyme, and bay leaf and bring to a simmer over medium-high heat. Reduce the heat to low and cook the beans for 45 to 50 minutes or until they are tender but not mushy, maintaining just a bare simmer and stirring occasionally. Remove the sprigs of thyme and the bay leaf. Leave the beans in the pot to cool in their own cooking liquid.

3. Place the julienned onion, wine, and saffron in a small heavy-bottomed nonreactive saucepan and cook over medium-high heat for about 5 minutes or until the onion is just limp and bright yellow from the saffron, but not browned at all. There should be approximately 1 tablespoon of liquid remaining in the pan. Remove from the heat.

4. Sauté the bacon in a large heavy-bottomed sauté pan over medium-high heat for about 8 minutes or until it is crisp. Remove the bacon and discard all but 1 tablespoon of the grease. Apple-smoked bacon is leaner than regular bacon, so there shouldn't be much grease in the pan. Drain the beans and add to the bacon grease along with the onion and bacon. Heat thoroughly. Add the greens and heat them, stirring, for 2 to 3 minutes or until they wilt. Stir gently so the beans don't get mashed. Stir in the sesame oil. Season with salt and pepper to taste. Keep warm while cooking the tuna.

5. Remove the tuna fillets from the refrigerator about 15 minutes before you are ready to cook them, so that they can come to room temperature. Rub both sides of the fillets with the pepper.

6. Heat a heavy skillet over medium-high heat until very hot. Add the oil and heat until hot but not smoking. Add the tuna fillets 2 at a time and sear for 2½ minutes. Turn the fillets over and sprinkle them with ¼ teaspoon of the salt. After another 2½ minutes, turn the fillets back over and sprinkle that side with ¼ teaspoon of the salt. For a rare fillet, remove from the pan immediately. For a well-done fillet, cook about 3 minutes longer on each side.

7. Divide the greens and beans among 4 plates and top with a serving of seared tuna. Serve immediately.

# CHARLESTON RED RICE WITH CHICKEN AND SAUSAGE

Rice is always present in the Lowcountry, and many people will not let a day pass without at least one serving. This recipe is a variation of the rice pilau of Pawleys Island. It's a great dish for a lot of people, but it can't sit too long or the rice overcooks and becomes unpleasantly mushy.

Serves 6 people.

¼ cup peanut oil
6 chicken thighs, skin on but trimmed of any fat
Salt and freshly ground black pepper to taste
½ cup finely chopped yellow onion
1 tablespoon minced garlic
1 pound smoked sausage, cut into ¾" pieces (if using links, divide in a sensible way)
1⅓ cups uncooked converted long-grain white rice (I use Uncle Ben's)
2⅔ cups chicken stock (see page 5)
⅔ cup crushed tomatoes
1 tablespoon Tabasco sauce

1. Preheat the oven to 350°F.

2. Heat the peanut oil over medium heat in a medium-size ovenproof pot with a cover. Add the chicken thighs and sauté them for about 2 minutes per side or until they are nicely browned. Remove the thighs, season them with salt and pepper, and reserve. Pour off all of the oil and juices except for 2 tablespoons.

3. Add the onion and garlic to the oil and sauté over medium heat for about 3 minutes or until the onion is translucent. Add the sausage and sauté for 4 to 5 minutes or until nicely browned, stirring occasionally. Add the rice and stir to coat well with oil.

4. Meanwhile, in a small saucepan, heat the stock to a simmer. Return the chicken to the pot with the rice and add the hot stock, tomatoes, and Tabasco. Stir well to combine. Add salt and pepper to taste. Cover tightly and bake in the preheated oven for 20 to 30 minutes or until the chicken and rice are cooked and the liquid is absorbed. (Note that this is a moist dish, not one where the grains of rice are dry and fluffy.) Check seasoning for salt and pepper.

5. Serve immediately or set aside to cool to room temperature. You may refrigerate for up to 2 days. To reheat, cover with aluminum foil and bake in a 325°F oven, stirring occasionally, for 20 to 30 minutes or until heated through.

# PANNED QUAIL WITH PAN GRAVY

Quail is a favorite on most Southern tables, probably because quail hunting has a long tradition in the Lowcountry. The largest quail farm in the world is located in South Carolina, making the bird readily available to us in all seasons.

Quail freezes very well and is available frozen in most food stores. It typically comes whole or semi-boneless. Semi-boneless, which we use in our quail recipes, has the rib cage removed but the leg and wing bones intact and is ready for stuffing, roasting, grilling, or simply sautéing, as in this recipe. If the quail are not semi-boneless and removing the rib cage is a chore you'd prefer not to do, simply cut the quail in half down the center of the breast and through the backbone. This method will require more "hand eating," but it's perfectly acceptable. And if the quail were "home shot," look out for buckshot as you chew.

Serves 4 people.

**FOR THE QUAIL:**

8 semi-boneless quail
3 cups buttermilk
2 large egg yolks
2 cups all-purpose flour
½ teaspoon baking soda
1 tablespoon salt
2 teaspoons freshly ground black pepper, or to taste
1 cup peanut oil

**FOR THE PAN GRAVY:**

½ cup all-purpose flour
2 cups chicken stock (see page 5)
3 cups whole milk
1 cup plus 1 tablespoon heavy cream
1 sprig fresh thyme or ¼ teaspoon dried thyme
2 bay leaves
Salt and freshly ground black pepper to taste

1. Rinse the quail under cold running water. Pat dry. Put the quail and buttermilk in a large nonreactive bowl, cover, and marinate in the refrigerator for at least 4 hours or overnight, turning the quail occasionally.

2. Just before cooking, remove the quail and add the egg yolks to the buttermilk, whisking lightly to incorporate them. This allows for a little heavier breading and also helps the crust to brown. Return the quail to the buttermilk and yolk mixture.

3. In a medium bowl, mix the flour, baking soda, salt, and pepper. Remove the quail from the buttermilk and dredge them lightly in the flour, shaking well to remove any excess flour.

4. Put the peanut oil in a cast-iron skillet. The exact amount will be determined by the size of your pan. You don't want the oil to cover the quail; you want just enough to come about halfway up the quail, so that turning them once will cook them. Heat the oil over medium-high heat to 300°F on a frying thermometer or until very hot but not smoking.

5. Add the quail, but no more than 4 at a time. Putting too many in the pan will bring the temperature of the oil down, resulting in greasy quail. Panfry them for about 3 minutes breast side down, then turn them over and continue for 3 minutes more on the back side, rotating them 180° once on each side. They should be nicely browned yet still a little pink in the center.

6. Drain the quail on paper towels. Remove them to a platter and keep them warm in a 200°F oven while cooking the gravy. Be sure to move quickly so they don't dry out.

7. Pour off all but ¼ cup of the peanut oil from the pan used for the quail. Be careful to leave all of the browned bits in the pan, because they add extra flavor to the gravy.

8. Add the flour to the pan, stirring to prevent lumps. Be sure to scrape up any of the browned bits that are stuck to the bottom of the pan. Cook the flour over medium heat for a few minutes to brown it, stirring occasionally. Don't be timid. You want a nice rich brown color.

9. Increase the heat to high and whisk in the chicken stock, milk, and cream. Add the thyme and bay leaves. Season well with salt and pepper. Reduce the heat to a simmer. Stir the gravy constantly with a whisk to prevent lumps. At this point, the gravy should be light to medium brown and a little thicker than cream. Simmer the gravy for about 15 minutes or until it is thick enough to coat a spoon. Remove the sprig of thyme and bay leaves. If the gravy is lumpy, strain it into a fresh pan. Serve immediately or, if you want to hold the gravy, reserve a tablespoon of cream to spoon over the top to prevent a skin from forming. Then you may set the gravy aside until ready to serve. Reheat it gently just before serving, stirring the cream on top into the gravy.

NOTE: Traditionally, cream gravy uses pan drippings and therefore is made after the quail has been fried. It is easy to make the gravy in advance, however, using 2½ pounds of chicken backs and necks that have been dredged in seasoned flour and panfried in oil. When browned, continue with the gravy as described in this recipe. For extra flavor, return the backs and necks to the pan while you are simmering the gravy.

# DUCK BREASTS WITH ESPRESSO-INFUSED SAUCE AND CREAMY GRITS

We came up with this dish one morning during a cooking class held at the restaurant. It is really a version of our preserved duck with red-eye gravy, which is really a version of the classic country ham and red-eye gravy. We like to serve it with creamy grits.

Serves 4 people.

- 4 tablespoons rendered duck fat (see page 42)
- 4 large boneless duck breasts
- Salt and freshly ground black pepper to taste
- ¼ cup finely chopped shallots
- 1 carrot, peeled and finely chopped
- 1 large clove garlic, peeled and finely chopped
- 2 tablespoons crushed espresso beans (crush with a coffee grinder, nut grinder, or mortar and pestle)
- 2 cups duck stock (see page 6)
- ½ teaspoon minced fresh thyme or ¼ teaspoon crumbled dried thyme
- 2 tablespoons unsalted butter, at room temperature and cut into 8 pieces
- 1 recipe Creamy Grits (recipe follows)
- 2 sprigs fresh thyme for garnish (optional)

1. Heat 2 tablespoons of the duck fat in a large heavy-bottomed skillet over medium-high heat. Season the duck breasts with salt and pepper and place them in the skillet skin side down. Cook for 4 minutes, turn over, and cook about 2 minutes longer for medium rare. Transfer to a warm platter and tent with aluminum foil, shiny side down, to keep warm.

2. Heat the remaining duck fat in the skillet over medium-high heat until hot but not smoking. Add the shallots, carrot, and garlic and sauté for 3 to 4 minutes, stirring occasionally, until lightly browned. Stir in the crushed espresso beans. Stir in the stock and thyme and bring the mixture to a boil. Reduce the heat and simmer the sauce for 15 minutes or until it has reduced by half and has a strong coffee flavor. Pour the mixture through a fine sieve set over a medium saucepan, pressing hard on the solids.

3. Place the saucepan over medium-high heat and bring the sauce to a boil. Continue cooking until the sauce is reduced to ½ cup. Whisk in the butter 1 piece at a time. Season with salt and pepper to taste.

4. Thinly slice the duck breasts on the diagonal. Spoon the hot grits onto 4 warm plates. Place the slices of duck over the grits, spoon the sauce over the top, and garnish with the sprigs of thyme. Serve immediately.

## Creamy Grits

Makes 6 cups.

2 cups whole milk
2 cups water
1 teaspoon salt
1 cup uncooked quick grits *(not instant)*
4 tablespoons unsalted butter
1 cup heavy cream
2 teaspoons freshly ground black pepper

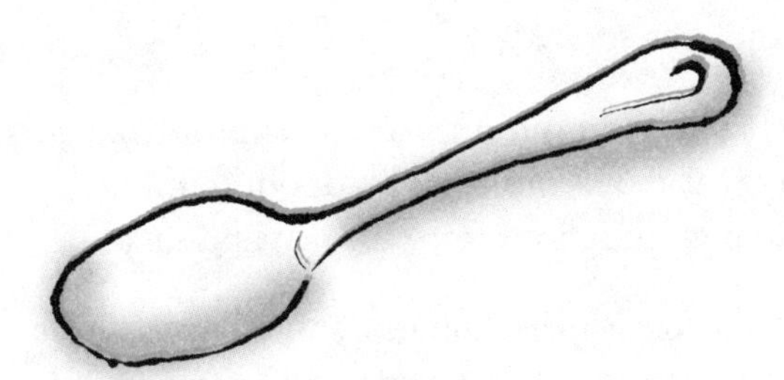

1. Bring the milk and water to a boil in a heavy-bottomed saucepan over medium heat. Stir in the salt. Slowly add the grits, stirring constantly. When the grits begin to thicken, turn the heat down to low and simmer for 30 to 40 minutes, stirring occasionally to prevent the grits from scorching.

2. Add the butter and cream, stirring to incorporate thoroughly, and simmer for 5 minutes. Stir in the pepper. Serve the grits immediately or keep them warm, covered, in a double boiler over simmering water.

NOTE: If the grits are too thick, stir in more cream or milk. Remember that grits solidify as they cool; they will get thicker once on the plates.

# OVEN-ROASTED VEAL CHOP

This recipe can be the center of a very elegant meal. Veal chops seem to be restaurant food as opposed to home food, even though they are an easy but impressive main course at home. To make them even easier, have the butcher prepare the chops for you, since cutting them from a bone-in loin can be a little tricky.

Serves 4 people.

4 tablespoons unsalted butter
4 tablespoons peanut oil
Four 10-ounce veal loin chops
1 cup thinly sliced shallots
2 cups dry white wine
1 cup veal stock (see page 9) or chicken stock (see page 5)
Salt and freshly ground black pepper to taste
1 teaspoon roughly chopped fresh thyme
1 teaspoon thinly sliced fresh tarragon

1. Preheat the oven to 375°F.

2. Heat the butter and oil in a large ovenproof skillet over medium-high heat. Add the veal chops and cook for about 6 minutes or until browned on both sides. Remove the chops from the pan and set aside.

3. Add the shallots to the liquids remaining in the pan and sauté over medium heat for about 5 minutes or until softened. Add the wine, increase the heat to high, and boil for about 6 minutes or until the liquids have reduced to ½ cup. Add the stock and return to a boil. Add salt and pepper to taste.

4. Place the veal chops on top of the shallots and put the skillet on the lower rack of the preheated oven. Cook to the desired degree of doneness, about 8 minutes for medium. Remove the chops from the pan and set aside.

5. Briskly reduce the cooking liquids remaining in the pan over medium-high heat for about 4 minutes or until they have thickened enough to coat the back of a spoon. Stir in the thyme and tarragon and taste for seasoning. Transfer the veal chops to warm serving plates and coat with the reduced sauce. Serve immediately.

# MUFFY'S MEAT LOAF DELUXE

Ron Roberts is a chef from north Georgia who now lives in Atlanta. Over the years, we've worked together in several restaurants. Ron is a gentle fellow with a predilection for baking. When he worked at the Pawleys Island Inn, he always had a big basket of muffins ready for the staff when the restaurant opened. Thus the nickname Muffy. Ron also came up with this meat loaf recipe for staff "family meals." It's a terrific recipe for what can otherwise be a mundane dish.

Serves 6 people.

4 tablespoons unsalted butter
1 cup chopped yellow onion
½ cup chopped green bell pepper
2 pounds lean ground beef (preferably chuck)
1 pound lean ground veal
1 pound lean ground pork
1 cup cottage cheese
1½ cups chili sauce
3 large eggs, lightly beaten
1 cup dried bread crumbs, made in a food processor from a sliced and dried baguette
½ cup red wine

8½" × 4" loaf pan

1. Preheat the oven to 350°F.

2. Heat the butter in a heavy-bottomed sauté pan over medium-high heat until hot but not smoking. Add the onion and bell pepper and sauté, stirring constantly, for 3 to 4 minutes or until the onion is wilted and translucent but not browned. Remove the pan from the heat.

3. In a large bowl, mix the beef, veal, and pork. Add the onion and green pepper along with the cottage cheese, ½ cup of the chili sauce, the eggs, and the bread crumbs. Combine well. Shape the meat loaf and place it in the loaf pan. Pour the red wine over it, then pour the remaining cup of chili sauce over it. Bake the meat loaf in the preheated oven for about 1 hour or until the juices run clear. A meat thermometer inserted in the center should read 155°F. Let the meat loaf rest in its pan for 10 minutes before slicing.

# ROASTED PORK LOIN WITH RED CABBAGE BRAISED WITH CHESTNUTS

Pork and cabbage somehow naturally go together, and the sweet richness of the chestnuts complements both of them. Be careful not to overcook the pork. Years ago it had to be cooked to 190°F, but I like it at 140°F, when it is medium, juicy, and tender.

Serves 6 people.

- ⅓ cup peanut oil
- 2-pound boneless pork loin
- 2 sprigs fresh thyme
- 2 sprigs fresh rosemary
- 2 sprigs fresh sage
- 2 sprigs fresh Italian parsley
- 2 bay leaves
- 1 tablespoon unsalted butter, melted
- ½ teaspoon salt
- ½ teaspoon freshly ground black pepper
- 1 recipe Red Cabbage Braised with Chestnuts (recipe follows)

1. Preheat the oven to 400°F.

2. Heat the peanut oil in a heavy sauté pan over high heat until it is just starting to smoke. Pat the pork loin dry and place it fat side down in the hot oil. Sear the loin, turning, until it is nicely browned on all sides.

3. Remove the pork loin from the pan. Place the herbs on a rack in a roasting pan and place the pork loin on top of them. Drizzle the melted butter over the loin, then season it with the salt and pepper. Roast the loin in the preheated oven for 30 to 40 minutes or until it has reached an internal temperature of 140°F. Let the pork rest for at least 10 minutes before slicing.

4. Place the hot cabbage, without too much cooking liquid, on a serving platter. Overlap the slices of pork on top of the cabbage and serve immediately.

# Red Cabbage Braised with Chestnuts

Serves 6 people.

- 3½ pounds red cabbage
- ¼ cup rendered duck fat (see page 42) or peanut oil
- ½ cup peeled and thinly sliced carrots
- 4 cups thinly sliced yellow onions (about 1¼ pounds)
- 1 cup red wine
- 3 cups chicken stock (see page 5)
- 1 tablespoon red wine vinegar
- 1 teaspoon salt
- ¾ tablespoon freshly ground black pepper
- 1 teaspoon sugar
- 1 bay leaf
- 1 sprig fresh parsley
- 1 sprig fresh thyme
- 4 cloves garlic, peeled and crushed
- 2 cups canned or cooked frozen unsweetened chestnuts, drained

1. Trim and core the cabbage. Slice it into ½"-thick ribbons. You need 14 cups. This seems like a lot, but it will cook down considerably.

2. Heat the duck fat or peanut oil in a heavy-bottomed nonreactive pot over medium-high heat. Add the carrots and onions and sauté, stirring frequently, for 8 to 10 minutes or until the onions are translucent. Add the cabbage and sauté, stirring, until it wilts.

3. Add the red wine, stock, vinegar, salt, pepper, and sugar. Tie up the bay leaf, parsley, thyme, and garlic in cheesecloth to make a bouquet garni and add it to the pot. Stir everything to combine. Adjust the heat as necessary to bring the mixture to a simmer and cook, uncovered, for ½ hour or until the cabbage is just tender. Add the chestnuts and nestle them down into the cabbage. Continue to simmer for ½ hour. Remove the bouquet garni before serving.

# QUICK BBQ PORK SANDWICH WITH SWEET AND SOUR ONIONS AND CUCUMBERS

Barbecue is one of my favorite foods, but it tends to become an all-day affair with the slow cooking and frequent basting it usually requires. I created this recipe for *Gourmet* magazine as a sandwich that could be made, start to finish, in 45 minutes or less. It turns out well, so if time is not on your side—or even if it is—this makes an excellent sandwich.

Serves 6 people.

**FOR THE PORK RUB:**

1 tablespoon paprika
1 tablespoon sugar
1 tablespoon minced garlic
1 tablespoon coarsely ground black pepper
2 teaspoons kosher salt
1½ pounds pork tenderloin

**FOR THE BASTING SAUCE:**

½ cup red wine vinegar
½ cup apple cider vinegar
1 tablespoon red pepper flakes
Juice of 1 lemon

**FOR THE SORGHUM AND ALE BARBECUE SAUCE:**

1 tablespoon peanut oil
2 tablespoons minced shallots
1 tablespoon minced garlic
1 tablespoon red pepper flakes
1 tablespoon ground cumin
½ tablespoon chile powder
8 ounces premium ale
⅓ cup sorghum or molasses
1 tablespoon tomato paste
2 teaspoons red wine vinegar
1 teaspoon kosher salt

**FOR THE ONIONS AND CUCUMBERS:**

½ cup thinly sliced red onion
½ cup peeled, seeded, and diced cucumber
1 tablespoon sugar
2 tablespoons red wine vinegar
Salt and freshly ground black pepper to taste

**FOR THE BARBECUED PORK:**

2 tablespoons peanut oil
The reserved pork tenderloin
6 kaiser rolls, sliced for sandwiches

1. To prepare the pork rub, combine the paprika, sugar, garlic, pepper, and salt in a small bowl. Rub the pork tenderloin with the mixture and reserve.

2. To prepare the basting sauce, combine all the ingredients in a small bowl and set aside.

3. To prepare the barbecue sauce, heat the peanut oil in a small heavy-bottomed saucepan over medium-high heat until the oil just begins to sizzle. Add the shallots, garlic, pepper flakes, cumin, and chile powder and cook over medium heat for 5 minutes or until lightly browned. Be careful that the mixture does not burn.

4. Add the ale, sorghum or molasses, tomato paste, vinegar, and salt and simmer for 10 to 15 minutes or until the sauce has thickened.

5. Meanwhile, combine the onion, cucumber, sugar, and vinegar in a small bowl. Set aside.

6. Preheat the oven to 350°F.

7. To finish preparing the pork tenderloin, heat the 2 tablespoons of peanut oil in an ovenproof skillet over medium-high heat until nearly smoking. Add the pork and sauté for about 4 minutes or until it is browned on all sides. Transfer the skillet to the preheated oven and cook for about 15 minutes. Remove from the oven and allow to rest for at least 7 minutes. Slice the pork thinly on the diagonal. Put the slices in a small bowl and add any pork juices that have accumulated from the slicing along with ¾ cup of the basting sauce.

8. Warm the kaiser rolls in the preheated oven. Drain the onion-cucumber mixture and season to taste with salt and pepper. Remove the rolls from the oven and layer with the pork. Spoon on the desired amount of the sorghum and ale barbecue sauce and top with the onion-cucumber mixture. Serve with a big portion of Plantation Slaw (see page 216).

# HERBED DUMPLINGS

This particular dumpling is my favorite, very much like a biscuit but a little softer. It goes especially well with Stewed Rabbit Smothered with Onions (see page 122) or it can be served as a side dish with gravy.

Serves 4 people.

- 8 cups stock (use the stock of the main dish you are serving or chicken stock [see page 5] or even water)
- 1½ cups self-rising flour
- ½ cup chopped fresh herbs, such as parsley, thyme, rosemary, chives, chervil, or basil
- ½ teaspoon freshly ground black pepper
- 1 teaspoon salt
- 2½ tablespoons unsalted butter, cut into ½" pieces and chilled
- 1 large egg
- ¾ cup buttermilk

1. Bring the stock to a simmer in a large pot with a lid.

2. Meanwhile, combine the flour, herbs, pepper, and salt in a large bowl and mix well. Add the chilled butter, working it into the flour with a pastry cutter, a fork, or your fingertips until the butter pieces are a little larger than an English pea, but smaller than a lima bean. If you are using your fingers, work quickly so that the heat of your hands won't melt the butter.

3. Combine the egg and buttermilk in a small bowl and mix well. Pour into the flour and, using light pressure, fold the mixture a few times with a plastic spatula until it just holds together. Do not overmix. In order to make light dumplings, work the dough as little as possible.

4. Spoon golf ball–size dumplings into the simmering stock and bring the liquid back to a simmer over medium heat. Cover the pot tightly and cook the dumplings for 8 minutes or until the centers are no longer moist batter. Remove with a slotted spoon. Reserve the stock. Serve the dumplings immediately or transfer them to a bowl, cover with plastic wrap, and set aside. When ready to serve, pour 2 cups of hot stock over the dumplings to reheat them. Serve in the stock or in another "soupy" medium such as gravy.

# STEWED APPLES

This buffet dish is great for a brunch or a game supper. When the writer John Egerton came to my kitchen to demonstrate the virtues of Kentucky country ham (via ABC's *Good Morning America),* this was his chosen accompaniment. Its sweet simplicity is the perfect foil for the salty, chewy complexity of country ham—one of the true glories of Southern culture. This side dish can also double as a dessert, especially after casual meals such as picnics or barbecues.

Serves 4 to 6 people.

2 pounds tart, firm apples such as Granny Smith, McIntosh, or Winesap
5 tablespoons unsalted butter
1⅓ cups sugar
8 fresh sage leaves or ¼ teaspoon rubbed sage
½ bay leaf
Salt to taste
Juice of 1 lemon

1. Peel, core, and quarter the apples.

2. Melt the butter in a heavy saucepan over medium heat. Add the apples, sugar, sage, and bay leaf. Stir to mix well and dissolve the sugar. Add salt to taste.

3. Cook the apples over medium heat for about 12 minutes. They should be tender but still mostly hold their shape. Remove the sage leaves, if fresh, and the bay leaf. Taste the apples to see if the addition of a few drops of fresh lemon juice would heighten the taste. (I like to add about a teaspoon.)

4. Transfer the apples and their juice to a warm serving dish and serve immediately or cool them to room temperature, cover, and refrigerate. Tightly covered, the apples will keep in the refrigerator for 2 days. When ready to use, warm the apples over medium heat, stirring occasionally so that they don't stick to the bottom of the pan.

5. If serving as a dessert, remove the apples from the juice with a slotted spoon and cook the juice for 5 minutes over medium heat to reduce and thicken it slightly. Pour it back over the apples and serve them warm, at room temperature, or cold.

# FENNEL GRATIN

■ This is a Thanksgiving dish that's hearty and at the same time very refreshing. It can be made ahead on a busy cooking day. The fennel bulb is the white, round part of the stalk. I especially like fennel for its crunch and faint taste of licorice or anise.

Serves 6 to 8 people.

⅓ cup fresh lemon juice
Salt
Freshly ground black pepper
6 fennel bulbs, trimmed and cut vertically into ¼"-thick slices
6 tablespoons unsalted butter
3 cups thinly sliced yellow onions (about ¾ pound)
2 cups heavy cream
1½ cups finely grated Swiss cheese

6" × 9" gratin dish or similarly sized baking dish, buttered

1. Preheat the oven to 375°F.

2. Bring 3 quarts of water, the lemon juice, and a pinch of salt and pepper to a boil in a large nonreactive saucepan. Lower the heat to medium and add the fennel slices. Blanch the fennel for 8 minutes or until just tender. Use care not to break the slices. Drain. Place the slices on paper towels to absorb any excess liquid.

3. Heat the butter in a large heavy-bottomed sauté pan over medium-high heat. Add the onions and gently sauté them, stirring occasionally, until lightly browned. Season with salt and pepper to taste. Place the onions in the bottom of the gratin dish.

4. Bring the cream to a simmer in a medium saucepan and season it with salt and pepper. While it is heating, pick through the blanched fennel slices and reserve the nicest of the tulip-shaped ones for the top layer of the gratin. Remove and discard the cores from the remaining slices. Roughly chop the remaining slices and distribute them over the onions. Sprinkle half of the cheese over the chopped fennel. Neatly place the reserved tulip-shaped slices of fennel on top of the cheese and pour the hot cream over them. Top with the remaining cheese.

5. Bake the gratin in the preheated oven for about 55 minutes or until the fennel is tender and the top is nicely browned. Watch carefully because it can quickly overbrown. Serve immediately.

# FRESH FENNEL AND RICE

This is a family favorite that we make often at home and at the restaurant. These are relatively unusual flavors for rice in the Lowcountry, but it tastes wonderful.

Serves 4 people.

2 cups chicken stock (see page 5)
3 tablespoons extra virgin olive oil
½ cup diced fennel bulb (reserve the fronds)
1 cup uncooked basmati rice
½ cup Pernod liqueur
1 cup peeled, seeded, and finely diced tomato
Salt and freshly ground black pepper to taste

1. Bring the chicken stock to a boil in a large saucepan.

2. Heat the olive oil in a large heavy-bottomed saucepan over medium-high heat. Add the fennel bulb and cook for 3 to 4 minutes, stirring, until it is limp and translucent. Add the rice and stir to coat well with the oil. Add the Pernod and continue to cook the mixture until the liqueur is absorbed. Add the hot stock and stir to combine well. Reduce the heat, cover, and simmer for 15 to 20 minutes or until the rice is cooked through and all the liquid is absorbed.

3. Gently stir in the diced tomato.

4. Pick the lacy leaves off the fennel fronds and chop enough to make ⅓ cup. Add to the rice and toss to combine. Continue to cook the fennel and rice only long enough to heat through. Season with salt and pepper to taste. Serve immediately.

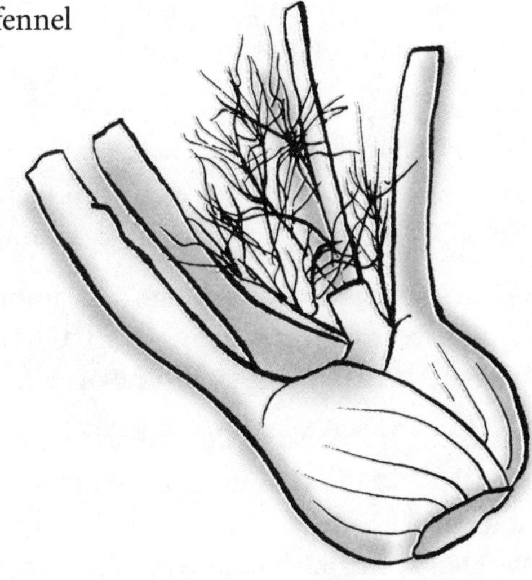

# BEER-BRAISED ONIONS

At the restaurant we use a lot of onions. When properly cooked, they are delicious. Sometimes I speculate that my fondness for onions stems from my father's disdain for them. When I was growing up, my mother always had to make two versions of dishes that contained them—one with and one without.

Boiler onions are medium-small onions—much larger (and easier to peel) than pearl onions. Most markets have a good supply of small yellow onions that make perfectly acceptable substitutes. Cipolline onions from Italy are small and rather flat, with a very sweet taste.

Serves 4 to 6 people.

3 tablespoons peanut oil
7 tablespoons unsalted butter
1 pound boiler onions or cipolline onions, peeled
2 cups veal stock (see page 9) or chicken stock (see page 5)
12 ounces dark beer (I use Beck's)
2 bay leaves
2 sprigs fresh thyme
6 sprigs fresh parsley
Sugar to taste
Salt and freshly ground black pepper to taste
½ cup chopped fresh parsley
2 tablespoons chopped fresh thyme

1. Heat the oil and 5 tablespoons of the butter in a heavy-bottomed sauté pan just large enough to hold the onions in a single layer. When the butter begins to sputter, add the onions and cook over medium-high heat for about 10 minutes or until they are nicely browned all over. Remove them from the pan and place on paper towels to drain. Discard the used oil and butter mixture and return the onions to the pan.

2. Add the stock, beer, bay leaves, thyme, and parsley. Bring the mixture to a boil. When it begins to boil, taste for bitterness. Most beers will add a little bitterness to the stock, which can be corrected by judicious use of a little sugar, but add it carefully, teaspoon by teaspoon, until the stock tastes as you prefer.

3. Reduce the heat to medium and simmer for about 15 minutes or until the onions are soft but not falling apart. Carefully remove the onions to a serving platter and keep warm in a 200°F oven.

4. Bring the cooking liquid back to a boil and reduce it until it thickens slightly. Add the remaining 2 tablespoons of butter and swirl it in. Add salt and pepper to taste. Strain the reduced juices over the onions. Sprinkle with the chopped parsley and thyme and toss to mix. Serve immediately.

# POTATO AND MUSHROOM GRATIN

■ As necessity is the mother of invention, we devised this particular gratin when we had an overabundance of wild mushrooms. Any variety of mushroom will do, as will rehydrated dried mushrooms. This is an earthy dish and goes well with most sautéed, roasted, or grilled meat and fowl.

Serves 8 people.

- 8 tablespoons unsalted butter
- 2½ cups diced white onions
- 4 cups thinly sliced shiitake mushroom caps (buy ½ pound and remove the stems)
- 2 tablespoons chopped fresh thyme
- 3 pounds baking potatoes
- Salt and freshly ground black pepper to taste
- 2 cups heavy cream

9" × 14" gratin dish or similarly sized baking dish, buttered

1. Preheat the oven to 350°F.

2. Heat 4 tablespoons of the butter in a heavy-bottomed sauté pan over medium heat. Add the onions and sauté, stirring occasionally, for about 3 minutes or until translucent. Add the shiitakes and thyme and sauté the mixture for 2 to 3 minutes or until the mushrooms are tender.

3. Peel the potatoes and slice very thinly lengthwise. Layer the slices in the gratin dish by overlapping them slightly in circles. Sprinkle with a quarter of the mushrooms. Season very lightly with salt and pepper. Continue to layer potatoes and mushrooms, and seasoning with salt and pepper, until all of the vegetables are used. Finish with a layer of potatoes. Press down lightly on the layers. Season lightly with salt and pepper and dot with the remaining 4 tablespoons of butter.

4. Bring the cream to a simmer. Pour it over the layered potatoes and mushrooms. Bake the gratin, uncovered, in the preheated oven for about 45 minutes or until there is no resistance when a small knife is inserted in the center. Let the gratin set for 5 minutes before serving.

# GREEN LENTILS

Try to find French green lentils for this recipe. They are superior in both taste and texture.

Serves 6 to 8 people.

- 3 cups dried green lentils
- 10 tablespoons unsalted butter
- 2 cups minced yellow onions
- 1 cup peeled and finely minced carrots
- ⅔ cup finely diced celery
- 4 cups chicken stock (see page 5)
- 6 cups water
- 1 cup mixed chopped fresh herbs, including parsley, thyme, rosemary, and oregano (I recommend using smaller amounts of rosemary and oregano, due to their stronger flavor)
- Salt and freshly ground black pepper to taste

1. Pick through the lentils for stones and imperfections. Rinse well in cold water and set aside to drain.

2. Heat 5 tablespoons of the butter in a heavy-bottomed saucepan over medium heat until hot but not smoking. Add the onions, carrots, and celery. Sauté, stirring occasionally, for 8 to 10 minutes or until lightly browned.

3. Add the lentils, stock, and water and stir to mix. Bring to a simmer, reduce the heat to low, and continue to cook, maintaining just a bare simmer, for 35 to 40 minutes or until the lentils are cooked but not mushy.

4. Drain any remaining liquid from the pan and discard. Stir in the remaining 5 tablespoons of butter and the herbs. Season to taste with salt and pepper. Serve immediately or cool to room temperature, cover, and refrigerate. Tightly covered, the lentils will keep in the refrigerator for 3 or 4 days. Gently reheat before serving.

# BUTTER PECAN ICE CREAM

This is everyone's favorite! I love the fragrance of the pecans cooking in the butter—it always reminds me of fall and family gatherings.

Makes 1½ quarts.

4 tablespoons unsalted butter
2 cups pecan pieces (about ½ pound)
4 cups half-and-half
6 large egg yolks
3 cups sugar
1 tablespoon pure vanilla extract

1. Heat the butter in a medium sauté pan over medium heat until melted. Add the pecans and cook them in the butter for 10 to 15 minutes or until they are roasted and aromatic. Stir frequently and adjust the heat if necessary to prevent scorching. Remove the pan from the stove and set aside.

2. Bring the half-and-half to a low boil in a heavy-bottomed saucepan over medium heat.

3. Meanwhile, put the egg yolks into the bowl of an electric mixer. With the whisk attachment, slowly beat the sugar into the yolks until the mixture lightens in color.

4. Prepare an ice bath by fitting an empty 3-quart bowl into a large bowl of ice.

5. Remove the half-and-half from the heat. Take 2 cups and slowly pour it into the bowl of the electric mixer, continuing to use the whisk attachment to combine it with the yolks and sugar. Slowly pour the mixture into the saucepan with the remaining half-and-half, now whisking by hand.

6. Return the saucepan to the stove. Stirring constantly with a wooden spoon or rubber spatula, gently cook the mixture over low heat for 5 to 10 minutes or until it is thick enough to coat the back of a spoon. You now have custard. Immediately strain the custard into the 3-quart bowl in the ice bath to avoid further cooking. Stir in the butter and nuts; while the mixture is still hot, the butter can be absorbed. Stir in the vanilla.

7. Chill the custard overnight in a covered container. When ready to churn, pour the chilled custard into a prepared ice cream maker and proceed according to the manufacturer's instructions.

# CHOCOLATE TEQUILA ICE CREAM

■ This is an adaptation of an ice cream made by Stephan Pyles, the chef of Star Canyon and AquaKnox in Texas. It's an interesting combination of flavors. We eventually made it part of a banana split that became a very popular dessert.

Makes 1½ quarts.

10 ounces bittersweet or semisweet chocolate, finely chopped
¾ cup gold tequila
½ teaspoon pure vanilla extract
3 cups half-and-half
2 cups heavy cream
½ cup honey
¼ cup plus 2 tablespoons unsweetened cocoa powder
Pinch of salt
6 large egg yolks
½ cup sugar

1. Put the chocolate, tequila, and vanilla in a 3-quart bowl and set aside.

2. Bring the half-and-half, cream, honey, cocoa, and salt to a low boil in a heavy-bottomed saucepan over medium heat.

3. Meanwhile, put the egg yolks into the bowl of an electric mixer. With the whisk attachment, slowly beat the sugar into the yolks until the mixture lightens in color.

4. Remove the half-and-half mixture from the heat. Take 2 cups and slowly pour it into the bowl of the electric mixer, continuing to use the whisk attachment to combine it with the yolks and sugar. Slowly pour the mixture into the saucepan with the remaining half-and-half mixture, now whisking by hand.

5. Return the saucepan to the stove. Stirring constantly with a wooden spoon or rubber spatula, gently cook the mixture over low heat for 5 to 10 minutes or until it is thick enough to coat the back of a spoon. You now have custard.

6. Pour the hot custard into the bowl with the chocolate, tequila, and vanilla and vigorously whisk the mixture until the chocolate completely melts. Strain the custard into a refrigerator container, cover, and chill overnight. When ready to churn, pour the chilled custard into a prepared ice cream maker and proceed according to the manufacturer's instructions.

# HONEY AND THYME ICE CREAM

■ On my first visit to France, I had a version of this ice cream at the then 3-star restaurant Moulin de Mougins. It was part of a trio of desserts that reflected the flavors indigenous to the chef Roger Vergé's locale. After that meal, I was able to better understand the relationship between food and location, which is as important to cooking as the microclimate is to wine making.

Makes 1 quart.

2 cups half-and-half
½ cup sugar
4 sprigs fresh thyme
12 large egg yolks
¾ cup honey
⅓ cup heavy cream, chilled

1. Bring the half-and-half, ¼ cup of the sugar, and the thyme to a low boil in a heavy-bottomed saucepan over medium heat.

2. Meanwhile, put the egg yolks into the bowl of an electric mixer. With the whisk attachment, slowly beat the remaining ¼ cup of sugar into the yolks until the mixture lightens in color.

3. Prepare an ice bath by fitting an empty 2-quart bowl into a large bowl of ice.

4. Remove the half-and-half mixture from the heat and carefully remove the thyme sprigs. Take 1 cup and slowly pour it into the bowl of the electric mixer, continuing to use the whisk attachment to combine it with the yolks and sugar. Slowly pour the mixture into the saucepan with the remaining half-and-half mixture, now whisking by hand. Set aside.

5. Place the honey in a small saucepan and warm it over low heat.

6. Meanwhile, return the saucepan with the half-and-half mixture to the stove. Stirring constantly with a wooden spoon or rubber spatula, gently cook the mixture over low heat for 5 to 10 minutes or until it is thick enough to coat the back of a spoon. You now have custard. Immediately remove the custard from the stove, stir in the warm honey and chilled cream, and strain into the 2-quart bowl in the ice bath to avoid further cooking. Chill the custard overnight in a covered container. When ready to churn, pour the chilled custard into a prepared ice cream maker and proceed according to the manufacturer's instructions.

# OLD-FASHIONED BANANA PUDDING

Banana pudding is the ultimate comfort food of my childhood. My mother usually made it once a week. It's quick and easy, and I've added bourbon for another taste dimension. You may leave it out if you prefer, as the pudding is good either way. You may serve this banana pudding in an old-fashioned Pyrex pie dish with a scalloped rim (it fits perfectly), in individual serving dishes, or in a suitable decorative dish of your choosing.

Serves 8 to 10 people.

8 large eggs, separated
1¾ cups sugar
5 cups whole milk
1 cup heavy cream
½ cup plus 2 tablespoons cornstarch
¾ cup best-quality bourbon (optional)
½ teaspoon pure vanilla extract
1 cup water
½ teaspoon cream of tartar
1 box Nabisco Nilla Wafers
4 bananas, peeled and sliced into ¼"-thick rounds

1. Put the egg yolks and ½ cup of the sugar in the bowl of an electric mixer and, using the whisk attachment, beat them until they are light in color and form a ribbon.

2. Combine ½ cup of the sugar and the milk and cream in a nonreactive saucepan and bring them to a simmer over medium-high heat.

3. Sift the cornstarch over the egg yolk mixture and incorporate by hand.

4. Whisk 2 cups of the hot milk mixture into the egg yolk mixture by hand. Whisk the egg yolk mixture into the remaining hot milk mixture in the saucepan. Reduce the heat to medium and cook, stirring constantly, for 2 to 3 minutes or until the custard is bubbly and thick. Remove the pan from the heat, add ½ cup of the bourbon and the vanilla, and cool to room temperature.

5. Combine ¼ cup of the sugar, the remaining ¼ cup of bourbon, and the water in a small bowl and set aside.

6. Clean the bowl of the electric mixer, making sure there are no traces of grease in it. Place the egg whites and cream of tartar in the bowl and beat the egg whites until they form soft peaks. Gradually beat in the remaining ½ cup of sugar. The egg whites should still form peaks that can be shaped with a spoon.

7. Preheat the oven to 400°F.

8. One by one, dip vanilla wafers into the bourbon-water mixture and lay them on the bottom of your chosen serving dish. Cover the wafers with a layer of custard (use about a third of the custard). Follow with a layer of banana slices, placing them in circles. Cover the bananas with custard (about another third) and then add another layer of vanilla wafers that have been dipped in the bourbon-water mixture. Add a thin layer of custard, then the remaining banana slices. Cover with the remaining custard.

9. Spread the meringue over the top of the custard, being sure to cover the edges. Take a spoon and make little peaks in the meringue so that it won't be flat when baked. Place a ring of vanilla wafers, rounded side up, around the edge of the pudding, pushing them down just enough so that there appears to be a "crown" of wafers.

10. Bake the pudding in the preheated oven for 4 minutes or until the meringue feels set and the little peaks have browned. You may serve the pudding right away, cool it to room temperature and serve, or refrigerate it and serve the next day.

# GINGERED PEAR TARTE TATIN

This unusual combination of flavors makes for a nice fall dessert. Ginger is a savory accompaniment to the sweetness of the pears and its subtle heat is a nice counterpoint. We've made this tart for many years (since about 1982, I think) and it's always a welcome addition to the menu. This recipe works best with ripe but firm pears, such as comice or Bosc, as they hold their shape better when cooked.

When you make this tart there will be a good amount of wonderful, syrupy juice, which will come out when you invert it onto a plate. Be sure to select a large enough plate to accommodate the juice. This tart will not cut into neat slices, but is meant to be a home-style presentation of loose pears and delicious pastry.

Serves 12 people.

2⅓ cups sugar
½ cup water
16 tablespoons unsalted butter, cut into 16 pieces
3 tablespoons peeled and minced fresh ginger
8 ripe but firm Bosc or comice pears, peeled, cut in quarters lengthwise, and cored
1 recipe Best Pie Dough (see page 28), unbaked
1 recipe Caramel Sauce (see page 38)
1 recipe Crème Fraîche (see page 33)

10" pie pan

1. Preheat the oven to 425°F.

2. Combine 2 cups of the sugar and the water in a heavy-bottomed saucepan over medium-high heat. Bring the mixture to a boil, stirring only until the sugar dissolves. If there are any sugar crystals on the sides of the pan, brush them down with a clean pastry brush that has been dipped in water. Watching carefully, let the sugar continue to boil until it is a dark golden color. It is now caramelized sugar and must be treated carefully, because it is extremely hot and will stick to your skin if it splatters on you. Carefully pour the caramel into the pie pan, tilting and rotating the pan until the sides are coated as well as the bottom. Set the pan aside. (You will probably think there is too much caramel, but it really takes this much to properly caramelize the pears on the bottom.)

3. Place the butter, the remaining ⅓ cup of sugar, and the ginger in a large heavy-bottomed sauté pan over medium-high heat and stir until the sugar is dissolved. Add the pears and continue to stir for 8 to 10 minutes or until the mixture is hot and the pears have begun to soften a little. Pour the pear mixture out on a baking sheet with sides and set aside to cool.

4. Remembering that the tart is going to be inverted when you serve it, carefully arrange the cooled pear quarters in the pie pan, round side down. Beginning at the outside edge, place the quarters like the spokes of a wheel. Decoratively arrange pear quarters to fill the center. Cut the remaining pear quarters into 4 pieces each, mix them back into the butter and sugar mixture, and pour the mixture over the decorative layer of pears.

5. On a lightly floured surface, roll out the pie dough into a circle that is 1" wider than the pie pan. Place the circle on top of the pears and tuck the overhanging edge down inside the sides of the pan. Cut 3 1" air vents in the crust.

6. Place the tart in the preheated oven with a foil-lined baking sheet on the rack below to catch any drippings. Bake the tart for 45 to 50 minutes or until the crust is very crisp. Let it set at room temperature for 5 minutes before inverting.

7. Place a serving plate, inverted, on top of the pie crust. Quickly, decisively, and carefully invert the tart and serving plate together so that the crust ends up on the plate and the pears are on top of the crust. Be careful, keeping in mind all of the extra juice. Let the tart set at room temperature for 5 minutes. Serve with the caramel sauce and crème fraîche, passed separately.

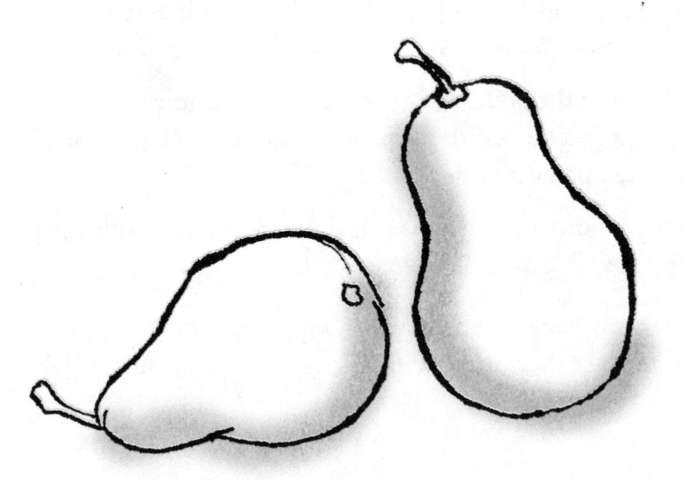

# PAWLEYS ISLAND PIE

When we took over the Pawleys Island Inn in 1980, this pie—the creation of our manager Susan Felder—was on the menu. Susan went on to open her own restaurant, the Rice Paddy, in Georgetown, South Carolina, and is now making the pie there, where it's still getting rave reviews. It is a quick and simple pie to make, but it has a particular, strong appeal.

Serves 8 to 10 people.

½ recipe Best Pie Dough (see page 28), baked
1 cup all-purpose flour
2 cups sugar
¼ teaspoon salt
2 cups semisweet chocolate chips
2 cups walnut pieces
4 large eggs
16 tablespoons unsalted butter, melted and cooled to room temperature
1½ teaspoons pure vanilla extract
1 cup heavy cream

12" tart pan or 10" Pyrex deep-dish pie pan

1. After baking the crust according to the recipe for Best Pie Dough, remove the crust from the oven to cool and reduce the temperature to 325°F.

2. Combine the flour, sugar, and salt in a large bowl, mixing by hand. Add the chocolate chips and walnut pieces and stir to combine well.

3. In a separate bowl, mix the eggs and butter together with a spoon. Add the vanilla and stir to combine well. Add the egg mixture to the flour mixture, again mixing by hand so that you will not have bubbles. Spoon the mixture into the baked crust.

4. Bake the pie in the preheated oven for 40 to 45 minutes if in a tart pan (50 to 60 minutes if in a deep-dish pie pan) or until the filling has set. Let the pie cool to room temperature before cutting.

5. Whip the cream until it forms soft peaks. Serve alongside the pie or garnish each piece with a dollop.

NOTE: If you are using a tart pan with a removable bottom, place a foil-lined baking sheet on the rack below it in the oven in case the filling leaks.

# PECAN PIE WITH RUM CREAM

This is one of the classic desserts of the South. The rum cream is a nice counterpoint to the pie's rich sweetness. If you can serve this when it is still warm, it will heighten the flavor of the nuts and provide a great contrast to the cool cream.

Serves 8 to 10 people.

**FOR THE PIE:**

- 1 recipe Sugar Dough (see page 31), baked
- 3 tablespoons unsalted butter, melted
- 1½ cups light corn syrup
- ¾ cup sugar
- ¾ cup packed light brown sugar
- 4 large eggs plus 2 large egg yolks
- 1 cup pecan pieces
- 1½ cups pecan halves

12" tart pan or 10" Pyrex deep-dish pie pan

**FOR THE RUM CREAM:**

- 2 cups heavy cream
- ¼ cup sugar
- Dark rum to taste (I use Myers's)

1. After baking the crust according to the recipe for Sugar Dough, remove the crust from the oven to cool and reduce the temperature to 350°F.

2. Pour the butter into the bowl of an electric mixer. Add the corn syrup, sugar, brown sugar, eggs, and additional egg yolks. Beat with the flat beater until all of the ingredients are thoroughly combined.

3. Spread the pecan pieces over the bottom of the pie shell. Cover them with the pecan halves and pour in the filling.

4. Bake the pie in the preheated oven for 40 to 50 minutes if in a tart pan (55 to 60 minutes if in a deep-dish pie pan) or until the filling has set. If you are using a tart pan, be sure to remove the pie from the pan while it is still warm; when the pie cools, the filling will stick to the pan anywhere it touched it. Let the pie cool to room temperature before cutting.

5. To make the rum cream, whip the cream with the sugar until it forms soft peaks. Fold in rum to taste. Serve alongside the pie or garnish each piece with a dollop.

**NOTE:** If you are using a tart pan with a removable bottom, place a foil-lined baking sheet on the rack below it in the oven in case the filling leaks.

# WARM CHOCOLATE SOUFFLÉ CAKE WITH A MOLTEN CENTER

Our version of the popular chocolate dessert. This is quick, easy, and can be prepared in advance and baked when you're ready to serve it. Most people think that it's tricky to make, so be sure to serve it when you're entertaining.

Serves 10 people.

- 1¼ cups unsalted butter
- 10 ounces bittersweet chocolate, chopped into small pieces
- 10 large eggs
- 1 cup sugar
- 2 vanilla beans, split lengthwise
- ½ cup cake flour
- 1 recipe Vanilla Ice Cream (see page 37)
- 1 recipe Kahlúa Fudge Sauce (see page 40)

Ten 6-ounce ramekins, buttered and sprinkled inside with sugar

1. Preheat the oven to 400°F.

2. Melt the butter and chocolate in the top of a double boiler over barely simmering water. Cool to room temperature and set aside.

3. Combine the eggs and sugar in the bowl of an electric mixer. With the side of a spoon, scrape the seeds out of the vanilla bean pods and add them to the egg mixture. Reserve the pods for another use. Using the whisk attachment, whip the mixture until it triples in volume.

4. Fold the cooled chocolate into the egg mixture. Sift in the flour. Combine thoroughly but gently by hand. Fill the ramekins half full. Place them on a baking sheet and bake in the preheated oven for 8 to 10 minutes. When the soufflés are done, they will easily pull away from the edge of the ramekins.

5. Unmold the hot soufflé cakes by carefully running a knife around the edge of the ramekins and inverting them onto dessert plates. Place a small scoop of vanilla ice cream on top of each cake and garnish the plate with 3 spoonfuls of Kahlúa fudge sauce. Serve immediately.

NOTE: The uncooked soufflés can be covered and held in the refrigerator for up to 2 days. Take the soufflés out of the refrigerator, bring to room temperature, and bake as directed. If you bake them straight from the refrigerator, add 2 or 3 minutes to the baking time.

# CORN CAKE WITH SORGHUM BUTTERCREAM

We came up with this dessert to take to the James Beard House years ago. It goes on our menu annually in the fall, the time of year that reminds me of cornmeal and sorghum making. Carl Garret, a friend and bluegrass musician, let me help one fall with the making of his sorghum. I have to admit that the music we played was more fun than boiling the sorghum. This cake is easier to slice when it's cold, but the flavor is at its height when near room temperature. Slice the cake ahead of time and let it warm up before serving.

Serves 10 people.

- 1 pound unsalted butter, at room temperature
- 3 cups sugar
- 10 large eggs, broken into a bowl but not beaten
- 1 tablespoon pure vanilla extract
- 2 cups stone-ground yellow corn-meal
- 2 cups all-purpose flour
- 1 tablespoon baking powder
- 1 teaspoon salt
- 1 recipe Sorghum Buttercream (recipe follows)
- 1 recipe Frangelico Strawberries (see page 97)
- 1 recipe Buttermilk Ice Cream (see page 219)

12" springform pan, buttered and sprinkled inside with sugar

1. Preheat the oven to 375°F.

2. Put the butter and sugar in the bowl of an electric mixer and beat with the flat beater until the mixture is fluffy and light in color. Add the eggs 1 at a time, scraping down the bowl after every 2 eggs. Add the vanilla and beat until the mixture is light and well mixed. Transfer to a large mixing bowl.

3. In a separate bowl, sift together the cornmeal, flour, baking powder, and salt. Gently but thoroughly stir the dry ingredients into the butter mixture.

4. Spoon the batter into the springform pan and bake in the preheated oven for about 1 hour or until a cake tester inserted in the middle comes out clean. Be careful not to overcook the cake or it will be dry. Cool in the pan for 10 minutes. Remove from the pan and cool on a rack to room temperature.

5. Slice the cake into 3 equal layers. Spread the sorghum buttercream between the layers. (It is not supposed to cover the top or sides.) Refrigerate the

cake until the buttercream has hardened. When it is cold, the filled cake can be wrapped tightly in plastic wrap and refrigerated for up to 2 days.

6. Slice the cake while still cold, leaving enough time for it to come to room temperature before serving. Place the slices of cake on plates with the outside edge down and the inside tip pointing up. Spoon the juice from the Frangelico strawberries around the cake, add a scoop of buttermilk ice cream, and garnish the plate with the strawberries.

## Sorghum Buttercream

This is a rich buttercream that will melt in extreme heat and harden with refrigeration. If you don't use it immediately, put it in the refrigerator, but be sure to let it come to room temperature before spreading.

Makes enough to fill a 12" Corn Cake.

- 2 cups sorghum
- 8 large egg yolks
- 2 pounds unsalted butter, cut into 32 pieces and refrigerated until 15 minutes before starting the recipe
- 1 tablespoon pure vanilla extract

1. Heat the sorghum in a heavy-bottomed nonreactive saucepan over medium heat until it comes to a boil.

2. Meanwhile, put the egg yolks in the bowl of an electric mixer and, using the whisk attachment, whip them until they lighten in color. With the mixer at medium speed, slowly pour the hot sorghum into the egg yolks. Increase the speed to high and continue to whip until the mixture has tripled in volume. Cool to room temperature.

3. With the mixer speed on medium, begin to add the butter 1 piece at a time, waiting to add another piece until the previous piece is mostly incorporated. Continue to add the butter until all of it is incorporated, stopping to scrape the bottom of the bowl several times. Reduce the speed to low and add the vanilla. Use immediately or cover and refrigerate.

**NOTE:** You may order sorghum from the Guenther Family Sorghum Mill, 4064 Muddy Pond Road, Muddy Pond, Tennessee 38574 (615-445-3589).

# FRANGELICO STRAWBERRIES

Although strawberries are thought of as seasonal to spring, they are now available all year. This recipe is so good with Corn Cake with Sorghum Buttercream (see page 95) that we fudge a little and serve strawberries in the fall, when sorghum is boiled. These berries exude juices, which we spoon around the cake as well.

Serves 4 people.

1 pint fresh strawberries
1 cup sugar
2 tablespoons Frangelico liqueur
2 tablespoons water

1. Wash the strawberries, remove the stems, and set aside.

2. Mix the sugar, Frangelico, and water in a small heavy-bottomed saucepan and bring to a boil over medium-high heat.

3. Place the strawberries in a bowl and pour the Frangelico syrup over them. Stir and set aside to cool. The berries will look glazed. When at room temperature, cover and keep in a cool place or refrigerate for up to 2 hours before using.

# Four Suggested Winter Menus



Oysters with Champagne Mignonette Sauce /108
Roasted Mushroom Broth /105
Christmas Goose and Gravy /117
Sweet Potatoes with Bourbon and Blue Cheese /135
Esau's Winter Greens /132
Rum Cake with Caramelized Bananas /140

Pâté of the South with Flatbread /109
Salad of Smoked Fish and Field Greens with a Cognac Vinaigrette /104
Leg of Lamb with Winter Fruits and Nuts /124
Buckwheat Groat Fritters /129
Jack Daniel's Chocolate Ice Cream with Warm Fudge Sauce /137

Brown Oyster Stew with Benne Seeds /106
Grouper with Rice and Green Chiles /111
Wild Mushroom Ragout /133
Butterscotch Pudding /138

Smoked Salmon Rillettes /103
Seared Duck Breasts with Buttery Savoy Cabbage /116
Chad's Mom's Sweet Potato Soufflé /134
Buttermilk Bread Pudding /139

## Winter in the Lowcountry

Frost may be infrequent in the Lowcountry, and snow still rarer, but even slightly cool weather is a very welcome occasion to enjoy some heartier foods. This is motivated in part by the hunting season, which lasts until January's end for waterfowl and through February for small animals. Although any chance to dine on rabbit, duck, or squab is welcome, my favorite recollections are the huge "hunt breakfasts" I used to prepare for plantation owners along the Waccamaw and Black Rivers.

Just outside Georgetown, South Carolina, there is an artery named Plantation Row. Here there is a succession of manor homes that remain in the ownership of private individuals. Although some of these properties were established by eighteenth-century rice planters, others were bought in the nineteenth century as winter hunting preserves for their owners, many of whom resided in the Northeast. It was not uncommon for these plantations to be boarded up for ten months of the year and used only briefly in late fall and early winter, during game season. In more modern times, the lucky plantation owners are able to meet the high cost of maintaining these residences by leasing hunting rights to private individuals and clubs. Sometimes after a hunt, I'd be invited to come over with my kitchen crew and prepare a lavish breakfast, which often included one of the duck, rabbit, or sausage recipes in this cookbook.

As in many other regions of the world, we tend to change our cooking techniques in the winter, turning to braises, stews, and roasts. In Charleston, rice is never out of season, but in winter we make chicken bog, or pilau. Historians of the South Carolina Lowcountry can tell you that the society was based on rice growing for nearly two centuries, until 1860 when the industry reached its pinnacle, and that pilau is the quintessential rice dish. As Karen Hess tells it in *The Carolina Rice Kitchen,* one seventeenth-century Englishman described pilau as "rice boiled so artfully that every grain is singly, without being added together, with spices, intermixt and a boil'd fowl in the middle." Indeed, pilau is still considered a great delicacy and any tampering with the simple, pristine ingredients of the original recipe is surely heresy.

By winter, even the long growing season of the Lowcountry produces very little other than tubers and greens. For generations, Charleston cooks have found that, in winter, dried fruits and nuts are savory and satisfying foodstuffs, and benne seeds (known elsewhere as sesame seeds) are commonly used. They are most frequently used in confections and my addition of them to oyster stew is somewhat unusual, but the seeds provide a distinctive complexity to what otherwise could be a rather dull offering.

Although the brief Lowcountry winter may provide fewer fresh vegetables and fruits, there is no shortage of delectables to savor, and certainly no lack of riches at the table. I am certain that you will find much here to enjoy in winter and you will discover, too, that dining based on seasonal availability is far better than turning to the lackluster and tasteless hothouse produce used in some kitchens.

# SMOKED SALMON RILLETTES

Easily prepared ahead and stored until ready to use, rillettes make a great cocktail snack or first course for an elegant meal.

Serves 20 people as a cocktail hors d'oeuvre or 8 people as a first course.

- 1½-pound fresh salmon fillet, skinless
- 1 small sprig fresh thyme or ¼ teaspoon dried thyme
- 1 cup fish stock (see page 8)
- ½ pound plus 2 tablespoons unsalted butter, at room temperature
- 1 tablespoon minced shallot
- ¼ teaspoon ground nutmeg
- ½ pound skinless smoked salmon, cut into small pieces

1. Place the fresh salmon fillet and thyme in a heavy-bottomed saucepan and cover with the fish stock. Gently heat the stock to a simmer and cook the fillet, turning it once, for 8 to 10 minutes or until just cooked through. It will still be somewhat translucent in the center. It is very important not to overcook the salmon. If your fillet isn't uniformly thick, you may want to cut off the thin end so that you can remove it from the stock while the thicker part finishes cooking.

2. Let the salmon cool in the stock to room temperature. Cover and refrigerate.

3. Melt 2 tablespoons of the butter in a heavy-bottomed sauté pan over medium heat. Add the shallot, nutmeg, and smoked salmon and sauté, stirring occasionally, for about 2 minutes or until the salmon turns mostly opaque. Remove the salmon from the pan, place on a plate, cover lightly, and refrigerate until thoroughly cooled.

4. Remove the cold poached salmon fillet from the fish stock and pat it dry. Cut it into slices about ¼" thick. Place the slices, the cold smoked salmon plus any of its juices, and the remaining ½ pound of soft butter on a baking sheet with sides. With 2 forks, gradually mix all of the ingredients together, using long pulling motions. When you finish, you should have slender pieces of salmon held together by creamy butter.

5. Place the rillettes in a crock and refrigerate for at least 4 hours or overnight. Tightly covered with plastic wrap, they will keep for 3 days in the refrigerator. Remove from the refrigerator at least 1 hour before serving.

6. If an hors d'oeuvre, serve the rillettes with toast points or crackers. If a first course, place each serving of rillettes on a few lightly dressed baby lettuce or watercress leaves and pass the toast points or crackers separately.

# SALAD OF SMOKED FISH AND FIELD GREENS WITH A COGNAC VINAIGRETTE

This is a pretty salad, and rather unusual. A mix of assertive greens such as arugula, radicchio, and frisée stands up best to the robust combination of flavors. It is essential that you taste the finished dressing for proper balance. A good many of the ingredients can vary in taste and strength. Doubling up on the greens and fish will make the salad into a rather special lunch dish.

Serves 4 people.

- 1 tablespoon red wine vinegar
- 2 tablespoons cognac
- ½ teaspoon sugar
- 1 large egg yolk
- 1 tablespoon Dijon mustard (I use Grey Poupon)
- 2 tablespoons peanut oil
- 4 tablespoons walnut oil
- 3 cups mixed baby greens, gently washed and dried
- 1 cup chopped fresh herbs, such as Italian parsley, chervil, chives, oregano, or tarragon
- 1 cup mixed smoked fish and/or shellfish, such as smoked salmon, sturgeon, mackerel, trout, scallops, oysters, mussels, or clams

1. Put the vinegar, cognac, sugar, egg yolk, and mustard in a small nonreactive bowl, a blender, or a food processor. Whisk or process the ingredients until well combined.

2. Slowly whisk in the peanut oil and walnut oil or very slowly pour them into the blender or food processor, teaspoon by teaspoon. Be careful not to add them too quickly or you will break the emulsion.

3. In a large bowl, toss the greens with the dressing, using as much or as little dressing as you like. Divide the greens among 4 serving plates. Toss the herbs in the large bowl and sprinkle them over the greens. Top the salads attractively with the smoked fish. Serve immediately.

NOTE: According to the American Egg Board, 1 tablespoon of vinegar has sufficient acid to kill any bacteria present in a raw egg.

# ROASTED MUSHROOM BROTH

This recipe was originally devised as a sauce base, but now I serve it as a comforting broth. The earthy flavor of the fresh mushrooms is intensified by the addition of dried mushrooms, and the final soup is capable of warming people on even the frostiest evening.

Serves 2 people.

1 fresh portobello mushroom
8 fresh shiitake mushrooms
1 large shallot, peeled and cut in half
1 large clove garlic, peeled
4½ tablespoons extra virgin olive oil
1 teaspoon kosher salt
1 teaspoon chopped garlic
¼ cup sliced shallots
2 sprigs fresh thyme or ½ teaspoon dried thyme
¼ cup dried chanterelles
4 cups chicken stock (see page 5)

1. Preheat the oven to 375°F.

2. Put the portobello mushroom, shiitake mushrooms, halved shallot, and whole garlic clove in a bowl. Toss with 3 tablespoons of the olive oil and the salt. Spread the mixture out on a baking sheet and roast in the preheated oven for about 15 minutes or until the mushrooms are tender and lightly browned.

3. Heat the remaining 1½ tablespoons of oil in a small heavy-bottomed stockpot until hot but not smoking. Add the chopped garlic, sliced shallots, and thyme. Cover and cook over low heat, stirring occasionally, for 3 to 4 minutes or until the shallots are translucent.

4. Add the chanterelles, chicken stock, and roasted mushroom mixture. Bring to a boil. Reduce the heat to medium and maintain a slow boil for about 1 hour or until the liquid is reduced by half. Skim off any fat or impurities that rise to the top in a foam.

5. Strain the broth through a sturdy sieve, pressing hard on the solids to extract all of their flavors, then pass the broth through a fine mesh sieve. Chill the broth for about 2 hours and spoon off any fat that rises to the top. Reheat when ready to serve. Tightly covered, the broth will keep in the refrigerator for 5 days.

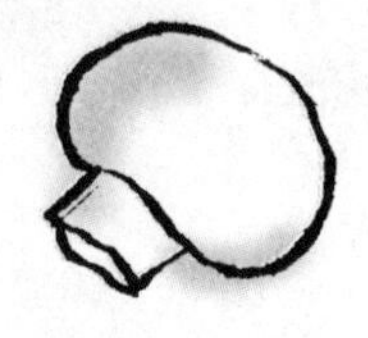

# BROWN OYSTER STEW WITH BENNE SEEDS

This is a very old recipe that comes from a plantation in Georgetown County, and it is one of the restaurant's most popular winter soups. The benne plant, more commonly known as the sesame plant, was brought to the Lowcountry from Africa and was thought to be lucky.

The number of oysters in the stew can vary because of their size and your taste. The oysters may be big singles or little ones from clusters, in which case add as many more as you like.

Serves 4 people.

- 4 tablespoons benne seeds
- 2 tablespoons peanut oil
- 2 tablespoons (about 1 ounce) very finely diced pancetta (If pancetta is not available, substitute bacon sliced crosswise into ¼"-thick strips)
- 2 tablespoons very finely minced yellow onion
- 2 tablespoons all-purpose flour
- 1¼ cups heavy cream
- 24 fresh oysters, shucked, but with their liquor strained and reserved
- 1¾ cups fish stock (see page 8) or bottled clam juice
- 1 teaspoon chopped fresh thyme
- 1 tablespoon fresh lemon juice
- 1 teaspoon sesame oil
- 2 tablespoons chopped fresh chervil or Italian parsley or a combination of both
- Salt and freshly ground black pepper to taste

1. Place the benne seeds in a small heavy-bottomed sauté pan over medium heat and dry roast them by cooking them for about 9 minutes or until they become dark and fragrant. Remove from the stove. Roughly crush half of the benne seeds with a spoon and reserve.

2. Heat the oil in a heavy-bottomed saucepan over low heat. Sauté the pancetta for about 5 minutes or until crisp and lightly browned. Remove the pancetta with a slotted spoon and place on paper towels to drain. Leave the oil and any fat from the pancetta in the saucepan.

3. Add the onion and crushed benne seeds to the saucepan and sauté for about 3 minutes, stirring frequently. When the onion is lightly browned, add the flour, stir well to combine, and cook for 2 minutes.

4. In a separate pan, heat the cream to just below a simmer.

5. Add the reserved oyster liquor, fish stock, and thyme to the onion and simmer, stirring with a whisk, for about 2 minutes or until the mixture is without lumps. Add the warm cream and simmer for 5 minutes. Add the oysters and the whole benne seeds, along with the lemon juice, sesame oil, and chervil or parsley. Leave the stew on the heat until the oysters just begin to curl. Quickly remove the saucepan from the heat and add salt and pepper to taste.

6. Divide the stew among 4 warm soup bowls. Garnish with the reserved pancetta and serve immediately, along with oyster crackers or buttered toast fingers. At the table, the stew should be hot and steamy and the oysters plump and juicy.

# OYSTERS WITH CHAMPAGNE MIGNONETTE SAUCE

■ Oysters are always best when just opened, but if you open them ahead of time, store them on a bed of ice in the refrigerator, covered with plastic wrap. They will keep for an hour. (Be sure that the ice doesn't melt and soak the oysters.) If possible, serve the oysters on ice—it makes for a wonderful, crispy oyster and a fine presentation. If you are eating really good briny oysters, this will be a great occasion to splurge a little on a superior flinty French Chablis.

Makes enough sauce for 12 oysters.

½ cup champagne vinegar
½ cup dry white wine
2 tablespoons minced shallot
¼ cup cracked black pepper
12 fresh oysters

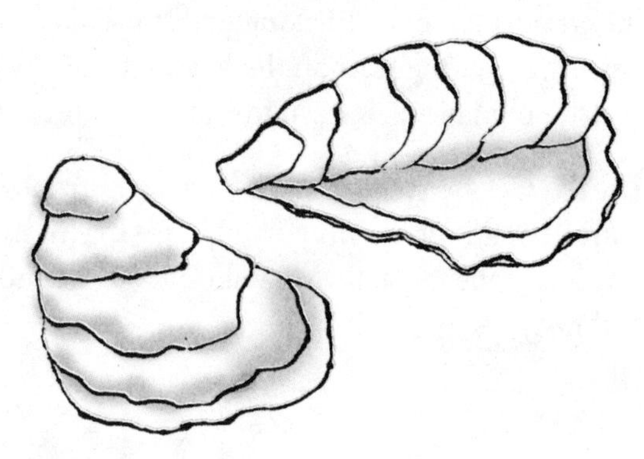

1. Combine the vinegar, wine, shallot, and pepper in a small nonreactive bowl. Cover and chill for at least 2 hours or overnight.

2. Carefully open the oysters, leaving them on the deep bottom shell. Be sure to slide a knife under the oyster to loosen it completely.

3. Top each oyster with a small spoonful of mignonette sauce, using more for larger oysters. Pass the rest of the sauce at the table.

# PÂTÉ OF THE SOUTH

When I was growing up, a pimento cheese sandwich was very much a Southern lunch-box staple, as well as a popular party hors d'oeuvre. In the sixties, with the emergence of convenience foods, this great Southern delicacy faded into store-bought mediocrity. There are dozens of prepared versions of pimento cheese available, but none rise to the greatness of an honest homemade batch. Nathalie Dupree, the cookbook author and chronicler of all Southern food, tagged it the "pâté of the South" to indicate just how important the concoction is to Southern culture. We serve it as our bar specialty at Louis's, accompanied by freshly baked flatbread (see page 24).

Serves 12 to 16 people as an hors d'oeuvre.

1½ pounds sharp Cheddar cheese, grated
4 ounces cream cheese, at room temperature
¾ cup mayonnaise (I use Hellmann's)
1 tablespoon grated yellow onion
1 teaspoon cayenne pepper
7 ounces whole peeled pimentos, drained and quartered

1. Place the Cheddar cheese, cream cheese, mayonnaise, onion, and cayenne pepper in the bowl of an electric mixer and beat with the flat beater for 1 or 2 minutes on medium speed. You only want to mix the ingredients, not make them smooth.

2. Add the pimentos and continue mixing until they are shredded and the mixture is somewhat smooth. Still, be careful not to overmix. The mixture should not be homogenized.

3. Pack the cheese in crocks, cover with plastic wrap, and refrigerate overnight. Remove from the refrigerator at least 45 minutes before serving. Tightly covered, it will keep in the refrigerator for 3 to 4 days.

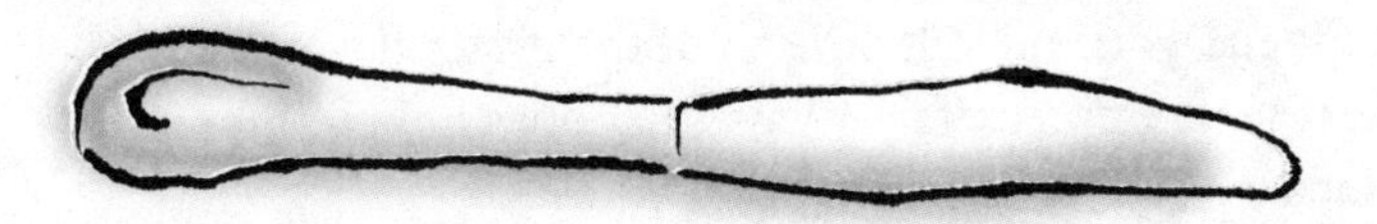

# OYSTER PIE

When I was a youngster living at home, this oyster pie used to be a Thanksgiving favorite. I noticed, however, that the Lambert family's oyster pie was a little better than ours. Later I found out why. When Helen Lambert made the pie, she used the tiny oyster crackers we call oysterettes, while my family used saltine crackers. It's hard to believe the difference a cracker can make.

Serves 6 people.

4 cups oyster crackers
4 cups oysters, drained, but with their liquor strained and reserved
Salt and freshly ground black pepper to taste
½ cup heavy cream
8 tablespoons unsalted butter

10" Pyrex deep-dish pie pan

1. Preheat the oven to 400°F.

2. Coarsely crumble the oyster crackers and layer the bottom of the pie pan with 1 cup of them. Top with a layer of oysters, using 1 cup of them. Sprinkle with salt and pepper. Repeat with 3 more layers each of oyster crackers and oysters, remembering to season each oyster layer with salt and pepper.

3. Pour the oyster liquor into a glass measuring cup and add as much cream as necessary to make 1 cup. Pour over the oysters. Dot the top with the butter. Let the pie set for 10 minutes.

4. Place the pie in the top third of the preheated oven and bake for about 15 minutes or until the top begins to brown and the oysters are plump and hot. Turn up the heat and broil the oyster pie for 4 minutes or until the top is completely browned. Be careful not to overcook the oysters or they will expel all of their juices. If this happens, you will still have all of the oyster flavor, but not finely textured oysters. Serve immediately. (This "pie" does not cut into neat wedges; you'll get a looser home-style serving.)

# GROUPER WITH RICE AND GREEN CHILES

This spicy dish is another great use of rice in the Lowcountry tradition. The chiles add a little heat and perk up the dish to make it special, while the shiitake mushrooms add a little Asian flair and punch. Don't despair if you can't find shiitakes; the dish works equally well with button mushrooms.

Serves 4 people.

**FOR THE RICE:**

- 3 tablespoons unsalted butter
- ¼ cup minced shallots
- 2 small green chiles, seeded and minced
- 1 cup uncooked converted long-grain white rice (I use Uncle Ben's)
- ¼ cup dry white vermouth
- 1¾ cups fish stock (see page 8) or chicken stock (see page 5), heated
- 1 sprig fresh thyme
- ½ bay leaf
- ¼ cup chopped fresh Italian parsley

**FOR THE GROUPER:**

- Four 6-ounce grouper fillets
- Salt and freshly ground black pepper to taste
- 2 tablespoons unsalted butter
- 2 tablespoons peanut oil
- 2 tablespoons extra virgin olive oil
- 1 cup thinly sliced shiitake mushrooms (buy about 2 ounces and remove the stems)
- 1 large clove garlic, peeled and sliced lengthwise into 2 pieces
- ½ cup chicken stock (see page 5)
- 1 sprig fresh thyme

1. To prepare the rice, heat the butter in a medium skillet over medium-high heat until it bubbles. Add the shallots and chiles and sauté, stirring occasionally, for about 5 minutes or until softened. Add the rice and cook, stirring constantly, for 2 to 4 minutes or until all the grains are well coated with butter. Add the vermouth and cook until it is absorbed.

2. Add the hot stock, thyme, and bay leaf and stir well. Bring to a simmer, reduce the heat to low, cover the skillet, and continue cooking at the barest simmer for about 18 minutes or until the stock is mostly absorbed and the rice is tender. Remove from the stove, stir in the parsley, and keep warm while cooking the fish.

3. Preheat the oven to 275°F.

4. Season the grouper fillets with salt and pepper. Heat the butter and peanut oil in a nonstick skillet over medium-high heat until hot but not smoking. Add the fillets and sauté for about 1 minute or until the skin is golden brown. Carefully turn the fillets over with a spatula and sauté the other side for about 30 seconds or until golden.

5. Remove the fillets to a baking sheet big enough to hold all of them in a single layer. Bake on the middle rack of the preheated oven for about 3 minutes or until just cooked through. The fillets should be opaque in the center and just firm to the touch. Remove from the oven and tent with aluminum foil, shiny side down, to keep warm.

6. While the grouper is baking, heat the olive oil in a heavy-bottomed sauté pan over medium-high heat until hot but not smoking. Add the mushrooms and garlic and cook, stirring occasionally, for about 4 minutes or until the mushrooms are barely tender.

7. Add the chicken stock and thyme and bring to a boil, stirring constantly. Simmer the mixture for 2 minutes or until reduced slightly, continuing to stir. Season with salt and pepper to taste. Remove the garlic pieces and thyme sprig.

8. Divide the rice among 4 plates and top each serving with a grouper fillet. Spoon the mushrooms around the grouper and drizzle with some of the mushroom broth. Serve immediately.

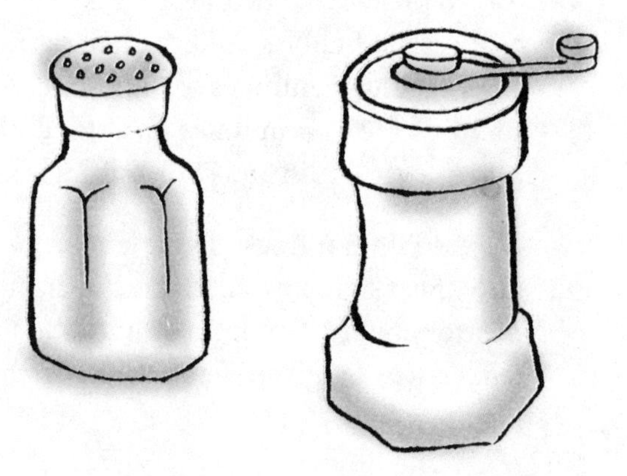

# SAUTÉED SNAPPER WITH A CURRIED VEGETABLE VINAIGRETTE

Michael Foley, a pioneer in regional cooking and a great friend, brought this unusual dish to us a few years back. It demonstrates how very flavorful a dish can be while still being light.

Serves 4 people.

**FOR THE CURRIED VINAIGRETTE:**

- 3 tablespoons unsalted butter
- 1 cup cleaned, very thinly sliced cremini mushroom caps (buy 6 ounces and remove the stems)
- ¼ cup very thinly sliced scallions, white and green parts
- ¼ teaspoon salt
- ¼ teaspoon freshly ground black pepper
- ⅓ cup zucchini, diced into ¼" pieces
- ⅓ cup yellow squash, diced into ¼" pieces
- 1 fennel bulb, trimmed, green fronds removed, and diced into ¼" pieces
- 1 red onion, peeled and diced into ¼" pieces
- 1 tomato, peeled, seeded, and diced into ¼" pieces
- ¾ cup extra virgin olive oil
- ¼ cup walnut oil
- 1 tablespoon curry powder
- 1 tablespoon ground coriander
- ¼ cup white wine vinegar
- 1 tablespoon shredded fresh basil

**FOR THE SNAPPER:**

- ½ cup all-purpose flour
- 2 teaspoons salt
- 2 teaspoons freshly ground black pepper
- Four 6-ounce red snapper fillets, skinned
- ½ cup peanut oil

1. To prepare the vinaigrette, heat the butter in a medium skillet over medium-high heat just until it begins to sizzle and the foam subsides. Quickly add the mushrooms, scallions, salt, and pepper. Stir well and cook for about 4 minutes or until the mushrooms have just wilted.

2. Add the zucchini, yellow squash, fennel, onion, tomato, olive oil, and walnut oil. Cook, stirring, over moderate heat for about 3 minutes or just until the vegetables are barely softened and heated through. Add the curry powder, coriander, vinegar, and basil. Remove from the stove and set aside while cooking the fish.

3. In a small bowl, mix together the flour, salt, and pepper. Dredge the snapper fillets in the mixture and shake to remove any excess flour.

4. Heat the peanut oil in a large skillet over high heat until hot but not smoking. Carefully place the fillets in the skillet, being careful not to overcrowd them. Putting too many in the pan will cause the temperature of the oil to drop and will result in greasy fish. Cook in batches if necessary. Adjust the heat so that the fillets continue to sauté gently without burning for 3 to 5 minutes or until the underside is brown. Gently turn them over with a spatula and continue cooking for 4 to 5 minutes or until they are opaque in the center and just firm to the touch.

5. Remove the fillets to warm serving plates. Stir the vinaigrette and spoon over the fillets. Serve immediately.

# LOWCOUNTRY CHICKEN BOG

When I first arrived in the Lowcountry from Atlanta in 1979, I was hungry for knowledge about its rather legendary food. I was quick to learn that the Lowcountry has some legendary folks as well. Dickie Creighton is one such person. Dickie is now in his eighties, and a legend in Pawleys Island. He was a merchant marine and at one time owned an island in the Pacific Northwest, in partnership with Mae West. (There are stories about that, too, but you'll have to find Dickie to hear those in person.) Anyway, Dickie and his dog Homelite were about the first souls we met when we opened our new restaurant. They came by every morning and Dickie would lay a fire in the big fireplace in the dining room. One day he brought over a big dish of his leftover chicken bog and we had it for breakfast. I'll never forget the comfort of its warm simplicity.

Serves 6 people.

- 3 ripe large tomatoes or 9 ripe plum tomatoes
- 3 tablespoons extra virgin olive oil
- Freshly ground black pepper to taste
- 2 tablespoons unsalted butter
- 2 tablespoons peanut oil
- 6 chicken thighs, bone in and skin on, but trimmed of any fat
- Salt to taste
- 1 cup finely chopped yellow onion
- 1 cup finely chopped celery
- ½ teaspoon minced garlic

- 2 cups uncooked converted long-grain white rice (I use Uncle Ben's)
- 4 cups chicken stock (see page 5)
- 1 large sprig fresh thyme
- 2 small bay leaves
- 2 teaspoons Tabasco sauce

1. Preheat the oven to 350°F.

2. Bring a large saucepan of water to a boil. Drop in the tomatoes and leave them for about 30 seconds (do this in 2 two batches if necessary). Remove the tomatoes from the saucepan and drop into ice water to cool. Drain and peel off the skin. Remove the cores and seeds from the tomatoes and dice the meat into ½" pieces. Toss the diced tomato with the olive oil and season with pepper to taste. Reserve at room temperature until ready to use.

3. Heat the butter and peanut oil over medium heat in a medium ovenproof pot with a cover. Add the chicken thighs and sauté for about 2 minutes per side or until nicely browned. Remove the thighs, season with salt and pepper to taste, and reserve. Pour off all the butter, oil, and juices except for 2 tablespoons.

4. Add the onion and celery to the butter and oil and sauté over medium heat for about 3 minutes or until translucent. Add the garlic and rice and sauté, stirring, for about 3 minutes or until the garlic is soft and the rice is translucent.

5. In a small saucepan, heat the stock to a simmer. Return the chicken to the pot with the rice and add the hot stock, the reserved tomatoes, the herbs, and the Tabasco. Stir well to combine. Add salt and pepper to taste. Cover tightly and bake in the preheated oven for 30 to 35 minutes or until the chicken and rice are cooked and the liquid is absorbed. (Note that this is a moist dish, not one where the grains of rice are dry and fluffy.) Remove the sprig of thyme and bay leaves. Check the seasoning for salt and pepper and serve immediately.

# SEARED DUCK BREASTS WITH BUTTERY SAVOY CABBAGE

This recipe demonstrates the versatility of this fine bird. The duck and cabbage combine to produce a tasty, earthy dish. If you have it on hand from other recipes, toss in a little shredded preserved duck during the last few minutes of the cooking of the cabbage. It will add a marvelous flavor to the succulent cabbage.

Serves 6 people.

- 6 large boneless duck breasts, skinned and trimmed of any fat or silver membrane
- 3 tablespoons extra virgin olive oil
- 1 tablespoon freshly ground black pepper
- 2 tablespoons peanut oil
- Salt and freshly ground black pepper to taste
- 8 tablespoons unsalted butter
- 2 small heads (about 2 pounds) Savoy cabbage, washed, cored, and diced into ¾" pieces

1. Rub the duck breasts with the olive oil and tablespoon of pepper. Wrap each breast tightly in plastic wrap and refrigerate overnight.

2. When ready to cook the duck breasts, heat a large heavy-bottomed skillet over medium-high heat until it is very hot but not smoking. Add the peanut oil and let it heat for a few seconds.

3. Remove the plastic wrap from the duck breasts and sprinkle them lightly with salt and pepper. Lay them in the hot oil and sear for 1 minute on each side. Reduce the heat to medium and continue to sauté the breasts until they are as done as you like them, turning once (estimate 3 minutes per side for rare and 5 minutes per side for medium rare).

4. Remove the breasts to a platter and keep them warm in a 200°F oven while preparing the cabbage.

5. Add the butter to the skillet over medium-high heat, scraping the bottom to pull up any browned bits left from sautéing the duck breasts. When the butter is hot, add the cabbage.

6. Let the cabbage cook undisturbed for 2 or 3 minutes or until the bottom has started to brown. Then turn it over and brown the other side lightly. If necessary, sauté the cabbage for 1 or 2 minutes more or until tender but just wilted.

7. Add any juices from the platter of duck breasts to the cabbage and toss to combine. Season to taste with salt and pepper.

8. Divide the cabbage among 6 serving plates. Slice the duck breasts into 4 slices each and place on top of the cabbage. Spoon the wonderfully buttery juice from the pan around the cabbage and serve immediately.

# CHRISTMAS GOOSE AND GRAVY

A fine, fat goose is certainly a long-standing Christmas tradition. Don't be afraid to go into unknown waters if you haven't cooked one before—it'll be worth the effort. And be sure to save the goose fat that is rendered during the cooking process—it's a great roasting medium for potatoes. If a frozen goose is the only kind you can obtain, it is important to thaw it properly. Unwrap the goose, place it in a pan, lightly cover the pan, and put it in the refrigerator to thaw. This will take from 24 to 36 hours.

Serves 6 to 8 people.

One 9- to 12-pound goose
8 tablespoons unsalted butter, at room temperature
Salt and freshly ground black pepper to taste
½ cup dry white wine
4 cups chicken stock (see page 5)
½ cup sliced yellow onion
1 carrot, peeled and thinly sliced
2 stalks celery, thinly sliced
1 small sprig fresh thyme
1 clove garlic, peeled and crushed
1 bay leaf
1 tablespoon cornstarch
⅓ cup Madeira or port

1. Preheat the oven to 350°F.

2. Rinse the goose with cold water. Remove the neck, gizzard, heart, and liver. Reserve the neck and gizzard; discard the heart and liver. Clip off the wing tips, crack them in 3 places, and reserve. Cut out and discard any fat deposits remaining in the cavity. Pat the goose dry and rub it with the butter. Salt and pepper it inside and out and place it on a rack in a roasting pan.

3. Basting every 15 minutes, roast the goose in the preheated oven for about 1 hour and 25 minutes or until a meat thermometer inserted into the thickest part of the thigh registers 175°F. Be careful not to let the thermometer touch the bone. At this point, the legs of the goose will be a little pink.

4. Remove the goose from the oven and cover it lightly with aluminum foil, shiny side down, to keep it warm while it is "reposing." Be sure to time the whole operation so that the goose can repose for ½ hour at room temperature before carving. This will aid in the carving and keep the slices of goose moist. If you don't like the meat pink, after the goose has reposed for 15 minutes, quickly cut the leg-and-thigh quarters off, each in a single piece, and put them back in the 350°F oven, uncovered, for 12 minutes.

5. While the goose is cooking, combine the reserved neck, gizzard, and wing tips with the wine, stock, onion, carrot, celery, thyme, garlic, and bay leaf in a heavy-bottomed nonreactive pot. Bring to a simmer and cook, stirring occasionally, for 1 hour.

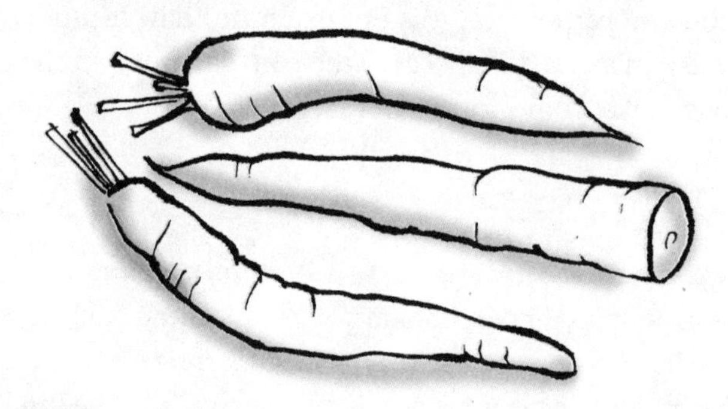

6. Pour the mixture through a fine sieve set over a medium saucepan, pressing hard on the solids. Spoon any fat off the top.

7. Mix the cornstarch with the Madeira or port in a small bowl, stirring until the cornstarch dissolves. Add the mixture to the pot, stir well, and simmer for 5 minutes. Add salt and pepper to taste. Strain the gravy once more. Keep the gravy warm on the back of the stove or gently reheat it when needed. Serve separately in a sauceboat.

NOTE: If you decide to stuff your goose, it will add about 35 minutes to the cooking time. Be sure to put the stuffing into the goose just as it is ready to go into the oven. Stuffing the goose in advance can cause food poisoning.

# ROASTED SQUAB WITH WILD RICE AND A SHALLOT AND GARLIC CONFIT IN A CABERNET SAUCE

Sumter, South Carolina, is home to the Palmetto Pigeon Plant, the largest squab farm in the world, so our restaurant is able to get these succulent little birds year-round on a day's notice. Squab are now being distributed through other suppliers as well, so their availability is quickly expanding. Look for them in specialty food stores. If they are not in stock, they probably can be special ordered.

Serves 4 people.

**FOR THE WILD RICE:**

- 1¼ cups uncooked wild rice
- 3 cups chicken stock (see page 5)
- 1 tablespoon unsalted butter or rendered duck fat (see page 42) or bacon fat
- ¼ cup peeled and very finely diced carrots
- ¼ cup finely diced onion
- ¼ cup dry white wine
- 1 sprig fresh parsley
- 1 sprig fresh thyme
- 1 bay leaf
- Salt and freshly ground black pepper to taste

**FOR THE SHALLOT AND GARLIC CONFIT:**

- 1½ cups peeled whole shallots
- ½ cup peeled whole cloves garlic
- 1½ cups extra virgin olive oil

**FOR THE SQUAB:**

- 4 squab (reserve the wing tips, necks, and gizzards; discard the hearts and livers)
- Salt and freshly ground black pepper to taste
- Reserved olive oil from the shallot and garlic confit

**FOR THE SAUCE:**

- 2 cups chicken stock (see page 5)
- ¼ cup peanut oil
- Reserved wing tips, necks, and gizzards from the squab
- ⅓ cup peeled and very finely chopped carrots
- ⅓ cup very finely chopped onion
- 1 cup plus 2 tablespoons Cabernet Sauvignon wine
- 1 sprig fresh parsley
- 1 sprig fresh thyme
- 1 bay leaf
- 1 tablespoon sugar
- 1 tablespoon red wine vinegar
- Reserved shallot and garlic confit
- ¼ teaspoon salt
- 1 tablespoon unsalted butter

1. Place the wild rice in a sieve, rinse with cold water, and set aside to drain. Heat the stock in a medium saucepan.

2. Meanwhile, heat the butter or fat in a heavy-bottomed pot over medium heat until hot but not smoking. Add the carrots and onion and sauté, stirring occasionally, for 3 to 4 minutes or until the onion is translucent. Add the wild rice and sauté for an additional 2 minutes, stirring constantly.

3. Deglaze the pot with the wine and cook for 5 to 6 minutes or until it evaporates, stirring constantly. Add the hot stock. Tie the parsley, thyme, and bay leaf in cheesecloth to make a bouquet garni and add to the pot. Season to taste with salt and pepper.

4. Bring the rice to a boil, reduce the heat to low, cover, and let simmer for 35 minutes or until the grains have opened and softened. They should not be mushy. Remove the bouquet garni. Drain the rice in a colander, cover, and keep warm over gently simmering water until ready to use.

5. While the rice is cooking, prepare the confit. Place the shallots, garlic, and olive oil in a small saucepan, bring the mixture to a slow simmer, and cook for 25 minutes. Strain and reserve both the confit—that is, the now preserved shallots and garlic cloves—and the oil, which will be used for basting the squab.

6. Preheat the oven to 350°F.

7. Sprinkle the squab with salt and pepper and place them on a rack in a roasting pan. Roast them in the preheated oven, basting with the oil from the shallot and garlic confit every 5 minutes, for about 25 minutes or until the juices run clear. Allow the squab to rest for about 10 minutes before carving.

8. While the squab are roasting, make the sauce. Heat the chicken stock in a medium saucepan.

9. Meanwhile, heat the peanut oil in a heavy-bottomed nonreactive pot over medium heat until hot but not smoking. Crack each wing tip in 3 places to allow more flavor to escape. Add the wing tips, necks, gizzards, carrots, and onion and, stirring occasionally, sauté for about 10 minutes or until the squab parts are nicely browned but not burned. Deglaze the pot with 1 cup of the wine, scraping up any browned bits from the bottom. Rapidly simmer the mixture for 4 to 6 minutes or until the wine is reduced to 2 tablespoons, stirring occasionally.

10. Add the hot chicken stock. Tie the parsley, thyme, and bay leaf in cheesecloth to make a bouquet garni and add to the pot. Bring the mixture to a rapid simmer and cook for about 20 minutes or until the liquid is reduced to 1 cup. Strain the liquid, pressing down on the solids. Reserve the liquid and discard the solids. Let the liquid cool until the fat rises to the top. Skim off the fat.

11. Combine the sugar, vinegar, and remaining 2 tablespoons of wine in a sauté pan. Bring the mixture to a boil over medium-high heat and cook for 6 to 8 minutes or until it is very syrupy and starting to caramelize. Stir in the reserved shallot and garlic confit so that it will reheat as the sauce is finished. Add the salt and the reserved cup of liquid. Rapidly simmer the mixture for about 5 minutes or until it is as thick as cream. Stir in the butter. Keep the sauce warm on the back of the stove or in a double boiler until ready to serve.

12. Carve the squab by slicing the breast meat off the bone and slicing off the leg-and-thigh quarters. Divide the warm rice among 4 plates, placing it in a mound on each plate. Arrange the breast meat and leg quarters of 1 squab over each mound of rice. Spoon the Cabernet sauce with the warm confit around the squab. Serve immediately.

# STEWED RABBIT SMOTHERED WITH ONIONS

When I was a child, the neighborhood rabbit supplier would come by on Saturday mornings with his offerings of personally hunted rabbit and squirrel. My mother would always take a couple of rabbits and occasionally a squirrel. We would feast on fried rabbit and gravy, but she alone would eat the stewed squirrel.

Serves 6 to 8 people.

Two 3-pound rabbits
24 ounces dark beer (I use Beck's)
½ cup julienned yellow onion (cut off the root and slice the onion top to bottom and it will make a natural julienne)
⅓ cup peeled and thinly sliced carrots
2 cloves garlic, peeled and thinly sliced
3 sprigs fresh thyme or ½ teaspoon dried thyme
1 small sprig fresh rosemary or ⅛ teaspoon dried rosemary
2 tablespoons lightly crushed black peppercorns
2 tablespoons sugar
4 tablespoons peanut oil
8 tablespoons unsalted butter
6 cups thinly sliced yellow onions (about 1½ pounds)
3 tablespoons all-purpose flour
1 tablespoon minced garlic
1 cup chicken stock (see page 5)
Bouquet garni of 2 bay leaves, 6 sprigs fresh parsley, and 3 sprigs fresh thyme
1 teaspoon salt

1. To prepare the rabbits, remove the back leg/thigh sections using kitchen shears and a cleaver or large French knife. Follow the pelvic bone closely to keep from losing too much meat. Remove the pelvic bone (located between the 2 back legs) from the saddle (the backbone loin section). Remove the flank flaps (thin pieces of skin) from the saddle. Cut the saddle into 2 portions of equal size.

2. Cut each front leg/shoulder portion from the rib cage by lifting it up, exposing the triangle-shaped bone under the front leg, and cutting underneath the bone to get a nice large portion. Altogether you will have 6 portions from each rabbit: 2 back legs/thighs, 2 front legs/shoulders, and 2 saddle portions. (You can turn this into 8 portions by separating the leg and the thigh.) The pelvic bones and rib cages can be used to make rabbit stock, but be sure to remove the hearts, livers, and kidneys.

3. Combine the beer, julienned onion, carrots, sliced garlic, thyme, rosemary, peppercorns, and sugar in a large nonreactive bowl. Add the rabbit pieces, cover, and refrigerate for at least 2 hours or overnight, turning them often.

4. When ready to cook the rabbit, preheat the oven to 350°F.

5. Remove the rabbit pieces from the marinade and pat them dry. Strain the marinade through a fine mesh sieve, reserving the liquid and discarding the solids.

6. In a large, heavy sauté pan, heat the peanut oil and 4 tablespoons of the butter over medium-high heat. When the fat is hot but not smoking, begin to brown the rabbit pieces, allowing about 1 minute per side. Be careful not to crowd the pan or the pieces will steam instead of brown. As you remove each piece, replace it with another to keep the heat balanced. Don't let the temperature drop. (If you'd rather, you can grill the rabbit.)

7. When you have finished browning all of the rabbit, remove the pieces to a platter and pour off the liquid fat, but retain all of the solid pan drippings.

8. Place the sauté pan back on the stove over medium heat. Add the remaining 4 tablespoons of butter and when hot, add the sliced onions. Sauté for 4 to 4½ minutes or until well cooked, stirring often. Sprinkle the flour over the onions, stir to combine, and cook for 3 minutes. Add the minced garlic, stir, and cook for 2 minutes. Add 1½ cups of the reserved marinade and the cup of stock and cook for 3 minutes. Add the bouquet garni to the pan and let the mixture simmer for 3 minutes, scraping the pan to release all of the browned bits.

9. Using the whole teaspoon, salt the rabbit pieces amply on both sides. Arrange the rabbit pieces in a single layer in a baking dish just large enough to hold the rabbit and the onions. Spread the onion mixture with its liquid over the rabbit. Top with a piece of wax paper, pressing down the sides to seal in the heat.

10. Bake the rabbit in the preheated oven for about 15 minutes or until the saddles are tender. Remove the saddles from the baking dish, place on a warm platter, and lightly cover with aluminum foil, shiny side down, to keep them warm while the rest of the rabbit finishes cooking. The other pieces should cook for about another 5 minutes. (It is easy to overcook rabbit, so watch carefully.) Remove the bouquet garni and place the back legs/thighs and front legs/shoulders on the serving platter with the saddles. Top with the onion mixture and serve immediately.

# LEG OF LAMB WITH WINTER FRUITS AND NUTS

■ This is a rather festive production, and it's not as difficult as it seems to prepare. It's perfectly suited for the holidays.

Serves 10 to 12 people.

2 cups dry white wine or fragrant tea such as Earl Grey
½ cup tart pitted dried cherries
½ cup pitted whole dates
½ cup dried apricots
⅔ cup walnut pieces
1½ cups pecan pieces
⅔ cup pistachio pieces
4 tablespoons unsalted butter, at room temperature
½ cup finely minced shallots

One 8-pound boned leg of lamb
1 tablespoon chopped fresh thyme or 1 teaspoon dried thyme
½ tablespoon chopped fresh rosemary or ½ teaspoon dried rosemary
1 teaspoon salt
1 teaspoon freshly ground black pepper
2 sprigs fresh thyme
2 sprigs fresh rosemary

Butcher's twine

1. Heat the wine or tea in a nonreactive saucepan. Roughly chop the fruits, place them in a bowl, and pour the hot wine or tea over them. Let the fruits steep for 20 minutes, then drain off the liquid.

2. Chop the nuts and mix them with the drained fruits. If you are not going to cook the lamb right away, refrigerate the filling. Do *not* put room-temperature filling in the lamb and then cook it later.

3. Preheat the oven to 450°F.

4. Heat 3 tablespoons of the butter in a heavy saucepan over medium heat. Add the shallots and sauté for 2 or 3 minutes or until softened. Set aside to cool slightly.

5. Place the leg of lamb on a work surface with the fat side down. Spread the cooled shallots over the lamb. Mix the chopped thyme, chopped rosemary, ½ teaspoon of the salt, and ½ teaspoon of the pepper and sprinkle over the shallots. Spread the fruit and nut mixture on top of the seasonings.

6. Very carefully roll the leg of lamb lengthwise back toward its natural shape. Tuck in the ends and tie with butcher's twine. It's very likely that some of the stuffing will fall out; tuck it as best you can back into the ends. Mix the remaining tablespoon of butter with the remaining ½ teaspoon of salt and ½ teaspoon of pepper and rub the mixture over the outside of the lamb. Slip the sprigs of thyme and rosemary under the twine on the bottom side of the lamb.

7. Place the lamb on a rack in a roasting pan. Reduce the oven temperature to 400°F. Roast the lamb for about 1 hour and 20 minutes for medium rare. A meat thermometer should read 130°F. Be sure to time the whole operation so that the lamb can "repose" for 10 to 15 minutes at room temperature before carving. When the leg of lamb is cooked to your liking, place it on a warm platter and lightly cover it with aluminum foil, shiny side down, to keep it warm while it is reposing and you are having a final glass of Christmas cheer.

# ANGUS STEAK WITH CLEMSON BLUE CHEESE SAUCE

Angus steak is my favorite type of beef. If you can't find Angus, any premium beef will substitute well. At the restaurant, after we buy the beef, we continue to age it for an additional 4 weeks before we trim and portion it. The steaks are consistently tender and the flavor is dramatically enhanced. It would be rather hard to age beef at home, but finding an expert butcher will give you the same results.

On his many visits to the coast, my father would always make a special trip to the sales counter at the agricultural department at Clemson University, to make sure that we had a constant supply of Clemson blue cheese on hand. The perk was that this same sales counter made the world's best milk shake. It's the same today. If you are ever close to Clemson, South Carolina, it's still worth a detour, both for the blue cheese and the milk shake. (I prefer chocolate.)

Serves 6 people.

- Six 10-ounce closely trimmed New York strip steaks
- 1 tablespoon crushed black peppercorns
- ½ cup dry white wine
- 2 tablespoons minced shallots
- ¼ cup veal demi-glace (see page 10)
- 1⅓ cups heavy cream
- 1 cup grated Clemson or other crumbly blue cheese
- Salt and freshly ground black pepper to taste
- 3 drops Tabasco sauce
- ⅔ cup crumbled Clemson or other crumbly blue cheese, at room temperature
- 1 tablespoon plus 1 teaspoon finely minced shallots
- 1 tablespoon plus 1 teaspoon finely minced fresh chives
- ¼ cup rendered duck fat (see page 42) or peanut oil

1. Remove the steaks from the refrigerator about 30 minutes before cooking, so that they can come to room temperature. Rub both sides of the steaks with the crushed black peppercorns.

2. Meanwhile, place the wine and 2 tablespoons of shallots in a heavy nonreactive saucepan. Bring to a boil over medium-high heat, reduce the heat to medium, and gently boil until only a syrupy glaze remains.

3. Add the veal demi-glace and continue to simmer the mixture over medium heat for about 5 minutes or until it is very thick and syrupy, watching the heat and stirring the sauce so that it will not scorch.

4. Add the cream and continue to simmer the mixture for another 5 minutes. Remove the sauce from the heat, add the cup of grated blue cheese, and stir until it dissolves. Season to taste with salt and pepper, remembering that the blue cheese itself will add salt to the sauce. Add the Tabasco and stir to mix well. Strain the sauce through a fine mesh sieve. Keep it warm on the back of the stove or in a double boiler over barely simmering water until time to serve.

5. In a small bowl, combine the ⅔ cup of crumbled blue cheese, finely minced shallots, and chives to make the topping. Set aside while cooking the steaks.

6. Heat the duck fat or peanut oil in a heavy skillet over medium heat until hot but not smoking. Add the steaks and sear for 3 minutes. Turn the steaks over and sprinkle with salt. After 3 minutes, turn the steaks again and sprinkle with salt. Finally, sear each side of the steaks for an additional 30 seconds. This will produce a finely seared and seasoned rare steak. For medium-rare steaks, increase the cooking time for the last searing to 1 minute per side.

7. Place the steaks on warm plates. Ladle a little of the sauce over each steak, sprinkle with the topping, and serve immediately.

# JOHN HENRY'S TEXAS SCHOOLHOUSE CHILI

John Henry Whitmire, a jeweler and bon vivant, is a great friend who resides in Pawleys Island. One Labor Day weekend, he burst into the restaurant kitchen during dinner like a tornado, asking for a little space to cook chili for the next day's picnic. On the busiest weekend of the year, John Henry was under everybody's feet borrowing knives and pots and pans and asking advice. When he finished with his chili, he asked the kitchen staff for its verdict. I declared that it was worse than the chili served at the schoolhouse on hot dogs. We all pitched in and repaired the chili so that the picnic could go on. Over the years we created a veal chili, naming it after John Henry, not for its taste, but for the good times and friends in Pawleys Island.

Serves 4 people.

- 2 tablespoons peanut oil
- 1½ pounds veal, hand-chopped top round or store-bought ground (beef may be substituted if desired)
- 3 tablespoons minced garlic
- ¼ cup plus 1 tablespoon chile powder
- 2 tablespoons chopped fresh oregano
- 1 teaspoon ground cumin
- 2 teaspoons salt
- ¼ cup masa flour (see note)
- 5 cups veal stock (see page 9) or beef stock (see page 4)
- 1 cup dark beer (I use Beck's)
- 1 tablespoon red wine vinegar
- 1 tablespoon Chili Paste with Garlic (see page 23)
- 2 teaspoons freshly ground black pepper

1. Heat the oil in a heavy-bottomed pot over medium-high heat until hot but not smoking. Add the veal and sauté for 5 to 6 minutes or until it turns light brown, stirring occasionally.

2. Add the garlic, chile powder, oregano, cumin, and 1 teaspoon of the salt. Stir to combine well. Reduce the heat to medium and cook for 5 minutes, stirring occasionally. Add the flour and stir to combine well. Cook for 5 minutes, stirring occasionally. Add the stock and stir to combine well. Bring the chili back to a simmer, reduce the heat to low, and cook, uncovered, for 30 minutes or until it has thickened, stirring occasionally.

3. Add the beer, stir to combine, and cook the chili for 20 minutes or until it thickens again. Add the vinegar, chili paste, pepper, and remaining teaspoon of salt. Stir well to combine. Serve immediately.

**NOTE:** Masa flour is made from dried kernels of corn that have been cooked in limewater, then soaked overnight in limewater. The flour is then ground from these wet kernels. Since it is used to make tortillas, it is available in many grocery stores.

# BUCKWHEAT GROAT FRITTERS

These are rich and earthy fritters. Native to Russia, buckwheat groats add a welcome European flavor to the American stew pot and are generally available in large supermarkets. These fritters go well with robust meats such as lamb and game and are especially suited for fall and winter.

Serves 4 people.

- 1 cup chicken stock (see page 5)
- 1 cup water
- 1 tablespoon extra virgin olive oil
- 1 cup uncooked buckwheat groats
- 3 large eggs, lightly beaten
- 1 cup all-purpose soft wheat flour, such as White Lily
- 1½ teaspoons baking powder
- ¾ teaspoon sugar
- ¾ cup whole milk
- 1½ teaspoons maple syrup
- 1 teaspoon salt
- ¼ teaspoon freshly ground black pepper
- 1½ teaspoons chopped fresh chervil
- Peanut oil

1. Combine the stock, water, and olive oil in a saucepan over medium-high heat and bring to a boil.

2. In a medium bowl, combine the groats and 1 lightly beaten egg, stirring to coat the groats well with the egg. Transfer the mixture to a deep skillet with a lid and toast the groats over medium-high heat, stirring and breaking up the lumps, for 2 to 4 minutes or until the grains are separated. Remove the skillet from the heat, slowly add the hot stock mixture (the mixture will spatter), and cover the skillet tightly. Reduce the heat to low and cook the groats for 10 to 15 minutes or until the liquid is absorbed. Remove from the heat and set aside to cool.

3. In a medium bowl, combine the flour, baking powder, and sugar. Mix well.

4. In a large bowl, whisk together the 2 remaining eggs and the milk and syrup. Add the salt, pepper, chervil, and flour mixture. Combine thoroughly. Fold into the cooled groats and let the batter stand for 15 minutes. The batter will be a slightly sticky liquid.

5. Heat ⅛" of peanut oil in a well-seasoned cast-iron or nonstick skillet over moderately high heat until it is hot but not smoking or until it registers 350°F on a frying thermometer. Working in batches, drop heaping tablespoons of the batter into the skillet, spreading them slightly. Fry the fritters for 2 to 3 minutes on each side or until they are golden brown. Remove with a slotted spoon and drain on paper towels. If necessary, you can keep the fritters warm in a 200°F oven for up to 30 minutes, but no longer. They are best served immediately.

# GARLIC CUSTARD

This savory custard goes well with lamb and most other meats. The consistency is soft and creamy, so it acts as a sauce of sorts. The custard can be made ahead and reheated.

Makes six 4-ounce servings.

½ pound garlic cloves, unpeeled
1 cup chicken stock (see page 5)
1 teaspoon unsalted butter
¼ teaspoon sugar
½ teaspoon red wine vinegar
½ teaspoon salt
¼ teaspoon ground white pepper
⅔ cup heavy cream
1 cup whole milk
2 large eggs plus 1 large egg yolk

Six 4-ounce ramekins

Baking pan deep enough to hold water around the ramekins to just under their tops

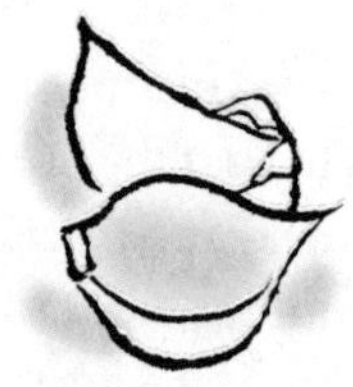

1. Preheat the oven to 300°F.

2. Place the garlic cloves in a small heavy-bottomed saucepan over medium-high heat, cover with cold water, and boil for 2 minutes. Drain the cloves and repeat the process a second time.

3. Peel the cloves when cool enough to handle. Return them to the saucepan. Add the stock, butter, sugar, vinegar, salt, and pepper and stir well to combine. Cook over medium-high heat, stirring frequently, until the liquid has evaporated and the garlic cloves have caramelized.

4. Put the garlic and ⅓ cup of the cream in a food processor and puree. Slowly add the remaining cream to smooth the puree; you may use some of the milk as well if necessary.

5. In a large bowl, lightly beat the eggs and the additional yolk. Whisk the garlic mixture and the milk into the eggs. Divide the mixture among the 6 ramekins. Place them in the baking pan and place the pan in the preheated oven. Carefully pour very hot water into the pan, filling it to just under the tops of the ramekins. Bake the custards for 1 hour or until a knife inserted in the center comes out clean.

6. Remove the ramekins from the baking pan and set them on paper towels. With a small knife, gently loosen the edges of the custards from the ramekins. Turn the custards out onto dinner plates and serve immediately.

# CHESTNUT SPOON BREAD

As is often the case, this dish was created because the restaurant had a few bags of chestnut flour left over from other preparations. We first served it with lamb medallions and found that it was a versatile side dish. Spoon bread has long been a Southern favorite, but the addition of the chestnut flavor really makes this version stand out.

Serves 6 to 8 people.

2 cups whole milk
½ cup heavy cream
4 tablespoons unsalted butter
¾ cup stone-ground white cornmeal
½ cup chestnut flour (available from Dean & DeLuca or other specialty food stores)
1¼ teaspoons baking powder
½ teaspoon baking soda
4 large eggs, separated
1 tablespoon sugar
¾ teaspoon salt

10" × 12" baking dish, buttered

Baking pan large enough to hold water around the baking dish to halfway up the sides

1. Preheat the oven to 350°F.

2. Combine the milk, cream, and butter in a heavy-bottomed saucepan over medium-high heat and scald the mixture by heating it until it is just about to boil. Remove from the heat and set aside.

3. Combine the cornmeal and chestnut flour in a large bowl. Pour the scalded mixture over them and mix until smooth. Let the mixture cool for

about 30 minutes or until lukewarm. Mix in the baking powder and baking soda. Lightly beat the egg yolks and mix them in.

4. In a medium bowl, beat the egg whites with the sugar and salt until stiff. Carefully fold them into the batter.

5. Pour the batter into the baking dish and place it in the larger pan. Put the pan in the preheated oven and pour very hot water into it until the water reaches halfway up the sides of the baking dish. Bake the spoon bread for 45 minutes or until it is set. Serve immediately. Don't worry if it falls—it's inevitable.

# ESAU'S WINTER GREENS

Esau Graham is a remarkable fellow, a tireless worker, and a cheerful colleague. He came up with this rendition of a Southern classic and it is now an extremely popular side dish at Louis's.

Serves 4 people.

1 tablespoon peanut oil
⅓ cup chopped apple-smoked bacon
½ cup finely chopped white onion
1 tablespoon minced garlic
16 cups thoroughly washed, stemmed, and chopped collard greens (about 2 large bunches)
¾ cup chicken stock (see page 5)
24 ounces light ale
1 teaspoon sugar
1½ tablespoons red wine vinegar
Salt
⅛ teaspoon cayenne pepper
¼ teaspoon freshly ground black pepper

1. Heat the oil in a heavy-bottomed nonreactive pot over medium heat. Add the bacon and cook for 4 to 5 minutes or until crisp. Remove the bacon and reserve.

2. Add the onion to the hot fat and cook, stirring occasionally, for 4 minutes or until it starts to soften. Add the garlic and cook for 1 minute.

3. Return the bacon to the pot and add the greens, stock, ale, sugar, vinegar, and 1 teaspoon of salt. Bring the greens to a rapid simmer and cook, stirring occasionally, for about 45 minutes or until they are thoroughly cooked and tender. Season with the cayenne pepper, black pepper, and more salt to taste. Serve immediately.

# WILD MUSHROOM RAGOUT

The term *ragout* refers to a thick, rich, well-seasoned stew. They are traditionally made of meat or poultry, but substituting mushrooms makes for an interesting variation. When finished, this dish will still have a lot of juice, which is okay, because it is meant to be served in a bowl or over grits or rice. If you want a thicker ragout—perhaps as a side dish for roasted chicken—strain the mushrooms and simmer the juice to reduce it to about 1 cup.

The mushrooms for this dish may include morels, cèpes (known in Italy as porcini), trumpets, hedgehogs, and shiitakes, depending on what is available. Do not use portobellos, as the black gills will fall apart when the mushrooms are sliced. Also, dried mushrooms that have been reconstituted can make up as much as half of the ragout.

A few mushroom tips:

- Rinse fresh morels, because they can be sandy.
- If you use shiitakes, remove the stems, as they are tough, and wipe the caps with a damp paper towel.
- When you reconstitute dried mushrooms, strain the liquid you use through a coffee filter, boil it to reduce it to a syrup, and add it to the dish you're preparing.

Serves 4 to 6 people.

¼ cup extra virgin olive oil
¾ cup minced shallots
¼ cup minced garlic
½ cup seeded and julienned poblano pepper
2 cups chicken stock (see page 5)
½ cup dry white wine
8 cups sliced wild mushrooms, cleaned and trimmed as necessary
2 tablespoons chopped fresh thyme or a pinch of dried thyme
⅛ teaspoon salt
⅛ teaspoon freshly ground black pepper

1. Heat the olive oil over medium heat in a heavy nonreactive stockpot until hot but not smoking. Add the shallots, garlic, and poblano pepper. Sauté over medium-high heat for 1 minute, reduce the heat to medium, and sauté for 5 to 7 minutes or until lightly browned, stirring frequently to make sure the mixture does not scorch. Lower the heat if necessary.

2. Meanwhile, heat the stock in a separate pan. Add the wine to the hot stock and briskly simmer for 5 minutes to reduce the volume.

3. Add the mushrooms and thyme to the shallot mixture and cook for 5 minutes, stirring well and often. Spoon off any oil that may rise to the top. Add the hot stock mixture and simmer for 8 to 10 minutes or until the ragout thickens somewhat. It will still have a lot of juice. Stir in the salt and pepper and serve immediately.

# CHAD'S MOM'S SWEET POTATO SOUFFLÉ

■ Chad Blackwelder worked with me while he was attending Johnson & Wales University in Charleston, and later he became my sous-chef. Chad is wonderfully creative and, like most gifted cooks, relies heavily on memories of his family's concoctions. This soufflé is a great example.

Serves 8 to 10 people.

**FOR THE TOPPING:**

- ½ cup packed light brown sugar
- ½ cup sugar
- 4 tablespoons all-purpose flour
- ⅓ cup pecan pieces
- ⅓ cup shredded coconut
- 4 tablespoons unsalted butter, cut into 12 pieces

**FOR THE SWEET POTATOES:**

- 4 large sweet potatoes, peeled and quartered
- 3 large eggs, lightly beaten
- 8 tablespoons unsalted butter, at room temperature
- 1 cup heavy cream
- 2 teaspoons ground cinnamon
- 1 teaspoon ground coriander
- Salt and freshly ground black pepper to taste

6" × 9" gratin dish or similarly sized baking dish, buttered

1. To prepare the topping, combine the brown sugar, sugar, flour, pecans, and coconut in a medium bowl until evenly mixed. Cut in the pieces of butter with a pastry cutter or 2 forks until the mixture forms pea-size pieces. Reserve.

2. Place the sweet potatoes in a heavy saucepan, cover with water, and bring to a boil. Boil over medium heat for about 20 minutes or until tender when

pierced with a fork. Drain the sweet potatoes and leave them to dry in a colander for about 10 minutes.

3. Preheat the oven to 325°F.

4. Put the sweet potatoes through a food mill. If you want to use a food processor instead, you may need to add a little of the cream to keep the mixture moving. Stop processing as soon as the potatoes are smooth. Too much processing will make them gummy.

5. With a whisk or large spoon, combine the sweet potatoes with the eggs, butter, cream, cinnamon, and coriander. Season with salt and pepper to taste. Pour the mixture into the gratin dish.

6. Distribute the topping evenly over the sweet potatoes and bake, uncovered, in the preheated oven for 30 to 40 minutes or until the top is nicely browned. Serve immediately.

# SWEET POTATOES WITH BOURBON AND BLUE CHEESE

■ This is the absolutely perfect pairing with a holiday turkey. With the tangy cheese and nutty bourbon, the sweet potatoes provide the right medley of tastes for a festive meal.

Serves 8 people.

8 medium sweet potatoes, skin on and washed
1 head garlic
2 tablespoons peanut oil
1 cup diced yellow onion
8 tablespoons unsalted butter
3 cups heavy cream or whole milk, depending on your taste
8 ounces crumbled Clemson or other crumbly blue cheese
½ teaspoon salt
½ teaspoon freshly ground black pepper
Light brown sugar to taste
2 tablespoons bourbon, or to taste

1. Preheat the oven to 400°F.

2. Pierce each sweet potato with a knife a couple of times to prevent them from exploding in the oven. Place them on a piece of aluminum foil in the preheated oven and bake for 45 minutes to 1 hour or until they are very soft.

3. Meanwhile, brush the head of garlic with a little of the peanut oil. Wrap tightly in foil and roast in the oven along with the potatoes. When soft, after about 30 minutes, remove from the oven, let cool enough to handle, and peel the cloves. Set aside.

4. Remove the sweet potatoes from the oven and turn off the oven. When they are cool enough to handle, peel and place in a baking dish. Cover with foil and return to the turned-off oven to keep warm.

5. Heat the remaining oil in a heavy-bottomed sauté pan over medium heat. Add the onion and sauté, stirring continuously, for 6 to 8 minutes or until it is a caramel brown. Lower the heat if needed to keep from scorching. Remove the onion from the pan and set aside. Discard the oil.

6. Place the butter and cream or milk in a saucepan and heat until the butter melts.

7. Place the garlic cloves, warm sweet potatoes, caramelized onion, and blue cheese in the bowl of an electric mixer. Using the flat beater, beat in the hot butter and cream or milk, mixing all of the ingredients together. Don't over-beat. There should still be texture from the potatoes and onion.

8. Add the salt and pepper. Add brown sugar to taste. Add the bourbon by the teaspoonful, tasting the potatoes as you go, until they taste right to you. If the potatoes seem too thick, add more cream or milk. Serve immediately.

# JACK DANIEL'S CHOCOLATE ICE CREAM

Jack Daniel's, a Southern favorite, adds a layer of genteel flavor to this ice cream. If you prefer, you can leave it out and substitute 1½ teaspoons of pure vanilla extract.

Makes 1 quart.

- 5 ounces semisweet chocolate, finely chopped
- 5 ounces unsweetened chocolate, finely chopped
- ½ cup Jack Daniel's or other good-quality whiskey
- 2 cups whole milk
- 2 cups heavy cream
- 8 large egg yolks
- ¼ cup plus 2 tablespoons sugar

1. Put both chocolates and the Jack Daniel's in a 3-quart bowl and set aside.

2. Bring the milk and cream to a low boil in a heavy-bottomed saucepan over medium heat.

3. Meanwhile, put the egg yolks into the bowl of an electric mixer. With the whisk attachment, slowly beat the sugar into the yolks until the mixture lightens in color.

4. Remove the milk mixture from the heat. Take 2 cups of the hot mixture and slowly pour it into the bowl of the electric mixer, continuing to use the whisk attachment to combine it with the yolks and sugar. Slowly pour the mixture into the saucepan with the remaining milk mixture, now whisking by hand.

5. Return the saucepan to the stove. Stirring constantly with a wooden spoon or rubber spatula, gently cook the mixture over low heat for 5 to 10 minutes or until it is thick enough to coat the back of a spoon. You now have custard.

6. Pour the custard into the bowl with the chocolate and Jack Daniel's and vigorously whisk until the chocolate completely melts. Strain the custard into a refrigerator container, cover, and chill overnight. When ready to churn, pour the chilled custard into a prepared ice cream maker and proceed according to the manufacturer's instructions.

# BUTTERSCOTCH PUDDING

This pudding is the quintessential "feel good" food; it never fails to remind me of my childhood. This particular recipe is simply irresistible, as my granddaughter, Abigail, will tell you.

Makes twelve 1-cup servings.

- 4½ cups whole milk
- 2 cups heavy cream
- 1 vanilla bean, split lengthwise
- 12 tablespoons unsalted butter, cut into 12 pieces
- 2½ cups tightly packed dark brown sugar
- ½ cup tightly packed cornstarch
- ½ teaspoon salt
- 6 large egg yolks, lightly beaten
- 1 tablespoon pure vanilla extract

1. Put 4 cups of the milk and all of the cream in a heavy saucepan. With the side of a spoon, scrape the seeds out of the vanilla bean pod and add both the seeds and the pod to the saucepan. Stir to combine the ingredients and bring the mixture to a simmer over medium-high heat.

2. Meanwhile, place the butter and brown sugar in another heavy saucepan over medium-high heat and stir until they melt. Reduce the heat to very low and cook for 8 minutes, stirring occasionally. Increase the heat to medium and whisk in the hot milk and cream. If the mixture breaks or looks curdled, take it off the heat and whisk until it smoothes out.

3. Combine the cornstarch and salt in a small bowl. Whisk into the remaining ½ cup of milk, making sure there are no lumps. Whisk the cornstarch and milk mixture into the hot milk and butter mixture. Bring to a gentle boil, whisking occasionally.

4. Slowly whisk 2 cups of the hot butter and milk mixture into the egg yolks. Whisk the mixture into the saucepan with the remaining hot butter and milk mixture and simmer for 1 minute or until it starts to thicken.

5. Strain the pudding and discard the vanilla bean pod. Add the vanilla extract. Pour into a decorative bowl or individual serving dishes. If using a single large bowl, place a piece of plastic wrap directly on top of the pudding. If using individual dishes, cover them tightly with plastic wrap, then pierce a small hole in each to allow steam to escape. Covering the pudding helps to prevent a skin from forming on top. Cool to room temperature and refrigerate. The covered pudding will keep in the refrigerator for 3 or 4 days.

# BUTTERMILK BREAD PUDDING

An updated version of a classic, the addition of buttermilk adds a certain piquancy to this rich dessert.

Serves 6 people.

8 large eggs
4 cups sugar
1 tablespoon pure vanilla extract
4 cups buttermilk (whole fat if available)
2 cups heavy cream
2 tablespoons red wine vinegar
4 cups ½" cubes egg bread, such as challah
Best-quality strawberry preserves
Confectioners' sugar
1 recipe Crème Anglaise (see page 33)

Six 8-ounce ramekins, buttered with 4 tablespoons unsalted butter and dusted with 4 tablespoons sugar

1. Whisk together the eggs and sugar in a large mixing bowl. Whisk in the vanilla, buttermilk, cream, and vinegar. Add the bread cubes and toss with your fingers to incorporate. Cover and refrigerate for at least 6 hours or overnight. The bread will absorb much of the liquid.

2. Preheat the oven to 350°F.

3. Divide the bread pudding among the 6 ramekins. It should be wet and gooey. Place the ramekins on a baking sheet and bake in the preheated oven for 20 to 25 minutes or until the tops are golden brown and the custard has set.

4. Divide the strawberry preserves among 6 plates. Loosen the bread puddings by running a small knife around the edges of the ramekins and invert them on top of the preserves. Dust the puddings with confectioners' sugar and spoon the crème anglaise around them. Serve immediately.

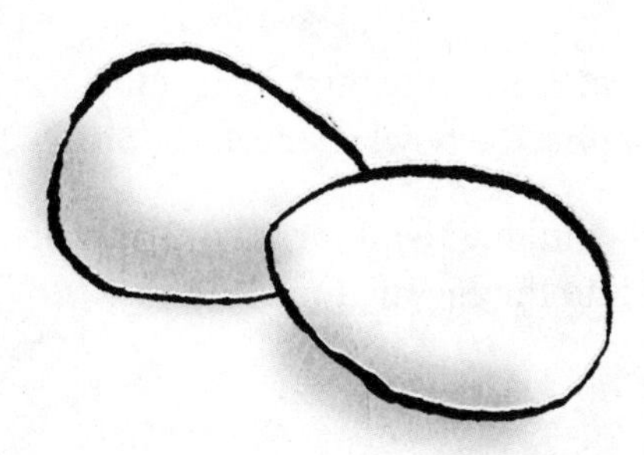

# RUM CAKE WITH CARAMELIZED BANANAS

This rum cake is a recipe from our pastry chef Deanie Cooper's grandmother. Deanie swears that her grandmother makes the best version, but I find it hard to believe that any version can be better than this one.

Serves 10 to 12 people.

**FOR THE CAKE:**

1¼ cups unsalted butter, at room temperature
1 cup pecan pieces
2 cups sugar
8 large eggs
2 teaspoons pure vanilla extract
2½ cups cake flour
1 tablespoon baking powder
1 tablespoon baking soda
1 teaspoon salt
1¼ cups dark rum (I use Myers's)

Bundt pan, buttered with 4 tablespoons unsalted butter and sprinkled with 2 tablespoons sugar

**FOR THE GLAZE:**

½ cup unsalted butter
½ cup packed dark brown sugar
½ cup dark rum (I use Myers's)

**FOR SERVING:**

1 recipe Vanilla Ice Cream (see page 37)
1 recipe Caramelized Bananas (recipe follows)

1. Preheat the oven to 350°F.

2. Heat 4 tablespoons of the butter in a sauté pan over medium heat until melted. Add the pecans and cook them in the butter for 10 to 15 minutes or until they are roasted and aromatic. Stir frequently and adjust the heat if necessary to prevent scorching. Set aside to cool.

3. Put the remaining butter and the sugar into the bowl of an electric mixer and beat with the flat beater until the mixture is fluffy and light in color. Add the eggs 1 at a time, scraping the bowl after each addition. Beat in the vanilla.

4. In a separate bowl, combine the flour, baking powder, baking soda, and salt and mix well. Fold into the egg mixture.

5. Pour the 1¼ cups of rum into the Bundt pan. Spoon the butter and pecans over it. Pour in the batter. Bake in the preheated oven for 35 to 45 minutes or until a cake tester inserted in the middle comes out clean. Remove from the oven and cool in the pan for 15 minutes. Invert onto a cake plate.

6. To make the glaze, put the butter, brown sugar, and rum in a small saucepan and heat until the butter is melted and the sugar is dissolved. Pour the hot glaze over the warm cake. Let the glaze cool and set before cutting the cake.

7. Serve each slice of cake with 2 scoops of vanilla ice cream and 3 pieces of caramelized banana. Drizzle some of the juices from the bananas around the cake.

## Caramelized Bananas

The bananas in this recipe are flambéed, which makes them wonderful, but you must do this carefully. Never pour alcohol out of a bottle into a hot pan when the pan is on the stove. It is possible that the fire may shoot back into the bottle, which can explode. Premeasure the rum in a metal cup and remove the hot pan from the stove before pouring in the rum.

- 1 cup unsalted butter
- 1 cup packed light brown sugar
- 4 bananas
- 1 cup dark rum (I use Myers's)

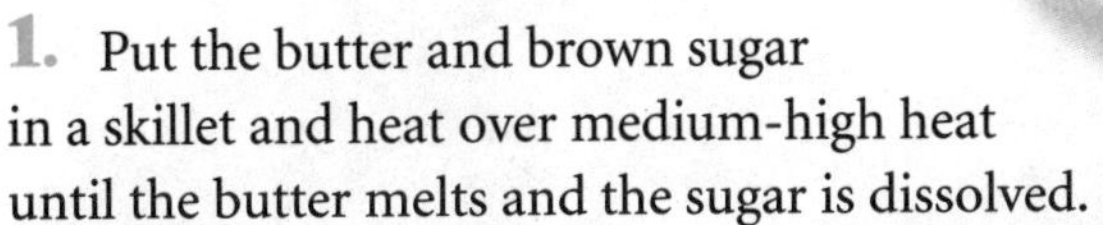

1. Put the butter and brown sugar in a skillet and heat over medium-high heat until the butter melts and the sugar is dissolved.

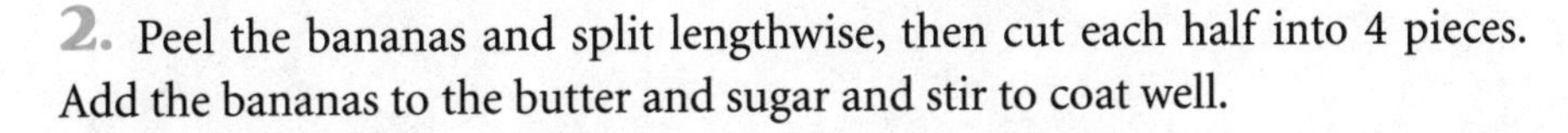

2. Peel the bananas and split lengthwise, then cut each half into 4 pieces. Add the bananas to the butter and sugar and stir to coat well.

3. Remove the pan from the heat and add the premeasured rum. Return the pan to the stove and shake it slightly. The heat may ignite the rum. When the flame dies, the bananas are ready. Otherwise, simmer for 30 seconds more. Both the bananas and pan juices should be served with the rum cake while still warm.

# Four Suggested Spring Menus

Sweet Onion and Goat Cheese Tart /147

Shad Roe with Bacon, Lemon Butter, and Capers /158

Creamy Grits /71

Lemon-Mint Ice Cream with Rosemary Sablés /181, 182

Soft-Shell Crab Salad with Candied Hazelnuts
and a Sherry Vinaigrette /152

Beef Tenderloin with Morels, Scallions, and Sugar Snaps /170

Mashed Potatoes with Sun-Dried Tomatoes /177

Blood Orange Crème Brûlée /183

Goat Cheese with Roasted Red Peppers /149

Mint-Encrusted Lamb Medallions /172

Asparagus and Morel Gratin /174

Buttermilk Tart with Fresh Raspberries /184

Salad of Watermelon, Watercress, and Scallions
with a Shallot-Citrus Vinaigrette /146

Cabbage Stuffed with Beer-Braised Rabbit /164

Baked Rice with Wadmalaw Sweets /176

Roasted Banana Ice Cream /179

## Spring in the Lowcountry

In antebellum years, early spring was Charleston's most brilliant social season, a time for theater, concerts, and elegant private parties and balls. Even now spring is a favored time here. The season is glorious, and visitors come to tour our homes and gardens. The season is heralded by the advent of showy azalea flowers, and spring fruits and vegetables begin to appear in the market.

The very earliest sign of spring in Charleston is shad roe. By early March, the roe, or eggs, of the plentiful shad fish found along our Atlantic seacoast are ready for harvesting. Long considered a great delicacy in the Lowcountry, Charlestonians eagerly await the arrival of shad roe on restaurant menus—as much for its distinctive taste as its signaling the beginning of the season. Not long after shad roe appears, soft-shell crabs are harvested. The blue crab, which is ubiquitous along our shoreline, sheds its skin, and before it has a chance to grow a new hard shell—just several days—enterprising fishermen and food enthusiasts catch soft-shell crabs. What a treat to enjoy the sweet meat without having to wrest it from its normally hard shell!

For me, cooking in springtime is a special pleasure. It is the beginning of the seasonal rhythm that governs the food we eat, and cooking with fresh, young vegetables provides renewed inspiration. As spring appears, we buy up the slender asparagus, the small new potatoes, the tender green beans, the little sweet carrots, and the young lettuces. Mint is soon available to dress up peas, Easter lamb, iced tea, and mint juleps. There are young leeks, fiddlehead ferns, and tender greens, especially spinach. You will find a whole host of recipes using Wadmalaw Sweets, which are available exclusively in spring, unlike most of the other sweet onions. (Maui and Walla Walla are year-round sweet onions that you may use when Wadmalaws—or Vidalias—aren't available.) I love cooking with these wonderfully perfumed, sugary onions. All of these young, fresh vegetables play an important part in my recipes for spring, and I hope you will use them as an inspiration to taste the best of spring's beneficence.

# SALAD OF WATERMELON, WATERCRESS, AND SCALLIONS WITH A SHALLOT-CITRUS VINAIGRETTE

I made this salad at the Celebration of Southern Chefs in Memphis in 1998 and served it with my Braised Black Angus Short Ribs Crusted with Wadmalaw Sweets (see page 208). It was a huge triumph, if I do say so myself. The refreshing flavor of the watermelon was the perfect counterpoint to the rich ribs.

Serves 6 to 8 people.

**FOR THE VINAIGRETTE:**

3 tablespoons minced shallots
2 teaspoons coarse Dijon mustard (I use Grey Poupon)
1 teaspoon honey, or to taste
2 tablespoons rice wine vinegar
2 tablespoons apple cider vinegar
1 tablespoon fresh blood orange juice (regular fresh orange juice may be substituted)
1 tablespoon fresh lemon juice
1 tablespoon fresh lime juice
½ cup extra virgin olive oil
½ cup peanut oil
Salt and freshly ground black pepper to taste

**FOR THE SALAD:**

½ teaspoon sesame oil
3 tablespoons sesame seeds
4 cups seeded watermelon pieces, about 1" each
6 cups fresh watercress leaves (about 1 bunch), gently washed and dried
¼ cup fresh Italian parsley, gently washed and dried
½ cup sliced scallions, white and green parts
½ cup fresh chervil tops (fresh oregano may be substituted)

1. To make the vinaigrette, put the shallots, mustard, honey, vinegars, and fruit juices in a small nonreactive bowl, a blender, or a food processor. Whisk or process the ingredients until well combined.

2. Slowly whisk in the oils or very slowly pour them into the blender or food processor, teaspoon by teaspoon. Be careful not to add them too quickly or you will break the emulsion. Add salt and pepper to taste. Tightly covered, the dressing will keep in the refrigerator for a week. If it separates, whisk to bring it back together.

3. To prepare the salad, heat the sesame oil in a small sauté pan until hot but not smoking. Add the sesame seeds and cook until the oil colors slightly. Pour off the oil and reserve the seeds.

4. Combine half of the sesame seeds with the watermelon, watercress, parsley, scallions, and chervil in a large bowl and toss with the vinaigrette to taste.

5. Divide the greens among individual salad plates, carefully saving the colorful watermelon pieces to place on top. Sprinkle with the remaining sesame seeds and serve immediately.

# SWEET ONION AND GOAT CHEESE TART

I have been told many times that I use a lot of onions in my restaurant preparations, and it's true. The onion is very versatile and can add layers of flavor to dishes. Wadmalaw Sweets, the local sweet spring onions, are grown on nearby Wadmalaw Island, and they further increase my predilection for this great vegetable.

Makes four 6" tarts or twelve 2½" tartlets.

- 4 tablespoons unsalted butter
- 6 cups finely sliced Wadmalaw Sweets or other sweet onions such as Vidalia or Maui (about 1½ pounds)
- Salt and freshly ground black pepper to taste
- ¼ cup goat cheese, at room temperature
- ¼ cup sour cream
- 1 tablespoon heavy cream
- 1 large egg yolk
- ¼ teaspoon chopped fresh thyme
- 1 teaspoon salt
- ½ recipe Best Pie Dough (see page 28), unbaked

1. Heat the butter in a heavy skillet over medium heat. Add the onions and sprinkle them with a little salt and pepper. Stir to combine. Reduce the heat to low and cook the onions, stirring occasionally, for about 30 minutes or until they begin to caramelize. As the liquid evaporates and the onions begin to caramelize, a thin glaze will cling to the bottom of the pan. When this happens, add a tablespoon or 2 of water to deglaze the pan. With a spoon or spatula, scrape up the glaze as it liquefies. The onions will absorb this liquid and its color. You may have to do this several times during the caramelization process. The onions should turn golden brown after about 15 minutes of this. Remove from the heat.

2. Preheat the oven to 450°F.

3. Whisk together the goat cheese, sour cream, heavy cream, egg yolk, thyme, and 1 teaspoon of salt in a medium bowl. Set aside.

4. On a lightly floured surface, roll out the dough to 1⁄16" thickness. Cut out either four 6" circles or twelve 2½" circles. Place the circles on baking sheets. For 6" circles, place ½ cup of the caramelized onions on each and spoon 1½ tablespoons of the cheese mixture on top, spreading evenly. For 2½" circles, use 2 tablespoons of the caramelized onions and ½ teaspoon of the cheese mixture. Don't attempt to spread out the cheese on the tartlets.

5. Bake the tarts in the preheated oven for about 15 minutes or until the pastry is baked and light brown. (Both sizes take about the same time to cook.) The 6" tarts can be quartered and served in slices. Serve immediately.

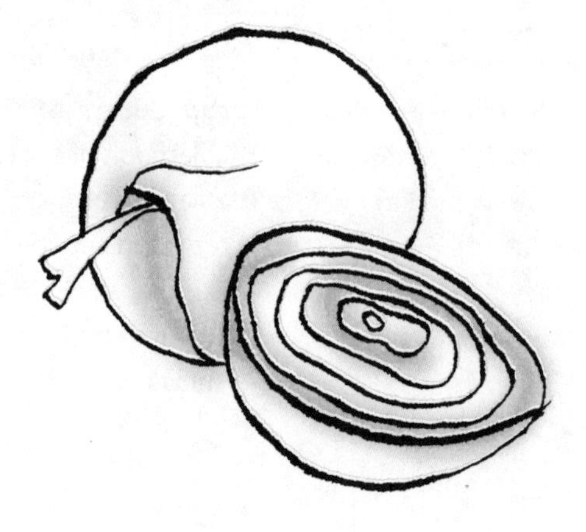

# GOAT CHEESE WITH ROASTED RED PEPPERS

■ This is probably the most popular salad I've ever served. It went on my menu in 1984 and it's still there today. It's a fairly simple salad, but for the best flavor, the goat-cheese rounds must be warm.

Serves 4 people.

3 medium red bell peppers
5 tablespoons extra virgin olive oil
3 large cloves garlic, peeled and very thinly sliced
Kosher salt and freshly ground black pepper to taste
1 log goat cheese (about 14 ounces)
⅓ cup all-purpose flour
1 large egg, lightly beaten
½ cup whole milk
1 cup dried unseasoned bread crumbs, made in a food processor from a sliced and dried baguette
4 tablespoons unsalted butter
1 tablespoon red wine vinegar
4 cups baby lettuce leaves, washed and gently patted dry

Wax paper

1. Preheat the broiler.

2. Rub the whole bell peppers with 1 tablespoon of the olive oil. Place them on a baking sheet lined with aluminum foil and broil for 15 to 20 minutes or until their skin blisters, turning regularly. They will get black spots, which won't hurt, but you don't want them to get black all over.

3. When the peppers have blistered, place them in a bowl and cover tightly with plastic wrap or place them in a brown paper bag and fold the top shut. When the peppers are cool enough to handle, peel off their skins. Core them and remove all of their seeds.

4. Quarter the peppers lengthwise, place in a bowl, and toss with 1 tablespoon of the olive oil, the garlic, and salt and pepper to taste. Cover and let sit at room temperature for at least 3 hours. (The peppers may be done a day ahead and refrigerated, but they should be brought back to room temperature before serving.)

5. Line a baking sheet with wax paper. Cut the goat-cheese log into 12 rounds. Dip the rounds in the flour and shake to remove the excess. In a small bowl, mix the egg and milk. Dip the rounds in this mixture, making sure they are completely covered. Dip the wet rounds into the bread crumbs, making sure they are fully coated. Place the rounds on the baking sheet and lightly cover with plastic wrap. Place the rounds in the refrigerator to dry for at least 30 minutes or overnight.

6. When ready to serve the salad, preheat the oven to 200°F.

7. Heat the butter in a heavy-bottomed sauté pan over medium-high heat. Sauté the goat-cheese rounds for 2 minutes per side or until golden brown. Keep the rounds warm in the preheated oven while you are finishing the salad.

8. Whisk the vinegar and remaining 3 tablespoons of olive oil together, adding the oil slowly, or put the vinegar in a blender and very slowly pour the oil into it, teaspoon by teaspoon. Add salt and pepper to taste.

9. Toss the greens with the dressing to just lightly coat them. Divide the greens among 4 salad plates, placing them on the top half of the plate. Working quickly, fan 3 pieces of red bell pepper on the bottom half of each plate, just touching the greens. Top each with warm rounds of goat cheese and serve immediately.

# SOFT-SHELL CRABS WITH A RAGOUT OF SPRING VEGETABLES

I think of this recipe as one that captures the changing of the seasons. It takes a little time because each of the green vegetables needs to be blanched separately, but the final dish is well worth the effort.

Serves 4 people.

- 1 cup haricots verts or baby green beans
- 1 cup diagonally sliced asparagus (slices should be about ⅓" long)
- 1 cup shelled sweet peas
- 1 cup snow peas, stem ends removed
- 1 cup fiddlehead ferns, skin removed
- 5 tablespoons unsalted butter
- 3 cups sliced sweet onions, such as Wadmalaw, Vidalia, or Maui (about 1 pound)
- 1 cup fresh morels
- 1 cup chicken stock (see page 5)
- ¼ cup heavy cream
- 1 cup mixed red and yellow sweet cherry tomatoes, halved
- 1 tablespoon chopped fresh chervil
- 1 tablespoon chopped fresh basil
- 1 tablespoon chopped fresh thyme
- 1 teaspoon salt, or to taste
- 4 panfried soft-shell crabs (see steps 1–4 on page 154)

1. To blanch the green vegetables, bring a saucepan of salted water to a boil. Drop in the haricots verts and gently boil for 1 minute to set their color. Remove from the saucepan with a slotted spoon and refresh by rinsing with cold water. Set aside to dry. Follow the same procedure with the asparagus, sweet peas, snow peas, and fiddlehead ferns.

2. Melt 2 tablespoons of the butter in a heavy-bottomed pan over medium heat. Add the onions and morels and sauté for 4 minutes, stirring occasionally. Add the blanched green vegetables and continue to sauté for 2 minutes. Add the chicken stock and cream and stir to combine. Raise the heat to medium-high and briskly simmer the mixture for about 7 minutes or until the liquid is reduced by half.

3. With the mixture still briskly simmering, add the remaining 3 tablespoons of butter, the tomatoes, and the herbs. Cook, stirring occasionally, for 5 minutes or until the mixture thickens. Immediately remove the pan from the heat. Add the salt and stir to combine well.

4. Divide the vegetables among 4 plates and top each with a crab. Serve immediately.

# SOFT-SHELL CRAB SALAD WITH CANDIED HAZELNUTS AND A SHERRY VINAIGRETTE

Our sous-chef Chad Blackwelder came up with this unusual salad. It became a seasonal specialty and is still on our spring menu, even after 12 years.

Serves 6 people.

**FOR THE CANDIED HAZELNUTS:**

2 large egg whites
¼ cup sugar
¾ pound toasted and skinned hazelnuts (see steps 1 and 2 on page 220, but do not crush the nuts)

**FOR THE SALAD:**

2 tablespoons minced shallots
2 teaspoons Dijon mustard (I use Grey Poupon)
1 teaspoon honey
3 tablespoons sherry wine vinegar
2 tablespoons red wine vinegar
⅓ cup hazelnut oil
⅔ cup peanut oil
Salt and freshly ground black pepper to taste
2 cups julienned zucchini
2 cups julienned yellow squash
2 cups peeled and julienned chayote squash
2 cups peeled and julienned jícama
2 cups julienned red bell peppers
3 cups blanched haricots verts or baby green beans
4 cups mixed baby greens, gently washed and dried

**FOR THE CRABS:**

6 cleaned soft-shell blue crabs
2 cups buttermilk
1 large egg
1⅔ cups bread flour
1 cup toasted and skinned hazelnuts (see steps 1 and 2 on page 220, but do not crush the nuts)
Pinch of kosher salt
Pinch of freshly ground black pepper
½ cup peanut oil plus extra as needed
4 tablespoons unsalted butter plus extra as needed

1. Preheat the oven to 350°F.

2. To prepare the candied hazelnuts, whip the egg whites and sugar to just below the frothy stage. Toss with the hazelnuts.

3. Place the nuts on a wire mesh rack on top of a baking sheet. Bake in the preheated oven for about 10 minutes, watching carefully to avoid scorching. Cool to room temperature. You will have to break the nuts off the rack when ready to use.

4. To make the salad, place the shallots, mustard, honey, and both vinegars in a nonreactive bowl, a blender, or a food processor. Whisk or process the ingredients until well combined.

5. Slowly whisk in the hazelnut and peanut oils or very slowly pour them into the blender or food processor, teaspoon by teaspoon. Be careful not to add them too quickly, which could break the emulsion. Add salt and pepper to taste. Reserve.

6. Put the zucchini, squashes, jícama, bell peppers, and haricots verts in a bowl, cover, and refrigerate. Refrigerate the greens in a separate bowl.

7. Place the crabs in a nonreactive pan. Mix the buttermilk and egg and pour over the crabs. Cover the pan with plastic wrap and refrigerate for 1 hour, turning the crabs occasionally.

8. Process the bread flour and 1 cup of hazelnuts in a food processor until the mixture resembles coarse cornmeal. Pour into a bowl and stir in the salt and pepper. Drain the crabs and carefully dredge them in this breading mixture, shaking off the excess. Place the crabs on a wire rack over a baking sheet.

9. Heat ½ cup of the peanut oil and 4 tablespoons of the butter in a heavy skillet over medium-high heat. When hot, carefully place 2 or 3 of the crabs, depending on their size, in the skillet with their white side down. Panfry the crabs for 1½ to 2 minutes on each side or until they are a nice golden brown. Transfer to a platter lined with paper towels. (You may hold the crabs in a 200°F oven while you finish frying the others, but be sure to move quickly so they don't dry out.) You may have to add more peanut oil and butter to the pan as you continue to fry the remaining crabs.

10. To serve, finely crush half of the candied hazelnuts. Toss the mixed greens with some of the vinaigrette and divide among 6 salad plates. Toss the other vegetables with some of the vinaigrette. Set aside a third of the vegetables and divide the rest among the salad plates. Top each salad with a crab. Sprinkle the reserved vegetables over the crabs. Sprinkle both the crushed and whole candied hazelnuts over the salads as a garnish. Serve immediately.

# PANFRIED SOFT-SHELL CRABS

This is the technique that the restaurant uses to panfry soft-shell crabs. It is an alternative to deep-frying that uses less fat and is a good bit simpler. Panfrying also produces a lighter, more intensely flavored soft-shell crab than the traditional deep-frying method.

Serves 4 people.

- 8 cleaned soft-shell blue crabs
- 2 cups buttermilk
- 1 tablespoon Tabasco sauce
- 1 cup yellow cornmeal
- 1 cup all-purpose flour
- ½ teaspoon baking soda
- 1¼ teaspoons salt
- 1¼ teaspoons freshly ground black pepper
- ½ cup peanut oil plus extra as needed
- 4 tablespoons unsalted butter plus extra as needed
- ¼ cup plus 2 tablespoons water
- 2 tablespoons red wine vinegar
- ¼ cup plus 2 tablespoons fresh lemon juice
- 1 pound unsalted butter, cut into 16 pieces
- 2 tablespoons chopped fresh Italian parsley or chervil

1. Place the cleaned crabs in a nonreactive pan. Mix the buttermilk and Tabasco and pour over the crabs. Cover the pan with plastic wrap and refrigerate for 1 hour, turning the crabs occasionally.
2. Combine the cornmeal, flour, baking soda, 1 teaspoon of the salt, and 1 teaspoon of the pepper and mix well. Drain the crabs and carefully dredge them in this breading mixture, shaking off the excess. Place the crabs on a wire rack over a baking sheet.
3. Heat ½ cup of the oil and 4 tablespoons of the butter in a heavy skillet over medium-high heat. When hot, carefully place 2 or 3 of the crabs in the skillet, white side down. Panfry the crabs for 1½ to 2 minutes on each side or until they are a nice golden brown.
4. Transfer the crabs to a platter lined with paper towels. (You may hold the crabs in a 200°F oven while you finish frying the others, but be sure to move quickly so they don't dry out.) You may have to add more oil and butter to the pan as you continue to fry the remaining crabs.

5. When the last crab has been fried, carefully pour all the fat out of the skillet, retaining any small browned bits. Combine the water, vinegar, and lemon juice in a small bowl. Add to the skillet and simmer for 30 seconds. Add the remaining ¼ teaspoon each of salt and pepper and stir to combine.

6. Add the butter pieces to the skillet all at once and whisk to incorporate. Add the chopped parsley or chervil, stir, and pour into a sauceboat. Serve the crabs immediately and pass the sauce separately.

# SOFT-SHELL CRABS WITH WADMALAW SUCCOTASH AND PICKLED ONIONS

This dish uses local favorites that all come to the market in the spring. The rich crab, the ham- and herb-infused succotash, and the tart onions all combine for a spring supper to remember.

Serves 4 people.

**FOR THE PICKLED ONIONS:**

4 cups ⅛"-thick slices red onion (about 1¼ pounds)
2 teaspoons kosher salt
¼ cup plus 2 tablespoons red wine vinegar
Pinch of red pepper flakes
¾ tablespoon pickling spices (grocery-store variety is fine)
¼ cup sugar

**FOR THE SUCCOTASH:**

6 ears sweet corn, husks on
2 cups chicken stock (see page 5)
2 cups water
4 ounces country ham, diced into ¼" pieces
1 cup minced yellow onions
2 sprigs fresh thyme
1½ pounds shelled butter beans
¾ cup heavy cream
12 tablespoons unsalted butter
1 cup diced yellow onions
1 cup diced plum tomatoes
3 ounces diced prosciutto
Kosher salt and freshly ground black pepper to taste

**FOR THE CRABS:**

8 panfried soft-shell crabs (see steps 1–4 on page 154)

1. To prepare the pickled onions, toss the onion slices with the salt and allow them to sit for 30 minutes. Put the slices in a bowl of cold water for 15 minutes. Drain well in a colander.

2. Combine the vinegar, pepper flakes, pickling spices, and sugar in a small saucepan over medium-high heat. Bring to a boil, reduce the heat to medium, and let simmer for 10 minutes.

3. Place the onions in a bowl and pour the vinegar mixture over them. Cool to room temperature and cover.

4. To make the succotash, preheat the oven to 350°F.

5. Roast the corn in its husks in the preheated oven for 20 minutes. Let cool and shuck. Slice the kernels off the cobs with a sharp knife. The corn should have a nice yellow color and still be crisp.

6. Bring the stock and water to a boil in a heavy-bottomed pot over medium-high heat. Add the ham, minced onions, thyme, and butter beans. Reduce the heat to low and briskly simmer, uncovered, for 30 minutes or until the beans are tender but not mushy. Drain and remove the ham and sprigs of thyme.

7. Put the cream in a small heavy-bottomed saucepan over medium heat and bring to a simmer. Simmer for about 1 hour or until the cream is reduced by half.

8. Heat the butter in a saucepan over medium heat, add the diced onions, tomatoes, and prosciutto, and stir to combine. Reduce the heat to low, cover, and "sweat" the mixture for 5 minutes, stirring occasionally. Add the corn and butter beans. Add the reduced cream and stir to combine. Season to taste with kosher salt and freshly ground black pepper.

9. To serve, spoon the succotash onto 4 serving plates, top each with 2 crabs, and mound a little of the pickled onions on top for a garnish. Serve immediately.

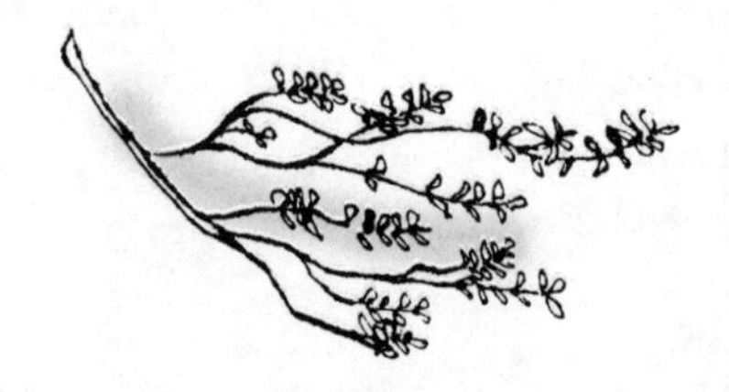

# SHRIMP PILAU

It is thought that the recipe for pilau, probably a rendition of the Oriental dish rice pilaf, came to Charleston in the late seventeenth century, shortly after rice arrived. Pilau is defined as a blend of rice with chicken or shrimp, and although other ingredients may be added for flavor, purists will tell you that anything other than stock and some seasoning is an aberration. Of course, there are about as many versions of pilau as there are of Southern barbecue.

Serves 4 people.

- 1 pound fresh shrimp, shelled and cleaned, but shells reserved
- 4 cups chicken stock (see page 5)
- 2 bay leaves
- 5 sprigs fresh thyme or ¼ teaspoon dried thyme
- 2 tablespoons peanut oil
- ½ cup diced bacon
- 2 cups diced sweet white or yellow onions (about ½ pound)
- 1⅓ cups diced green bell peppers
- 2 tablespoons hot green pepper, cored, seeded, and minced
- 1 cup thinly sliced scallions, green parts only
- 1 cup uncooked converted long-grain white rice (I use Uncle Ben's)
- Salt and freshly ground black pepper to taste

1. Place the reserved shrimp shells along with the stock, bay leaves, and thyme in a nonreactive pot over medium-high heat and bring to a simmer. Simmer for 20 minutes and strain. Measure the stock. If there are more than 2½ cups, briskly simmer until it is reduced to 2½ cups. Reserve.

2. Preheat the oven to 350°F.

3. Heat the peanut oil over medium-high heat in an ovenproof pan with a cover. When hot, add the bacon and sauté, turning occasionally, until it is lightly browned. Remove the bacon from the pan and place on a paper towel to drain.

4. Remove all but 4 tablespoons of fat from the pan and reserve. Add the onions, bell peppers, hot green pepper, and scallions to the pan. Sauté until lightly browned, stirring occasionally to prevent scorching. Add the rice and stir for 2 minutes or until it is coated with fat and begins to color slightly. Add the reserved stock and bring to a simmer. Stir in the reserved bacon. Cover and bake in the preheated oven for 15 minutes or until the rice is cooked and the liquid is absorbed.

5. Meanwhile, pat the shrimp dry and salt and pepper them lightly. Heat 4 tablespoons of the reserved fat in a heavy-bottomed sauté pan over medium heat. Add the shrimp and sauté, turning once, for 2 to 3 minutes or until they turn pink and begin to curl. Be careful—you want the shrimp to be done but not overcooked. Remove the pilau from the oven, fluff the rice with a fork, place the shrimp on top, and serve immediately.

# SHAD ROE WITH BACON, LEMON BUTTER, AND CAPERS

Charlestonians always look forward to the first-of-the-season shad roe to appear in the fish markets. The size of shad roe varies greatly, which is a major factor in how long it should be cooked. For that reason, cooking shad roe is one of those times when the old cast-iron skillet borders on being a necessity, because its heavy weight affords an even cooking surface. In this recipe, the roe is incredibly rich and delicious, the bacon adds a crunchy texture, and the capers and lemon add just the right touch of piquancy. The only improvement to this spring favorite would be to put a big dollop of creamy grits on the plate as well.

Serves 4 people.

- 4 sets medium to large shad roe
- 3 cups whole milk
- Tabasco sauce to taste (optional)
- 8 slices bacon, diced into ¼" pieces
- ⅔ cup all-purpose flour
- ¾ teaspoon salt
- ½ teaspoon freshly ground black pepper
- 9 tablespoons unsalted butter, 1 tablespoon reserved for sautéing, the rest cut into 12 pieces
- ¾ cup fresh lemon juice
- 1 cup chopped fresh Italian parsley
- 4 ounces small capers, drained
- ¼ cup water
- Salt and freshly ground black pepper to taste
- 1 recipe Creamy Grits (see page 71)

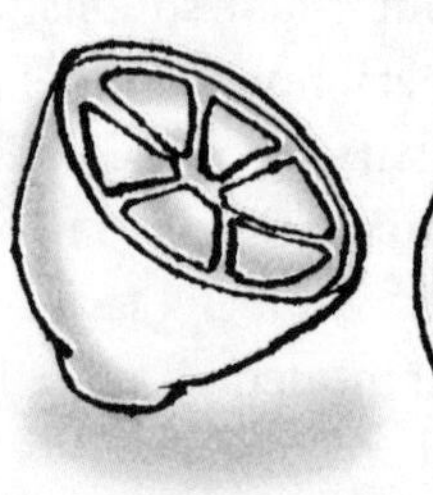

1. Cutting carefully, separate the sets of roe. You will see that there is a logical place to do this close to the center. Be sure not to puncture the membrane, as it holds in the eggs. Place the roe in a nonreactive pan and add enough milk to cover. Add a couple dashes of Tabasco to the milk if you like. Cover the pan and refrigerate for 2 hours.

2. Cook the bacon in a cast-iron skillet over medium heat until very crispy, turning it as it cooks. Remove to a paper towel to drain, leaving the rendered bacon fat in the pan.

3. Mix the flour, ¾ teaspoon of salt, and ½ teaspoon of pepper in a small bowl. When ready to cook the roe, drain carefully and dredge in the seasoned flour, shaking off the excess.

4. Add the reserved tablespoon of butter to the bacon fat in the skillet and heat over medium heat. When the butter starts to foam and the bubbles begin to subside, add the roe with the blue vein up. Sauté over medium heat, watching carefully. Shad roe has a tendency to cause the fat to pop and sputter as it cooks. The timing for cooking roe is important and delicate: in the center it should be cooked about medium, not rare, but not dry and crumbly either, and on the outside it should be slightly crusty. A 5" piece needs about 4 minutes on each side. When cooked, remove the roe to a platter lined with paper towels and cover loosely with aluminum foil while finishing the sauce.

5. Remove the skillet from the heat. Discard the fat but do not wipe or wash the skillet before proceeding. Add the lemon juice, parsley, capers, and remaining 8 tablespoons of butter. Place the skillet back on the heat and add the water. Shake the skillet as the butter melts. This should take about 3 minutes and the sauce should be slightly thickened. Take the skillet off the heat and add the reserved bacon and then salt and pepper to taste. Stir to combine everything.

6. Place the shad roe on warm plates, spoon a couple tablespoons of sauce over it, and serve with the creamy grits.

# WHOLE ROASTED BABY FLOUNDER WITH SWEET ONION MARMALADE

Here I use the sweet onion for a fairly rustic dish. The flounder is both crunchy and tender, and the onions just seem to melt into a sauce. If the onions are too sweet, stir a few drops of lemon juice into the sauce just before serving. Sometimes we serve the flounder with the sauce on top, directly on a bed of mashed potatoes. It's a little messy, but a delicious combination.

Serves 4 people.

**FOR THE MARMALADE:**

- 12 cups finely sliced Wadmalaw Sweets or other sweet onions, such as Vidalia or Maui (about 3 pounds)
- 1½ cups chicken stock (see page 5)
- 2 cups heavy cream
- ¼ teaspoon salt
- ¼ teaspoon freshly ground black pepper
- ¼ cup red wine vinegar

**FOR THE FISH:**

- Four 12- to 18-ounce dressed baby flounders
- 1 cup all-purpose flour
- 1 tablespoon salt
- 1 tablespoon freshly ground black pepper
- ¼ cup peanut oil
- 8 tablespoons unsalted butter

1. To prepare the marmalade, bring the onions and stock to a simmer in a heavy-bottomed saucepan over medium-high heat. Reduce the heat to low, cover, and let gently simmer for 1 hour, stirring occasionally.

2. Meanwhile, put the cream in a small heavy-bottomed saucepan and bring to a simmer over medium heat. Reduce the heat to low and simmer for 30 minutes or until the cream reduces by half.

3. Uncover the onions, add the salt and pepper, and increase the heat to medium. Cook the onions, stirring occasionally, for about 10 minutes or until the liquid begins to get syrupy. The onions should be very slightly browned. Stir in the reduced cream and simmer for about 20 minutes or until the mixture is a little thicker than heavy cream.

4. Add the vinegar, stir to combine well, and simmer for 1 to 2 minutes to meld the flavors. Keep warm while cooking the fish. (Cooled and then tightly covered, the marmalade will keep in the refrigerator for 2 to 3 days.)

5. Preheat the oven to 400°F.

6. Rinse the flounder and pat dry. In a shallow plate, combine the flour, salt, and pepper. Dredge both sides of the flounder in the seasoned flour, shaking to remove the excess.

7. Heat the oil and butter in a large skillet over medium-high heat until the butter begins to sizzle. One at a time, carefully lay the flounder in the skillet, white-skin side down. After 2 minutes, sneak a peek at the bottom side to make sure it is browning without burning, but don't be timid—a nice nutty brown is good. Carefully turn the flounder with a spatula and cook about 2 minutes or until browned. Transfer the fish to a baking sheet large enough to hold them all in a single layer.

8. Roast the flounder in the top third of the preheated oven for 6 to 8 minutes, depending on their size. Look closely: the inside of the fish should be just flaky and opaque. It is important not to overcook them. While the fish are roasting, warm the marmalade to a simmer. Place the fish on warm serving plates, top with the warm sauce, and serve immediately.

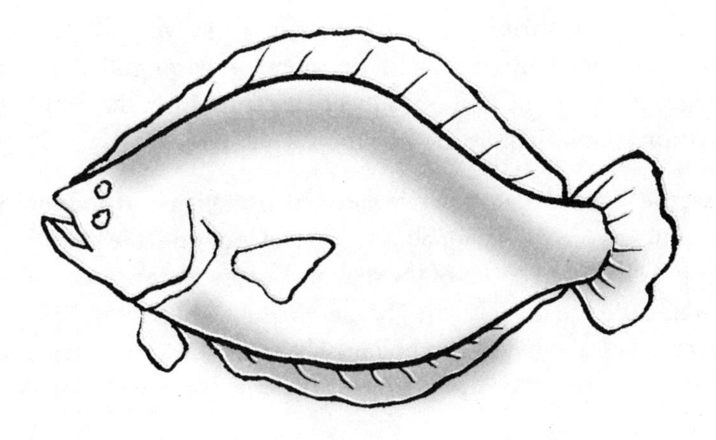

# ENCRUSTED RED SNAPPER WITH MORELS AND RED WINE

I expect that this dish falls into the fancy category, but it shouldn't. It's fairly easy to execute, though the flavors are complex and the finished product is something you can be proud of. This is a good example of combining red wine with fish, which is usually served with white wine. Use a light fruity red, such as a Burgundy or a good Beaujolais, in cooking the fish. Serve the same wine with the meal.

Serves 4 people.

**FOR THE SAUCE:**

- 2 cups dried morels
- 5 tablespoons minced shallots
- 2½ cups chicken stock (see page 5)
- 1½ cups plus 1 tablespoon red wine
- 2 teaspoons sugar
- 2 teaspoons chopped fresh thyme
- 2 crushed bay leaves
- Pinch of salt
- 3 grinds black pepper
- 1 tablespoon unsalted butter

**FOR THE SNAPPER:**

- 1 cup all-purpose flour
- 6 tablespoons porcini dust (made from 2 ounces dried porcini mushrooms; see note)
- 2 teaspoons salt
- Four 6-ounce red snapper fillets
- 2 tablespoons peanut oil
- 1 tablespoon unsalted butter

1. Reconstitute the dried morels by covering them with hot water and letting them soak for 30 minutes. Drain the morels, reserving all of the liquid except the sediment on the bottom. Squeeze the juice from the morels into the reconstituting liquid. Thinly slice the morels and reserve.

2. Place the liquid in a nonreactive saucepan over high heat and cook at a low boil, skimming as necessary, for about 15 minutes or until the liquid is reduced to a syrup. Add 3 tablespoons of the shallots along with the stock and 1½ cups of the wine. Add the sugar, thyme, bay leaves, salt, and pepper. Bring to a low boil over medium-high heat and boil briskly for about 15 minutes or until the mixture reduces to ½ cup. Strain. Reserve the liquid and discard the solids.

3. Heat the butter in a separate nonreactive saucepan and add the 2 remaining tablespoons of shallots. Cover and cook over medium heat until slightly translucent. Add the reserved morels and stir to combine. Add the remaining tablespoon of wine and the reserved ½ cup of liquid and stir to mix well. Keep the sauce warm while cooking the fish.

4. Mix the flour, porcini dust, and salt in a small bowl.

5. Lightly score the fillets on their skin side with diagonal cuts to keep the skin from shriveling. Dust the fillets with the seasoned flour, patting them lightly to remove the excess and leaving only a thin, delicate coating of flour.

6. Heat the oil and butter in a heavy skillet over medium-high heat until hot but not smoking. Place the fillets in the hot fat skin side up and sauté for about 3 minutes. Turn them over and sauté for about 5 minutes or until the fish are opaque in the center and just firm to the touch. The exterior color should be a deep, beautiful mahogany.

7. Place the snapper fillets on warm plates and pour a little sauce over each one, being sure to include a few of the mushrooms on each plate. Serve immediately.

TO MAKE PORCINI DUST: Using an absolutely dry food processor or blender, and working in batches as necessary, grind the dried porcini mushrooms until as fine as flour. The dust will keep for several months in a dry, airtight container.

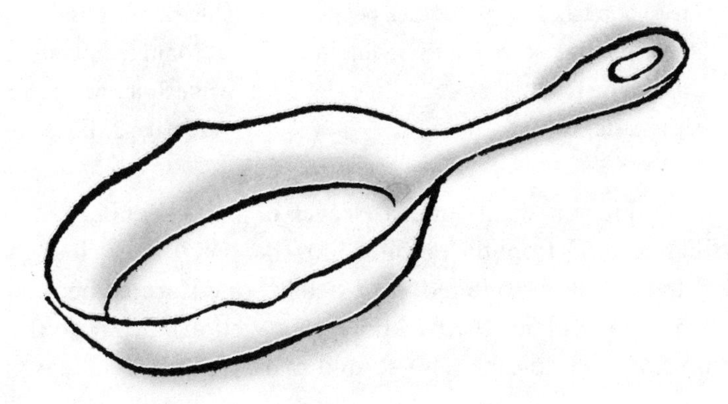

# CABBAGE STUFFED WITH BEER-BRAISED RABBIT

Both cabbage and rabbit are favorites of mine. For me, cabbage is the ultimate comfort food, and has been as long as I can remember. It is earthy and sweet and combines well with the cooking juices and tender meat of the braised rabbit, another favorite of my childhood.

Serves 4 people.

**FOR THE RABBIT:**

- One 3-pound rabbit
- 2 cups dark beer (I use Beck's)
- ½ cup yellow onion, peeled and sliced lengthwise
- ¼ cup peeled and thinly sliced carrots
- 4 sprigs fresh thyme or ¼ teaspoon dried thyme
- 1 bay leaf
- 2 tablespoons sugar
- 4 tablespoons peanut oil
- 3 tablespoons unsalted butter
- 1 cup chicken stock (see page 5)

**FOR THE CABBAGE:**

- One 2-pound head green cabbage
- 3 tablespoons unsalted butter
- ½ cup finely diced streak o'lean
- 1 cup reserved braising liquid from the rabbit
- 1 cup chicken stock (see page 5)

**TO ASSEMBLE:**

- ¼ teaspoon freshly ground black pepper
- 3 tablespoons reserved braising liquid from the rabbit
- Salt to taste
- 4 tablespoons unsalted butter, at room temperature
- 1 recipe Spicy Mole Sauce (see page 271)

1. Using kitchen shears and a cleaver or French knife, remove the back leg/thigh sections from the rabbit. Follow the pelvic bone closely to keep from losing too much meat. Remove the pelvic bone (located between the 2 back legs) from the saddle (the backbone loin section). Separate the saddle/loin section from the rib cage. This should make 3 portions: 2 leg/thigh quarters

and the saddle. The rib cage (with heart, liver, and kidneys removed) can be used to make rabbit stock.

2. Combine the beer, onion, carrots, thyme, bay leaf, and sugar in a nonreactive bowl. Add the rabbit pieces, cover, and refrigerate for at least 2 hours or overnight, turning them often.

3. When you are ready to cook the rabbit, remove the pieces from the marinade and pat them dry. Strain the marinade through a fine mesh sieve, reserving the liquid and discarding the solids.

4. In a large, heavy sauté pan, heat the oil and butter over medium-high heat. When the fat is hot but not smoking, brown the rabbit pieces, allowing about 1 minute per side. Be careful not to crowd the pan or the pieces will steam instead of brown. As you remove a piece, replace it with another to keep the heat balanced. Don't let the temperature drop.

5. Remove the browned rabbit to a platter. Pour off the fat from the pan, retaining all of the solid pan drippings.

6. Return the rabbit pieces to the pan. Add the chicken stock and 1½ cups of the reserved marinade. Bring to a simmer, scraping the pan to release all of the browned bits. Reduce the heat to low, cover, and gently simmer to braise the rabbit. The saddle will be cooked and tender in about 8 minutes; remove from the pan and reserve. The legs take longer—about 10 to 12 minutes.

7. Place all of the rabbit pieces in a bowl, strain the braising liquid over them, and let cool. When cool enough to handle, remove the meat from the bone, discarding any fat and tendon. Coarsely chop the meat. Reserve the meat and the braising liquid separately.

8. To prepare the cabbage, remove the tough dark green outer leaves. Reserve 4 of the nicest and discard the rest of the outer leaves. Cut the cabbage head into quarters. Cut out the core and discard it. Finely shred the quarters by hand or with the fine slicing blade of a food processor.

9. Melt the butter in a heavy-bottomed saucepan over medium-high heat. When the butter is hot, add the streak o'lean and stir. When the streak o'lean starts to brown and most of the fat is rendered, remove the meat from the pan and reserve, but leave the fat in the pan.

10. Increase the heat to high. Add the cabbage and sauté, turning once, for 3 minutes or until lightly browned. Add the cup of braising liquid and the chicken stock. Bring the cabbage to a simmer, reduce the heat, and simmer for 15 minutes or until the cabbage is tender but still a little crisp. Drain and transfer to a bowl to cool.

11. While the cabbage is cooling, bring 4 quarts of salted water to a boil. Add the 4 reserved outer leaves of the cabbage and gently simmer for 4 minutes. Remove from the pan and place in an ice bath. When the leaves are cool, drain well.

12. Preheat the oven to 375°F.

13. To assemble, place the rabbit meat in a bowl. Add the reserved meat from the streak o'lean and 3 cups of the shredded cabbage. Toss to combine. Add the pepper, 3 tablespoons of braising liquid, and salt to taste. Toss again.

14. Lay out the 4 blanched outer leaves and cut out the V-shaped piece of core. Divide the rabbit mixture among the leaves, placing it on one end. Carefully wrap each leaf around the mixture by folding in the sides, then rolling it up.

15. Place the packets of rabbit in a shallow baking pan. Using a small pastry brush, brush each packet with the butter. Bake the cabbage packages in the preheated oven for 15 minutes or until lightly browned.

16. Meanwhile, heat the mole sauce in a heavy-bottomed saucepan over medium heat, stirring occasionally to prevent scorching. Remove the cabbage packages from the oven and place each on a warm plate. Spoon the mole sauce around them and serve immediately.

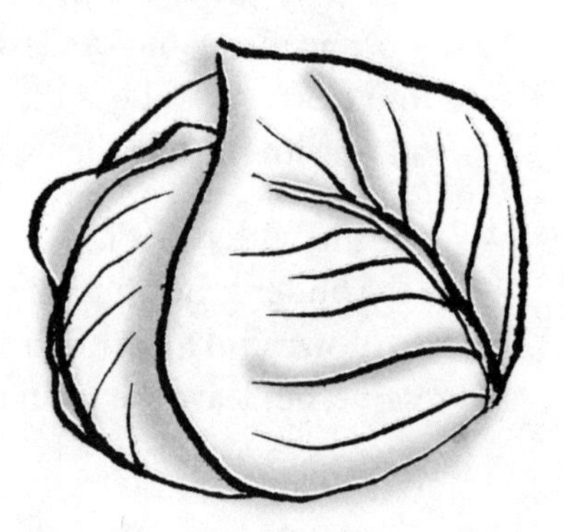

# BRAISED VEAL RIBS WITH GRILLED LEEKS

I was lucky enough to work for Chef François Delcros in my very first kitchen job. He was the owner of Le Versailles, which was Atlanta's very finest restaurant at the time. I give a lot of credit for my cooking to him, both as a teacher and a friend. Later, when we had the Pawleys Island Inn, François came to visit and ended up cooking with me. On one of those nights, the restaurant hosted a fund-raiser for the South Carolina governor's mansion. That dinner was the first time I served my veal ribs. As the ribs came out of the oven—a nice juicy medium rare—François quickly put them back in to cook to well done. I pulled them right back out, wanting them to be a little pink and very juicy. We almost came to blows. I expect this illustrates how American cuisine was beginning to evolve and finally shed the European shackles that had defined "fine dining" in this country for so long. Anyhow, the veal ended up going out mostly medium rare. I was happy, the governor was happy, and François was, well, mostly happy.

Serves 6 people.

**FOR THE GRILLED LEEKS:**

- 6 large leeks
- Extra virgin olive oil
- Salt
- Freshly ground black pepper

**FOR THE VEAL RIBS:**

- ⅓ cup peanut oil
- One 4-pound veal boneless rib roast, rolled and tied
- Salt and freshly ground black pepper to taste
- 1¼ cups peeled and finely diced carrots
- 2¼ cups finely sliced yellow onions (about ¾ pound)
- 1 cup dry white wine
- 3 cups veal stock (see page 9) or chicken stock (see page 5)
- 1 sprig fresh parsley
- 1 sprig fresh thyme
- 1 bay leaf

1. Shave the roots off the base of the leeks, keeping the base intact to hold the leek together. Cut off and discard the green part just above where the white part ends. Peel off the first outer layer of the white part. Starting 1" above the base of each, split the leeks down the middle. Soak in cold water to remove any sediment that is trapped between the layers. Drain and pat dry.

2. Heat the grill to medium-high. Rub the leeks with olive oil and sprinkle with salt and pepper. Turning and basting with olive oil, salt, and pepper, grill the leeks with the grill open for 30 minutes or until they are tender and browned along the edges of the middle and ends. Reserve until ready to serve.

3. Preheat the oven to 350°F.

4. To prepare the veal, heat the peanut oil in a large heavy-bottomed sauté pan over medium-high heat until just smoking. Put the veal in the pan, fat side down first. Sear all sides of the roast until nicely browned. Remove the veal, sprinkle with salt and pepper, and place in a large, heavy roasting pan.

5. Drain all but 1 tablespoon of fat from the sauté pan. Add the carrots and onions and cook, stirring frequently, for 4 to 5 minutes or until lightly browned. Deglaze the pan with the wine, scraping up any brown bits from the bottom of the pan. Add the stock and stir to mix well. Pour over the veal in the roasting pan.

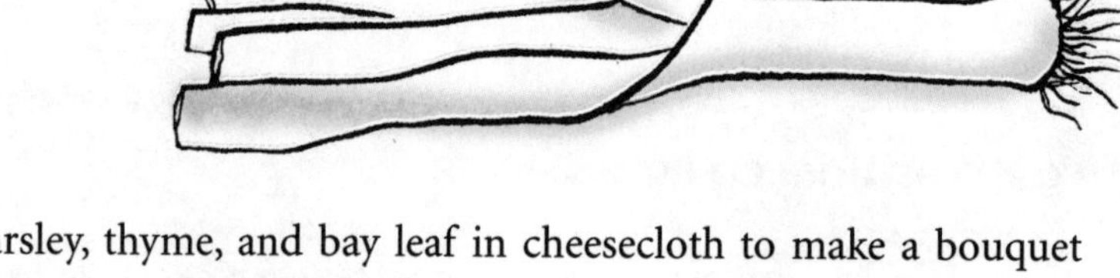

6. Tie the parsley, thyme, and bay leaf in cheesecloth to make a bouquet garni and add to the roasting pan. Put the pan over medium-high heat and bring the liquid to a boil. Cover the pan loosely by making a tent with a double layer of aluminum foil and place in the preheated oven.

7. Baste the veal with the pan juices every 15 minutes. Uncover the pan after 45 minutes. Check the temperature of the veal after 1 hour. It should register 125°F on a meat thermometer for medium rare. If it doesn't, continue to roast and baste the veal, checking its temperature every 10 minutes until the desired internal temperature is reached. Remove the veal from the pan and let it rest for 10 minutes before slicing. Strain the pan juices, remove the fat that rises to the top, and pour the juices into a sauceboat.

8. Remove the twine from the veal and carve it into slices about ⅓" thick. Arrange the slices on a warm platter and moisten with a small amount of the strained juices. Pass the rest in the sauceboat. The leeks may be served separately or on the platter with the sliced veal.

# VEAL SWEETBREADS WITH SWEET PEAS AND VIRGINIA HAM

Veal sweetbreads are very rich and creamy. They go well with the sweetness of the peas and the salty, savory flavor of the country ham. This recipe can be mostly done in advance and reheated for serving.

Serves 4 people.

- 6 tablespoons unsalted butter
- ⅓ cup peeled and minced carrots
- ⅓ cup minced yellow onion
- ⅓ cup minced celery
- 2 pairs veal sweetbreads, weighing about 1½ pounds per pair
- ½ cup white wine
- 2 cups veal stock (see page 9) or chicken stock (see page 5)
- 2 sprigs fresh Italian parsley
- 2 sprigs fresh thyme
- 1 bay leaf
- 1½ cups shelled fresh sweet peas (buy about 1 pound in the shell)
- ½ cup julienned country ham, fat removed
- ½ pound sliced shiitake mushroom caps (buy ¾ pound and remove the stems)
- ¼ teaspoon salt
- ½ teaspoon freshly ground black pepper
- ¼ cup port or Madeira

1. Preheat the oven to 350°F.

2. In a large ovenproof skillet with a cover, heat 4 tablespoons of the butter over medium heat until hot but not smoking. Add the carrots, onion, and celery and sauté for approximately 5 minutes or until the onion is slightly translucent, stirring occasionally.

3. Add the sweetbreads and sauté for about 10 minutes on each side, basting with the pan juices and turning only once, when their sides become white. Be careful when turning so that they don't break up.

4. Add the wine, stock, parsley, thyme, and bay leaf. Cover and bring to a boil. Reduce the heat until the mixture is just at a simmer and cover the top of the sweetbreads with wax paper. Cover with the lid, place on the middle rack of the preheated oven, and bake for 1 hour.

5. Meanwhile, blanch the sweet peas by placing them in a saucepan of boiling water for 2 to 3 minutes. Drain well and put in an ice bath. When cold,

drain well and set aside. (If using frozen peas, heat with 2 teaspoons of butter, a pinch of sugar, ¼ cup of water, ¼ teaspoon of salt, and a pinch of pepper until piping hot. Drain well.)

6. Remove the skillet from the oven. Remove the sweetbreads and vegetables, then strain the cooking liquid. Place the liquid in a small heavy-bottomed saucepan and boil over medium-high heat, skimming occasionally, until it has reduced to 1 cup and resembles heavy cream. Reserve.

7. Heat the remaining 2 tablespoons of butter in the skillet over medium heat until hot but not smoking. Add the ham and cook until slightly browned. Remove the ham from the pan and reserve. Add the mushrooms and sauté for 3 to 4 minutes or until just tender. Season with the salt and pepper. Add the reserved liquid to the pan. Add the sweetbreads and vegetables, ham, peas, and port or Madeira. Heat until warm and serve immediately.

# BEEF TENDERLOIN WITH MORELS, SCALLIONS, AND SUGAR SNAPS

This springtime preparation is great for a light lunch, despite what you might think about the heaviness of beef. Adding the vegetables and thinly slicing the meat lessen the intensity of the tenderloin.

Serves 4 people.

1 cup Green Chile Rub (see page 263)
One 2-pound piece beef tenderloin from the large end, trimmed
Salt and freshly ground black pepper to taste
¼ pound fresh morels
2 quarts water with 1 tablespoon salt
1 cup trimmed sugar snap peas (buy 6 ounces)
4 tablespoons unsalted butter
½ cup minced scallions, white and light green parts
2 sprigs fresh thyme
1 bay leaf
¾ cup chicken stock (see page 5)
3 tablespoons minced fresh parsley
1½ tablespoons minced fresh mint
1 large clove garlic, peeled and minced

1. Spread the green chile rub evenly over all sides of the tenderloin. Place in a large nonreactive baking pan, cover, and chill for at least 6 hours or overnight.

2. When ready to cook the tenderloin, preheat the oven to 400°F.

3. Place the tenderloin on a rack in a large roasting pan. Roast in the preheated oven for about 35 minutes for rare or until a meat thermometer inserted into the center registers 125°F. Remove from the oven, salt and pepper to taste, and cover with aluminum foil. Let stand for 10 minutes before slicing.

4. Halve the morels lengthwise or quarter them if they're large. Wash in a bowl of cold water and drain on paper towels.

5. Bring the salted water to a boil. Add the sugar snap peas and cook for 1 minute. Drain, refresh in an ice bath, and drain again.

6. Combine 2 tablespoons of the butter with the scallions, thyme, bay leaf, ¼ cup of the stock, and salt and pepper to taste in a large heavy-bottomed skillet over medium-high heat. Bring to a simmer, cover, and cook for 5 minutes. Add the morels and the remaining ½ cup of stock. Cover and simmer for 10 minutes or until the morels are tender. Add the sugar snaps, parsley, mint, and garlic. Cover and simmer for 1 minute.

7. Dice the remaining 2 tablespoons of butter and add to the skillet, stirring until the butter is just melted. Discard the bay leaf and season with salt and pepper to taste.

8. Slice the beef into ⅓"-thick slices, place on a warm platter, and surround with the vegetables and sauce. Serve immediately.

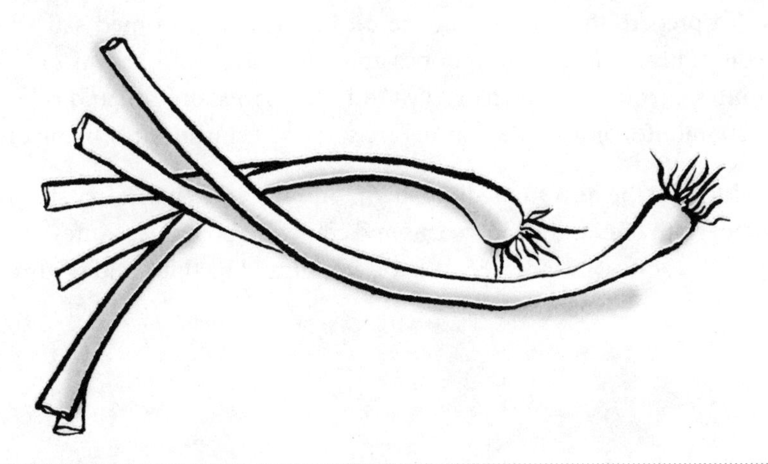

# MINT-ENCRUSTED LAMB MEDALLIONS

This dish was created to go with a Heitz Cellars Martha's Vineyard Cabernet Sauvignon for a wine dinner. The idea was that the mint and eucalyptus would mirror the characteristics of the wine. And they did.

Serves 4 people.

**FOR THE SAUCE:**

- 2 tablespoons peanut oil
- 1 pound lamb bones and trimmings
- ¾ cup peeled and thinly sliced carrots
- 1¼ cups thinly sliced yellow onions
- ½ cup thinly sliced celery
- ½ cup red wine
- 2 cloves garlic, peeled
- 2 large sprigs fresh Italian parsley
- 1 bay leaf
- 1 medium sprig fresh rosemary
- 2 sprigs fresh thyme
- 1 tablespoon black peppercorns
- 4 cups chicken stock (see page 5) or veal stock (see page 9) or water
- ¼ teaspoon salt
- 1½ tablespoons sugar
- 3 tablespoons red wine vinegar
- 2 tablespoons unsalted butter

**FOR THE LAMB:**

- 4 tablespoons extra virgin olive oil
- 1 cup finely chopped fresh mint
- ½ cup coarsely ground black pepper
- 4 tablespoons finely chopped fresh thyme
- 4 tablespoons minced garlic
- Two 1-pound boneless lamb tenderloins
- 3 tablespoons peanut oil

1. To prepare the sauce, heat the oil in a heavy-bottomed saucepan over medium heat, add the lamb bones and trimmings, and brown for about 20 minutes, turning to brown evenly. Add the carrots, onions, and celery. Cook for 20 minutes or until the onions are soft and translucent, stirring often.

2. Increase the heat to medium-high. Add the wine, garlic, parsley, bay leaf, rosemary, thyme, and peppercorns and cook for about 20 minutes or until the liquid has almost evaporated. What is left should be thick and syrupy.

3. Add the stock and salt and continue to cook the mixture over medium-high heat for about 1½ hours or until you have a lamb stock that is rich and dark. Skim off any fat or impurities that come up in a foam. Remove the stock from the heat and strain, pressing down on the solids to extract all of the juices. Reserve the liquid and discard the solids.

4. Mix the sugar and vinegar in a small nonreactive saucepan. Caramelize the mixture by cooking it over high heat, stirring constantly, for 8 minutes or until it is thick, syrupy, and beginning to brown.

5. Add the reserved lamb stock and, stirring to keep the mixture from scorching, cook over high heat for about 10 minutes or until the mixture is thick and syrupy. Skim the fat and impurities off the top as necessary. Remove the sauce from the heat and reserve until ready to use. When ready to serve, add the butter and reheat, whipping constantly until the butter melts into the sauce. You should have ½ cup of sauce.

6. To prepare the lamb, combine the olive oil, mint, pepper, thyme, and garlic in a food processor and process to a medium grind, about the size of rice grains. Coat the lamb with the mixture, cover, and refrigerate for 1 hour to dry.

7. Preheat the oven to 350°F.

8. Heat the peanut oil in a cast-iron skillet over medium-high heat until hot but not smoking. Reduce the heat to medium and brown each lamb tenderloin for 1 minute on each side. Transfer the skillet to the preheated oven and roast the lamb for 15 to 20 minutes or until a meat thermometer registers 135°F. Remove the lamb from the oven and let it "repose" for 7 to 8 minutes before carving.

9. Slice the lamb into ½"-thick slices. Divide it among 4 warm plates and spoon the sauce alongside it. Serve immediately.

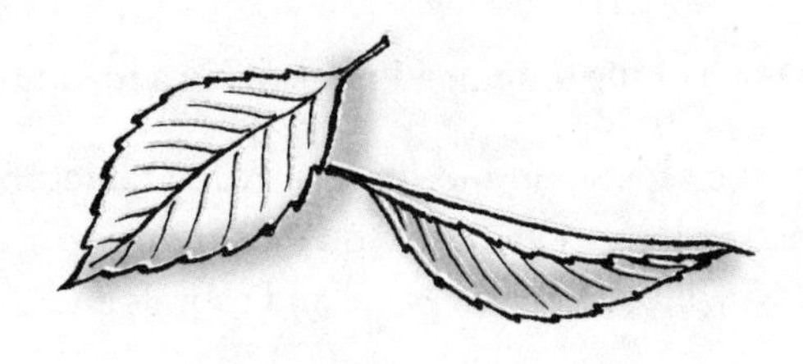

# ASPARAGUS AND MOREL GRATIN

There is an abundance of local asparagus in the Lowcountry in the spring and we like to use it as often as we can during its short season. This dish brings together 2 ingredients that seem to have a natural affinity for each other. It is also great to make ahead and reheat for a large group. We often serve it at spring receptions.

Serves 6 people.

**FOR THE TOPPING:**

½ cup bread crumbs, made in a food processor from fresh grocery-store white bread, crusts removed
¼ cup plus 2 tablespoons grated Parmesan cheese
¼ cup plus 2 tablespoons grated Swiss cheese
3 tablespoons chopped fresh Italian parsley
1 tablespoon chopped fresh basil
1 teaspoon chopped fresh thyme

**FOR THE ASPARAGUS AND MORELS:**

4 tablespoons unsalted butter
¼ cup sliced yellow onion
1 teaspoon finely minced garlic
3 cups fresh morels (about 6 ounces), whole if small and sliced lengthwise into thirds if large
1 tablespoon balsamic vinegar
1¾ cups heavy cream
1 cup chicken stock (see page 5)
1 tablespoon dry sherry, such as Dry Sack
2 tablespoons Madeira
½ teaspoon freshly ground black pepper
1 pound medium asparagus, peeled and cut on a 2" bias
Salt and freshly ground black pepper to taste

1. Mix together all of the topping ingredients in a medium bowl and set aside.

2. To prepare the asparagus and morels, heat 2 tablespoons of the butter in a saucepan over medium-high heat. Add the onion and sauté for about 4 minutes or until well wilted. Add the garlic and morels and sauté for 4 minutes.

3. Add the balsamic vinegar, cream, and stock. Stir to combine well. Bring the mixture to a simmer, reduce the heat to medium, and simmer for 5 minutes. Add the sherry and Madeira. Remove the morels with a slotted spoon and reserve. Simmer the mixture for 10 to 15 minutes or until thick enough to coat the back of a spoon. Add the ½ teaspoon of pepper. Remove from the heat but keep warm either on the back of the stove or in the top of a double boiler.

4. Bring a large saucepan of water to a boil over medium-high heat. Drop in the asparagus, reduce the heat to medium, and simmer for about 4 minutes or until just tender. Remove the asparagus with a slotted spoon and refresh in a bowl of ice water. Drain well.

5. Preheat the oven to 425°F.

6. Place the asparagus in the bottom of a small gratin dish and sprinkle lightly with salt and pepper. Add the morels. Pour the cream mixture over the vegetables, sprinkle with the topping, and dot with the remaining 2 tablespoons of butter.

7. Bake the gratin in the preheated oven for about 6 minutes. When it begins to bubble, change the heat to broil and broil the gratin for about 3 minutes or until the top is nicely browned. Watch carefully to be sure that the top doesn't burn. Serve immediately.

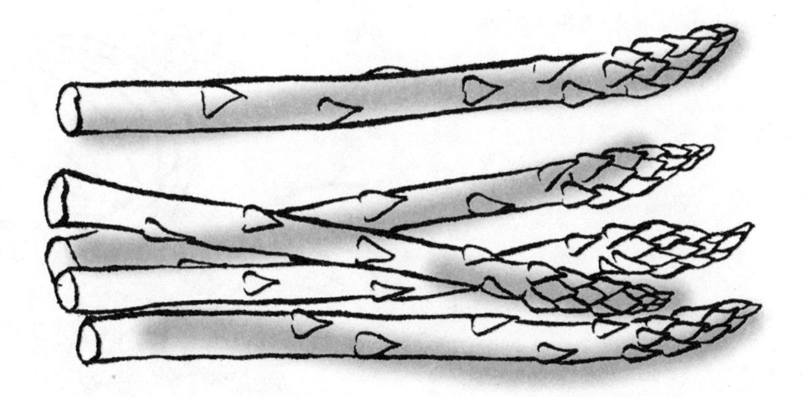

# BAKED RICE WITH WADMALAW SWEETS

What might at first appear to be too many onions for the rice cooks down to the taste of just their sweet essence. This dish goes well with lighter meats, such as chicken or veal, or delicate fish, like flounder or catfish.

Serves 6 to 8 people.

- 4 tablespoons unsalted butter
- 8 cups thinly sliced Wadmalaw Sweets or other sweet onions such as Vidalia or Maui (about 2 pounds)
- 2 cups minced shallots
- 1 bay leaf
- 2 sprigs fresh thyme
- 2 cups chicken stock (see page 5)
- 1 cup uncooked converted long-grain white rice (I use Uncle Ben's)
- Salt and freshly ground black pepper to taste

1. Preheat the oven to 350°F.

2. Heat the butter in an ovenproof nonreactive skillet with a cover over medium heat. Add the onions and shallots and sauté, stirring occasionally, for 5 minutes or until the onions are translucent. Add the bay leaf, thyme, and stock and bring to a simmer. Simmer for 5 minutes, stirring occasionally. Add the rice and stir to mix well.

3. Cover and transfer to the preheated oven for 18 to 20 minutes or until the rice is cooked through and the liquid is absorbed. Season to taste with salt and pepper. Place the rice in a serving dish, gently fluff with a fork, and serve immediately.

# MASHED POTATOES WITH SUN-DRIED TOMATOES

We always serve these potatoes with our Grilled Pork Porterhouse (see page 258). They're unusual in taste and texture. Be sure to measure the ingredients accurately; it's easy to add too many sun-dried tomatoes and overpower the rather delicate potato flavor. These are best when served right after they're made.

Serves 4 to 6 people.

2 pounds Idaho russet potatoes, peeled and each potato cut into 8 pieces
1 teaspoon salt
¼ cup extra virgin olive oil
4 tablespoons unsalted butter
¼ cup heavy cream
¼ teaspoon freshly ground black pepper
¼ cup drained and minced oil-packed sun-dried tomatoes

1. Cover the potatoes with water in a large heavy-bottomed saucepan, add ½ teaspoon of the salt, and bring to a boil over medium-high heat. Reduce the heat to a fast simmer and cook the potatoes for about 15 minutes or until they are just tender when pierced with a knife. Be careful not to overcook them.

2. Drain the potatoes in a colander. Place the colander over the empty saucepan in which the potatoes were cooked and place the saucepan back on the burner, which has now been turned off but still retains some residual heat. This will dry the potatoes a little, so the remaining ingredients will incorporate better.

3. Combine the oil, butter, and cream in a small heavy-bottomed saucepan and warm over medium heat to just below a simmer.

4. Pass the potatoes through a food mill or ricer or mash them roughly with a fork or potato masher. Put them in the bowl of an electric mixer and begin adding the warm oil and cream mixture, beating it into the potatoes with the flat beater. Be careful not to overbeat the potatoes or they will become pasty. (I leave mine on the lumpy side.) Gently beat in the pepper, sun-dried tomatoes, and remaining ½ teaspoon of salt. Serve immediately.

# GREEN BEAN AND POTATO SALAD

The combination of green beans and potatoes is a pretty old-fashioned idea, but I have dressed it up with the addition of walnuts, sweet onions, and balsamic vinegar. Elegant enough to accompany cold roasted sliced veal or lamb, it also makes a fine addition to a picnic. It can be served cold, but it is equally good served at room temperature.

Serves 4 people.

4 cups water
2 tablespoons salt
1 pound green beans, strings removed
½ pound small new potatoes, scrubbed clean
¼ cup white wine
6 tablespoons finely minced shallots
1 teaspoon chopped fresh thyme
Salt and freshly ground black pepper to taste
¼ cup balsamic vinegar
3 tablespoons red wine vinegar
½ cup walnut oil
1 medium sweet onion, such as Wadmalaw, Vidalia, or Maui, peeled and julienned
½ cup toasted walnut pieces

1. Bring the 4 cups of water and 1 tablespoon of the salt to a boil in a nonreactive saucepan and drop in the green beans. Gently boil for 6 to 7 minutes or until just tender. Drain, rinse with cold water to avoid further cooking, and drain again. Diagonally cut the beans into 1" pieces and reserve.

2. Combine the potatoes, enough water to cover them, and the remaining tablespoon of salt in a small saucepan over high heat. Bring to a boil, adjust the heat to maintain a simmer, and cook for about 15 minutes or until the potatoes are tender when pierced with a knife. Drain. When the potatoes have cooled just enough to handle, slice or quarter them, depending on their size and your preference. (Warm potatoes will absorb the flavorings better.)

3. Place the potatoes in a bowl and add the wine, shallots, thyme, and salt and pepper to taste. Toss well. Let cool to room temperature.

4. Whisk the vinegars and oil together, adding the oil slowly, or put the vinegars in a blender and slowly pour the oil into the blender, teaspoon by teaspoon. Add salt and pepper to taste. This mixture will not emulsify, so stir it well. Add to the potato mixture.

5. Combine the onion, green beans, and potatoes. Add salt and pepper to taste, sprinkle with the walnuts, and serve.

# ROASTED BANANA ICE CREAM

To make this ice cream the most flavorful, be sure to let the bananas overripen until their skins are mostly black.

Makes 1½ quarts.

- 2 tablespoons unsalted butter
- 1 cup pecan pieces
- 3 very ripe bananas
- 1½ cups whole milk
- 2 cups heavy cream
- 9 large egg yolks
- 3 cups sugar

1. Preheat the oven to 350°F.

2. Heat the butter in a medium sauté pan over medium heat until melted. Add the pecans and cook in the butter for 10 to 15 minutes or until they are roasted and aromatic. Stir frequently and adjust the heat if necessary to prevent scorching. Remove from the heat and set aside.

3. Place the bananas, still in their skins, on a baking sheet and roast in the preheated oven for about 20 minutes or until the skins are black and swollen. Remove from the oven and, when cooled to room temperature, peel and mash with a fork until they are the consistency of mashed potatoes. Set aside.

4. Bring the milk and cream to a low boil in a heavy-bottomed saucepan over medium heat.

5. Meanwhile, put the egg yolks into the bowl of an electric mixer. With the whisk attachment, slowly beat the sugar into the yolks until the mixture lightens in color.

6. Prepare an ice bath by fitting an empty 3-quart bowl into a large bowl of ice.

7. Remove the milk and cream mixture from the heat. Take 2 cups of the hot mixture and slowly pour it into the bowl of the electric mixer, continuing to use the whisk attachment to combine it with the yolks and sugar. Slowly pour the mixture into the saucepan with the remaining milk and cream mixture, now whisking by hand.

8. Return the saucepan to the stove. Stirring constantly with a wooden spoon or rubber spatula, gently cook the mixture over low heat for 5 to 10 minutes or until it is thick enough to coat the back of a spoon. You now have custard. Remove from the heat.

9. Stir the bananas into the hot custard. Immediately add the butter and nuts; while the mixture is still hot, the butter can be absorbed. Pour the mixture into the 3-quart bowl in the ice bath to avoid further cooking. Chill the custard overnight in a covered container. When ready to churn, pour the chilled custard into a prepared ice cream maker and proceed according to the manufacturer's instructions.

# LEMON-MINT ICE CREAM

■ This may very well be the most refreshing ice cream ever made! Be sure to serve it no more than 24 hours after you make it. The fresh flavor starts to wane quickly.

Makes 2 quarts.

1 bunch fresh mint
(about 20 1" sprigs)
1½ quarts heavy cream
6 large egg yolks
3 cups sugar
1 cup fresh lemon juice
Pinch of salt

1. Wash the mint and divide the bunch in half. Leave half whole and finely chop the other half (you will need 1 cup of chopped mint). Reserve both halves separately.

2. Put the cream and unchopped mint in a heavy-bottomed saucepan, bring to a simmer over medium heat, and cook for 30 minutes.

3. Meanwhile, put the egg yolks into the bowl of an electric mixer. With the whisk attachment, slowly beat the sugar into the yolks until the mixture lightens in color.

4. Prepare an ice bath by fitting an empty 3-quart bowl into a large bowl of ice.

5. Remove the cream from the heat. Take 2 cups and slowly pour it into the bowl of the electric mixer, continuing to use the whisk attachment to combine it with the yolks and sugar. Slowly pour the mixture into the saucepan with the remaining cream, now whisking by hand.

6. Return the saucepan to the stove. Stirring constantly with a wooden spoon or rubber spatula, gently cook the mixture over low heat for 5 to 10 minutes or until it is thick enough to coat the back of a spoon. You now have custard. Immediately strain the custard into the 3-quart bowl in the ice bath to avoid further cooking. Discard the whole mint. Stir in the lemon juice, salt, and chopped mint.

7. Chill the custard overnight in a covered container. When ready to churn, pour the chilled custard into a prepared ice cream maker and proceed according to the manufacturer's instructions.

# ROSEMARY SABLÉS

Our pastry chef Faison Cushman came up with these delightful confections. They're an unusual combination of flavors reminiscent of the south of France. We almost always have them with ice cream.

Makes approximately 10 dozen cookies.

1 pound unsalted butter, cut into ½" pieces
1¾ cups all-purpose flour
1¾ cups plus 1 tablespoon bread flour
2 cups sugar
4 large eggs, lightly beaten
1½ teaspoons pure vanilla extract
¼ cup finely chopped fresh rosemary

1. In a medium bowl, cut the butter into both flours with a pastry blender or 2 forks. Rub the butter and flour together with your fingertips until the mixture resembles coarse sand (the meaning of the French word *sable*). Mix in the sugar.

2. Add the eggs and vanilla to the bowl and work into the dough with your hands. Add the chopped rosemary and work into the dough. Shape the dough into a disk, wrap with plastic wrap, and chill for at least 1 hour or overnight.

3. Preheat the oven to 350°F.

4. On a lightly floured board, roll the dough out to ¼" thickness. Cut into 2" rounds. Place the cookies on a baking sheet lined with aluminum foil or baking parchment paper and bake in the middle of the preheated oven for 15 to 20 minutes or until lightly browned. Remove from the baking sheet and cool on a rack to room temperature. Store in an airtight container.

# BLOOD ORANGE CRÈME BRÛLÉE

■ Crème brûlée has been a staple of restaurant dessert lists for many years, since being canonized at New York's Le Cirque restaurant. When we opened the new Louis's, we decided to give it a twist. Much to our surprise, people loved it. Its pink color and very slight hint of orange seem to be a good choice for our new place. When blood oranges aren't available, we use whatever oranges are in the market.

Makes six 8-ounce servings.

4 cups heavy cream
2 cups fresh blood orange juice
12 large egg yolks
4 cups sugar

Six 8-ounce ramekins

Baking pan deep enough to hold water reaching about three-quarters up the sides of the ramekins

1. Preheat the oven to 325°F.

2. Combine the cream and juice in a heavy-bottomed nonreactive saucepan and heat to a simmer over medium heat.

3. Whisk the yolks and 3 cups of the sugar together in a large mixing bowl. Pouring slowly, whisk in the hot cream and juice. Strain through a fine mesh sieve.

4. Divide the mixture among the ramekins. Place in the baking pan and put in the preheated oven. Pour very hot water into the pan, filling it three-quarters of the way up the sides of the ramekins. Be careful not to splash any water into the ramekins. Cover the pan with aluminum foil and bake for 1 hour or until the custard reaches a semi-firm consistency. Remove the ramekins from the pan of water and cool to room temperature. Keep in a cool place or refrigerate until ready to serve.

5. When ready to serve, preheat the broiler. Sift the remaining cup of sugar evenly over the tops of the custards and place the ramekins as close to the broiler as possible. The sugar should get bubbly and dark and form a caramelized crust. You may need to turn the ramekins to cook the crust evenly. Serve immediately.

# BUTTERMILK TART WITH FRESH RASPBERRIES

During one summer break from college, I spent a wonderful time in Highlands, North Carolina, where I met a remarkable woman, Mary Cleveland. Mary owned—and cooked for—the Highlander. The Highlander served breakfast, lunch, and dinner; the food was honest mountain cooking and very excellent. It was there that I first tasted buttermilk pie, a rich, velvety variation of Southern chess pie. It was almost cloyingly sweet, but not quite. I later learned that the addition of vinegar was the reason for this. Mary baked all the restaurant's breads (her yeast rolls have never been equaled), and her cakes and pies were all baked by her from scratch as well. This is the kind of genuine Southern cooking that has almost died away, and the kind of cooking that inspires all cooks who strive for excellence.

Serves 8–10 people.

½ recipe Best Pie Dough (see page 28), unbaked
2½ cups sugar
3 tablespoons all-purpose flour
5 tablespoons unsalted butter, melted and cooled to room temperature
3 large eggs, lightly beaten
1½ cups buttermilk
1 teaspoon pure vanilla extract
1 teaspoon red wine vinegar
One 16-ounce jar apricot preserves
2 tablespoons cognac
2 pints fresh raspberries, gently rinsed and drained

12" tart pan with a removable bottom

1. Roll out the dough and bake in the tart pan according to the instructions for Best Pie Dough.

2. While the crust is baking, make the filling. Combine the sugar and flour in a large mixing bowl. Add the butter and mix well.

3. Place the eggs in a medium bowl and whisk in the buttermilk, vanilla, and vinegar. Whisk gently in order not to create any foam.

4. Stir the egg mixture into the sugar mixture, again mixing gently so that you will not incorporate any air. Pour the filling into the baked crust and bake in the 375°F oven for about 20 minutes or until the filling is delicately set in the middle. You may test it with a toothpick, which should come out dry. The tart will continue to set as it cools.

5. Place the tart on a rack and let it cool in the pan for 10 minutes. Remove the sides of the pan and let the tart cool to room temperature. Refrigerate until completely set, at least 1½ hours.

6. While the tart is refrigerating, make the glaze. Heat the preserves and cognac in a heavy-bottomed nonreactive saucepan over low heat until the preserves melt, stirring occasionally. Strain the glaze, discard any bits of fruit, and reserve.

7. Slide the tart onto a serving plate. Beginning at the outside edge of the tart, place the raspberries on the top in concentric circles until the top is completely covered. Gently brush the raspberries and the sides of the crust with the apricot glaze. If necessary, gently warm the glaze so it will brush easily.

8. Serve the tart immediately or keep in the refrigerator for up to 3 hours. It is better at room temperature, so remove it from the refrigerator 30 minutes before serving. The whole tart makes a very pretty presentation and you may want to slice it at the table.

# Four Suggested Summer Menus

Buttery, Garlicky Steamed Clams /198
Braised Black Angus Short Ribs Crusted with Wadmalaw Sweets /208
Sweet Corn and Morel Compote /212
Bittersweet Chocolate Semifreddo with Hazelnut Cream /220

McClellanville Lump Crab Cakes with a Whole-Grain Mustard Sauce /196
Red Snapper with Green Chiles, Sweet Corn, and Spinach /202
Green Beans with Sweet and Sour Onions /213
Fried Peach Pies with Butter Pecan Ice Cream /227

Charleston Chile-Pickled Shrimp /194
Spicy Chicken with Lemongrass and Fried Capellini /204
Fried Green Tomatoes /214
Toasted Corn Cake with Brandied Figs /228

Okra and Rice Soup /191
Deviled Crab Cakes /201
Plantation Slaw /216
Rustic Berry Tarts /224

## Summer in the Lowcountry

Charleston abounds with lovely outdoor settings. Few places are as alluring as a Charleston porch (or piazza, as the locals call it) for a relaxed summer dinner or an early-morning breakfast. Lowcountry beaches, riverbanks, and plantation gardens are delightful places to set out a picnic or a few tables and chairs. All these dazzling settings call for meals in turn with light summer appetites, such as a simple shrimp creole, some cool chile-pickled shrimp, or a big salad that can easily stand in for a meal.

Without a doubt, the quintessential summer moment for us is July 4. It's not only a huge holiday here, but it's also a fitting occasion for a generous family meal. When we lived in Pawleys Island, dinner followed the local parade. It wasn't a parade in the usual sense: the procession was really just a long march of local folks with their car tops down, waving the flag. Bicyclists, unicyclists, walkers, and kids on three-wheelers were also welcome. Our contribution to the hodgepodge was the upside-down margarita float. We rounded up an old pickup truck, hitched a flatbed to it, and installed a chair and the same margarita barrel that we used at our pig pickin's. It was considered a great success if no one fell off the truck.

After that we usually all proceeded to our house for dinner, where the porch, dining room, and living room were filled with tables. They'd be laden with piled-up bowls of Cindy's spicy slaw, just-pickled sliced tomatoes, corn on the cob, cornbread, and pickled onions and cucumbers. We'd all get busy over the grill cooking chicken and fish. At the end of the evening, we'd wind up with a big batch of homemade peach ice cream.

I've never forgotten the year we let our friend Warren Johnston experiment with a prune-Armagnac ice cream. Believing that more must be better, he increased the amount of Armagnac called for in the recipe. After several hours of churning, we realized that the alcohol content was too high for the custard to freeze. That night, dessert was a sweet cold soup. Although the Johnstons returned every year, it was (thankfully) *sans* ice cream recipes. After all, summer is the time for a heaping spoonful—not a mere sip.

Whatever the occasion, in summertime the eating is easy. Summer brings luscious ripe berries, juicy perfect peaches, and creek (pronounced "crick") shrimp—the tiny shrimp caught in our local waters. By late summer, tomato fever sets in. In the restaurant, we often prepare a simple salad of just-cut tomatoes dressed only with the freshest basil and a shallot vinaigrette, or a fresh tomato coulis with sautéed shrimp. At home, it's simpler still, as we relish sandwiches of sliced tomatoes and mayonnaise on white bread.

In some Lowcountry kitchens (mine in particular), corn now surpasses rice as the dominant influence. I love to serve it, cut off the cob, alongside fresh fish or added to soups, chowders, pancakes, puddings, and vegetable compotes. It's no less delicious when made as a confection, as in my toasted corn cake, served with summer's sweetest figs.

Many of the recipes I present here are simply favorites that I identify with summertime: fried green tomatoes, ice creams, and cobblers. Others take advantage of the Lowcountry's long growing season and the wonderful extravaganza of produce.

# OKRA AND RICE SOUP

Okra is one of the staples of Southern cooking, especially in the Lowcountry. Many people are put off by this vegetable, but in the initial sautéing in this recipe, the stickiness becomes a rich thickening agent for the soup.

Serves 4 people.

- 2 tablespoons peanut oil
- ½ pound fresh okra, ends trimmed and cut into ¼" pieces
- 1 yellow bell pepper, cored, seeded, and diced into ¼" pieces
- 1 red bell pepper, cored, seeded, and diced into ¼" pieces
- 1 poblano pepper, peeled, seeded, and finely chopped
- ½ teaspoon minced garlic
- 1⅓ cups peeled, seeded, and chopped ripe tomatoes
- ¾ cup uncooked long-grain rice (*not* converted)
- 1 bay leaf
- 3 sprigs fresh thyme
- 4 cups chicken stock (see page 5)
- Salt and freshly ground black pepper to taste
- Tabasco sauce to taste (optional)

1. Heat the oil in a heavy-bottomed nonreactive saucepan until hot but not smoking. Add the okra and peppers and sauté over medium-high heat for 3 to 5 minutes or until lightly browned. Add the garlic and sauté for 1 minute.

2. Stir in the tomatoes and cook for 1 minute. Add the rice, bay leaf, thyme, and stock. Stir well to combine and bring to a boil. Immediately reduce to a gentle simmer and cook until the rice is tender. Add salt and pepper to taste. In South Carolina, many people would add a couple dashes of Tabasco.

# JOHNS ISLAND SWEET CORN SOUP WITH LUMP CRABMEAT

There is no doubt that we have access to the finest, freshest crabmeat in the country, and probably the world. Couple that with the freshest sweet corn, onions, and peppers that are available from Johns Island's many truck farms and you've got what fine regional cuisine is all about.

Serves 10 to 12 people.

- 12 cups fresh, sweet corn kernels, 2 cobs reserved
- 4 cups chicken stock (see page 5)
- 1 small jalapeño pepper
- 1 sprig fresh cilantro
- 3 tablespoons unsalted butter
- 2 ounces pancetta, diced into ¼" pieces
- ¼ cup finely minced white onion
- ½ cup finely minced celery
- ⅓ cup finely minced leek, white part only
- 1 cup finely minced green bell pepper
- 1½ cups heavy cream
- 1 pound lump crabmeat, gently picked over to remove any shell without breaking up the big pieces of crab
- Salt and freshly ground black pepper to taste
- 2 tablespoons chopped fresh chives

1. Chop the reserved corncobs into 2" pieces. Combine the cobs, chicken stock, jalapeño pepper, and cilantro in a saucepan and bring to a boil. Reduce the heat to low and simmer for 30 minutes, partially covered. Measure the mixture. You want to have 3 cups; if there are less than 3 cups, add more chicken stock.

2. Meanwhile, melt the butter in a large heavy-bottomed saucepan over medium-high heat. Add the pancetta and cook, stirring occasionally, for 6 to 8 minutes or until lightly browned. Remove the pancetta with a slotted spoon and place on a paper towel to drain. Add the onion, celery, leek, and bell pepper to the fat rendered from the pancetta. Cover, reduce the heat to medium, and cook for 10 minutes, stirring occasionally. Add the corn kernels and stir to mix well. Cover and cook over medium heat for 5 minutes.

3. Strain the stock into the vegetable mixture, discarding the corncobs, jalapeño pepper, and cilantro. Stir and simmer for 15 minutes, partially covered. Strain the mixture, reserving the stock and the vegetables separately.

4. Cool the vegetables for 10 minutes, then puree them, using either a food processor or a food mill, adding a little liquid if necessary to keep the mixture moving. Whisk the puree back into the stock. Heat just to a simmer, add the cream, and return the soup to a simmer. At this point, if you are not going to serve the soup immediately, you may cool it to room temperature, cover, and refrigerate. Without the crabmeat, the soup may be kept in the refrigerator overnight.

5. Gently stir in the crabmeat, taking care not to break the lumps. Simmer for 3 to 4 minutes to heat the crabmeat through. Add salt and pepper to taste. Ladle the soup into bowls, garnish with the chives, and serve immediately.

# SHE-CRAB SOUP

This is Charleston's most famous dish. It is a regional variation on an English soup, adapted to local produce. John Martin Taylor, the owner of Hoppin' John's, a local cooking school and cookbook store, suggested the use of rice as the thickening agent for this soup. Frozen crab roe, from what Charlestonians call "she-crabs," is often available in fish markets. If you can't find it, you can substitute either chopped hard-boiled egg yolks or chopped toasted almonds, or both.

Serves 8 people.

- 4 tablespoons unsalted butter
- 1 cup finely chopped yellow onion
- ½ cup finely chopped celery
- 1 cup finely chopped leeks, white part only
- 1 bay leaf
- 1 sprig fresh thyme or 1 pinch of dried thyme
- ¼ teaspoon cayenne pepper
- 2 teaspoons salt
- ½ cup uncooked converted long-grain white rice (I use Uncle Ben's)
- 5 cups fish stock (see page 8) or crab stock or bottled clam juice
- 2 cups heavy cream
- 1 pound lump crabmeat, gently picked over to remove any shell without breaking up the big pieces of crab
- 6 tablespoons amontillado sherry
- ½ teaspoon fresh lemon juice
- ½ cup crab roe, finely chopped
- 2 tablespoons finely chopped fresh herbs such as parsley, tarragon, or chervil

1. Heat the butter in a heavy-bottomed soup pot over medium heat. Add the onion, celery, and leeks and gently sauté, stirring occasionally, for about 15 minutes or until very soft. Add the bay leaf, thyme, cayenne pepper, salt, rice, and stock and mix well. Bring the mixture to a simmer, reduce the heat to low, and simmer for 30 minutes, stirring occasionally.

2. Increase the heat to medium-high, add the cream, and bring the mixture to a boil. Immediately reduce the heat to medium and simmer for 5 minutes, stirring occasionally.

3. Remove the soup pot from the stove. When the soup has cooled enough to handle, remove the bay leaf and sprig of thyme. Put the soup through a food mill or puree it in a food processor. If you wish to present a more elegant soup, strain it through a fine mesh sieve, which will catch the minuscule bits of rice left from pureeing. Return the soup to the pot.

4. Place the pot over medium heat and add the crabmeat. Bring the soup to a boil, stirring gently to prevent scorching and being careful not to break up the lumps of crab. Stir in the sherry by the tablespoon to your taste and add the lemon juice.

5. In a small bowl, combine the crab roe and herbs for the garnish. Pour the soup into warm bowls, add the garnish, and serve immediately.

# CHARLESTON CHILE-PICKLED SHRIMP

■ Pickled shrimp, as well as a variety of pickled fish, have always been a Southern tradition. We decided to add a little spice to this perennial favorite without obliterating the elements that originally made it so popular. When making the pickling marinade, use whatever beer you would drink with these spicy shrimp.

Makes enough for 20 people as an hors d'oeuvre.

**FOR THE PICKLING BATH:**

- 1 gallon water
- 12 ounces dark beer (I use Beck's)
- ½ cup seafood seasoning (I use Old Bay)
- 6 tablespoons grocery-store variety pickling spices
- 2½ cups sliced yellow onions (about ¾ pound)
- 4 cloves garlic, peeled and crushed
- 2 tablespoons salt
- 2 tablespoons red pepper flakes
- 5 pounds large fresh shrimp, shells on

**TO ASSEMBLE:**

- 3 large tomatoes, cored, halved, and seeds and pulp squeezed out
- 2¾ cups thickly sliced yellow onions (about ¾ pound)
- 6 cloves garlic, peeled
- 2 medium red bell peppers, cored, seeded, and halved
- 2 medium green bell peppers, cored, seeded, and halved
- 4 medium jalapeño or poblano peppers, cored and halved
- ¼ cup plus 3 tablespoons extra virgin olive oil
- 2 teaspoons salt
- 3 tablespoons sherry wine vinegar
- ¼ cup drained capers
- ½ cup chopped fresh Italian parsley, leaves only

1. To pickle the shrimp, combine the water, beer, seafood seasoning, pickling spices, onions, garlic, salt, and red pepper flakes in a large pot. Bring to a boil over medium-high heat, reduce to medium, and simmer for 10 minutes.

2. Add the shrimp and cook for 2 to 3 minutes or until they turn pink and just begin to curl. Drain the shrimp and cool until they can be peeled. Set aside.

3. Preheat the oven to 500°F.

4. Toss the tomatoes, onions, garlic, and peppers in 3 tablespoons of the olive oil. Place on a baking sheet and roast in the preheated oven for about 15 minutes or until charred on top, wilted, and shriveled up. Remove from the oven and cool to room temperature. Puree the vegetables in a food processor, by batches if necessary. Stir in the salt.

5. Place the pureed vegetables in a large bowl. Whisk in the remaining ¼ cup of olive oil and the sherry wine vinegar. Add the capers, parsley, and shrimp. Stir to combine well. Chill the pickled shrimp, but remove from the refrigerator about 15 minutes before serving so that they won't be icy cold.

# MCCLELLANVILLE LUMP CRAB CAKES WITH A WHOLE-GRAIN MUSTARD SAUCE

Bob Kinkead, one of the country's very finest chefs, came up with the idea of dressing up crab cakes with lobster. This recipe is an adaptation of his presentation, using our very fine local crabmeat and New England lobster. Since we've put these crab cakes on the menu, we serve more of this appetizer than all others combined. They're easy to make, but be sure to sauté them in very hot oil using a heavy-bottomed sauté pan.

Makes twelve 2-ounce appetizer-portion crab cakes or six 4-ounce dinner-portion crab cakes.

- 1 cup best-quality mayonnaise (I use Hellmann's)
- 1 large egg white
- ¼ teaspoon cayenne pepper
- ¼ teaspoon seafood seasoning (I use Old Bay)
- ¼ teaspoon dry mustard (I use Colman's English mustard)
- 2 tablespoons fresh lemon juice
- 3 tablespoons extrafine cracker meal
- 1 pound lump crabmeat, gently picked over to remove any shell without breaking up the big pieces of crab, or ¾ pound crabmeat and ¼ pound lobster meat
- 1½ cups bread crumbs, made in a food processor from fresh grocery-store white bread, crusts removed
- ¼ cup peanut oil
- 2 tablespoons unsalted butter
- 1 recipe Whole-Grain Mustard Sauce (recipe follows)

1. Whisk the mayonnaise and egg white together in a small bowl until well blended. Add the cayenne pepper, seafood seasoning, dry mustard, lemon juice, and cracker meal. Whisk until well blended. Carefully fold in the crabmeat (and lobster, if using it).

2. Divide the mixture into 12 equal parts of 2 ounces each, or 6 equal parts of 4 ounces each, and gently pat each portion into the round shape of crab cakes. Gently coat the cakes with the bread crumbs. Place on a platter lined with wax paper, cover with plastic wrap, and refrigerate for at least 1 hour or until ready to cook. Do not hold for more than 4 hours.

3. When ready to serve, heat the oil and butter in a heavy-bottomed sauté pan over medium-high heat. Sauté the 4-ounce crab cakes for 1 minute and 45 seconds on each side, turning once. Sauté the 2-ounce crab cakes for 1 minute and 15 seconds on each side, turning once. The crab cakes will be nicely browned on the outside but still very moist and creamy on the inside. When cooked, drain the cakes briefly on paper towels. Serve immediately with the mustard sauce or keep warm in a 200°F oven for up to 15 minutes. If the crab cakes stay in the oven any longer, they will dry out.

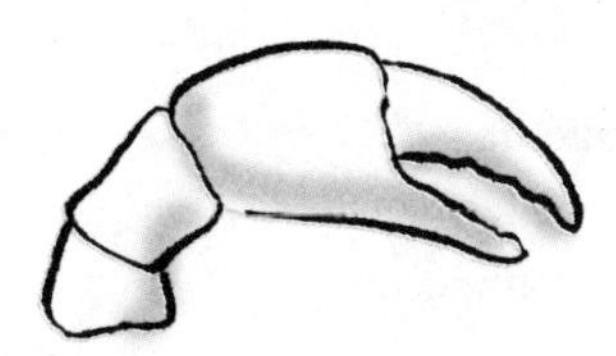

## Whole-Grain Mustard Sauce

Be careful not to boil this sauce once you add the mustard or it will become bitter. If you want a more assertive sauce, you may use as much as ⅓ cup of mustard.

Makes ¾ cup.

¼ cup dry white wine
2 tablespoons brandy
1 cup heavy cream
¼ cup whole-grain Dijon mustard (I use Grey Poupon)
Juice of ½ lemon
¼ teaspoon salt
Scant ¼ teaspoon freshly ground black pepper

1. Combine the wine and brandy in a small nonreactive saucepan and boil over medium-high heat until there is only about 1 tablespoon of liquid left. Whisk in the cream. Reduce the heat to medium and briskly simmer for 6 to 8 minutes or until the mixture thickens slightly.

2. Add the mustard and bring the mixture back to just a simmer. *Do not boil it.* Add the lemon juice, salt, and pepper. Keep the sauce warm on the back of the stove or over barely simmering water in the top of a double boiler until ready to serve.

# BUTTERY, GARLICKY STEAMED CLAMS

In our relatively warm Southern waters, we do not have the soft-shell clams found along Northern coastlines, but this quick and easy dish will rival any found north of the Mason–Dixon line. (And it works just as well with Northern clams.)

Serves 4 people.

- ¼ pound plus 1 tablespoon unsalted butter
- 4 tablespoons very finely minced garlic
- 2 cups finely sliced scallions, white and green parts
- 2 teaspoons crushed red pepper flakes
- 1 cup dry white vermouth
- 3 pounds littleneck clams, scrubbed and dried
- 1 cup roughly chopped fresh Italian parsley

A heavy-bottomed pan large enough to hold all of the clams

1. Put ¼ pound of the butter in the pan and heat over medium heat until hot but not smoking. Add the garlic, scallions, and red pepper flakes. Cook for 3 minutes, stirring occasionally, being careful not to let the garlic burn.

2. Add the vermouth, raise the heat to high, and cover the pan. Bring the mixture to a rapid boil and add the clams. Cover and continue to cook at a rapid boil, stirring occasionally. When the clams begin to open, which can be in as little time as 1 minute, remove the open ones as quickly as possible in order not to overcook them. (All of the clams should be cooked in no longer than 7 to 8 minutes.) Reserve the pan juices, including the garlic, scallions, and red pepper flakes.

3. Divide the clams equally among 4 bowls or place on a large platter. Add the parsley and remaining tablespoon of butter to the pan juices. Stir well to combine. Spoon the mixture over the clams. Serve immediately.

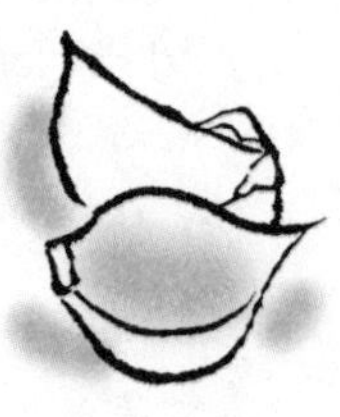

# CATFISH WITH ROASTED TOMATO, SAFFRON, AND BLACK OLIVES

This dish combines Mediterranean flavors with Southern catfish. We've found over the years that there are subtle similarities between Provence and the Lowcountry. Maybe the proximity to the sea, the hot weather, the strong sun, and good farming all create the same palate in some way. For whatever reason, these flavors go well with this fish.

Serves 4 people.

**FOR THE ROASTED TOMATOES:**

4 vine-ripe tomatoes, peeled, seeded, and chopped
1 cup peeled and chopped fresh plum tomatoes or best-quality canned plum tomatoes
2 cloves garlic, peeled and minced
⅓ cup very thinly julienned red onion
½ teaspoon chopped fresh thyme
1 tablespoon extra virgin olive oil
½ cup fish stock (see page 8) or good-quality bottled clam juice
Salt and freshly ground black pepper to taste

**FOR THE FISH:**

Olive oil–flavored cooking spray
4 tablespoons minced shallots
4 tablespoons white vermouth
2 sprigs fresh thyme or ½ teaspoon dried thyme
Salt and freshly ground black pepper to taste
Four 6-ounce skinless catfish fillets
⅓ cup brine-cured black olives, pitted and chopped
3 fresh basil leaves, finely sliced
2 tablespoons extra virgin olive oil
¼ cup tomato juice
4 tablespoons chopped fresh Italian parsley

1. Preheat the oven to 500°F.

2. Combine the vine-ripe tomatoes, plum tomatoes, garlic, onion, thyme, and olive oil in a bowl and toss to mix well. Pour the mixture onto a baking sheet and roast in the preheated oven until it begins to char. Return to the bowl, add the stock, and toss with salt and pepper to taste. (For a finer texture, place the mixture in a food processor and process to desired texture.)

3. Reduce the oven temperature to 375°F.

4. To prepare the fish, lightly coat the bottom of a shallow casserole dish with the cooking spray, then sprinkle with the shallots, vermouth, and thyme. Lightly salt and pepper the catfish fillets and place them in a single layer in the dish.

5. Mix the roasted tomatoes with the olives, basil, and olive oil. Spoon over the fillets. Cut a piece of wax paper or baking parchment paper to fit the casserole. Lightly coat 1 side with the cooking spray and place, sprayed side down, over the fillets. Bake in the preheated oven for 8 to 10 minutes or until the fillets are just cooked through. Watch carefully—the fillets will be opaque and just firm to the touch. It is important not to overcook the fish; the thickness of the fillets, the size and thickness of the casserole dish, and the oven will all create subtle (or not so subtle) differences in cooking times. When the fillets are cooked, carefully remove them to a warm serving platter, cover again with the wax paper, and keep warm near the stove while finishing the sauce.

6. Pour the ingredients remaining in the casserole into a saucepan and add the tomato juice. Simmer briskly over medium-high heat for 4 to 5 minutes or until the mixture thickens slightly. Stir in the chopped parsley, add salt and pepper to taste, and spoon over the fillets. Serve immediately.

# DEVILED CRAB CAKES

This is a spicier version of the lump crab cakes we serve in the restaurant. Add more or less seasoning, depending on your taste.

Makes ten 4-ounce dinner-portion crab cakes.

- 2 cups best-quality mayonnaise (I use Hellmann's)
- 2 large egg whites
- 1 teaspoon Tabasco sauce
- 1 tablespoon plus 1 teaspoon dry mustard (I use Colman's English mustard)
- 6 tablespoons minced shallots
- ¼ cup minced scallions, white and green parts
- 2 pounds lump crabmeat, gently picked over to remove any shell without breaking up the big pieces of crab
- 3 cups bread crumbs, made in a food processor from a sliced and dried baguette
- 2 tablespoons unsalted butter, melted and slightly cooled
- ½ cup peanut oil
- 4 tablespoons unsalted butter

1. Whisk the mayonnaise and egg whites together in a small bowl until well blended. Whisk in the Tabasco and dry mustard. Add the shallots and scallions and mix well. Carefully fold in the crabmeat so as not to break up the lumps. Gently fold in 2 cups of the bread crumbs.

2. Divide the mixture into 10 equal parts of 4 ounces each and gently pat each portion into the round shape of crab cakes. Mix the melted butter with the remaining cup of bread crumbs and gently coat each of the cakes.

3. Heat the oil and 4 tablespoons of butter in a skillet over medium-high heat. Sauté the crab cakes for 3 minutes on each side or until nicely browned, turning once. Watch the heat. If the fat gets too hot, the cakes will brown on the outside before they are cooked on the inside. When cooked, drain the cakes briefly on paper towels. Serve immediately or keep warm in a 200°F oven for up to 15 minutes. If the crab cakes stay in the oven any longer, they will dry out.

# RED SNAPPER WITH GREEN CHILES, SWEET CORN, AND SPINACH

This is a great combination of rather ordinary flavors that together produce an outstanding symphony. As my friend Bob Kinkead—the chef and owner of Kinkead's in Washington, D.C.—says of his skate wings, "It'll make you weep."

Serves 4 people.

**FOR THE CHILES, CORN, AND SPINACH:**

- 4 tablespoons unsalted butter
- ½ cup finely minced shallots
- 1 cup seeded and minced poblano chiles
- 1 seeded and minced serrano chile
- 4 cups fresh yellow corn kernels, cobs reserved
- 1 cup chicken stock (see page 5)
- ⅓ cup heavy cream
- ⅓ cup chopped fresh chervil
- 8 cups stemmed and washed fresh spinach
- Salt and freshly ground black pepper to taste

**FOR THE SNAPPER:**

- 1 cup all-purpose flour
- 1 teaspoon salt
- ¼ teaspoon freshly ground black pepper
- Four 6-ounce red snapper fillets, skin still on 1 side, scales off
- Salt and freshly ground black pepper to taste
- 1 tablespoon peanut oil
- 1 tablespoon unsalted butter

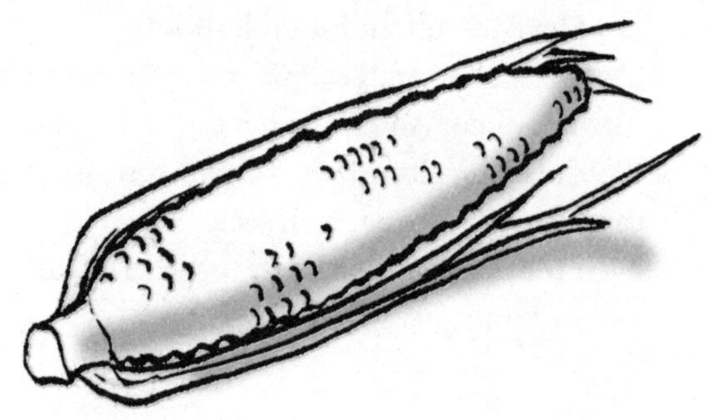

1. To prepare the vegetables, heat the butter in a heavy-bottomed saucepan over medium heat until hot but not smoking. Add the shallots and both types of chiles and cook, stirring occasionally, for 6 minutes or until the chiles are soft but not mushy.

2. Add the corn kernels. Run the back of a knife over the cobs to extract all of their milky juices and add to the saucepan. Continue to cook the mixture for another 5 minutes, stirring occasionally. Add the stock and cream, bring the mixture to a simmer, and cook for another 4 minutes, lowering the heat if necessary to prevent boiling. Stir in the chervil. Remove the saucepan from the heat and set aside.

3. Place the spinach in a heavy-bottomed pot over medium-high heat. (The water remaining on the spinach from washing is enough to cook it.) Tossing it occasionally, cook the spinach for 2 minutes or until just wilted. Season to taste with salt and pepper. Drain the spinach in a colander to get rid of any watery juices.

4. To prepare the snapper, mix the flour with the teaspoon of salt and ¼ teaspoon of pepper. Lightly score the fillets on the skin side with diagonal cuts to keep the skin from shriveling. Season them to taste with salt and pepper. Dredge the fillets in the seasoned flour, patting them lightly to leave only a very thin, delicate coating of flour.

5. Heat the peanut oil and butter in a heavy skillet over medium-high heat until hot but not smoking. Place the fillets in the skillet skin side up. Sauté for about 3 minutes on the first side, then sauté for about 2 minutes on the other side. Turn the heat down if the pan gets too hot so as not to burn the fish. When cooked, the fillets should be opaque in the center and just firm to the touch, with a nice golden brown color.

6. Warm the corn mixture and the spinach separately. Place equal amounts of the spinach in the middle of 4 plates. Put the snapper fillets, skin side down, to the side of the spinach and spoon the corn mixture around the fish. Serve immediately.

# SPICY CHICKEN WITH LEMONGRASS AND FRIED CAPELLINI

We added this dish to the menu when the Asian-fusion movement took hold in this country. It has a multitude of flavors, can be prepared mostly in advance, and will please those who like a lot of flavor in their food.

Serves 4 people.

**FOR THE SAUCE:**

- 2 cups chicken stock (see page 5)
- 2 tablespoons oyster sauce
- 1 tablespoon balsamic vinegar
- 1 tablespoon Chili Paste with Garlic (see page 23)
- 1 tablespoon sesame oil
- 2 tablespoons cornstarch
- ¼ cup peanut oil
- 1 tablespoon peeled and minced fresh ginger
- 1½ tablespoons minced garlic
- ¾ cup finely chopped lemongrass, white part only
- ½ cup julienned yellow onion
- 1 cup sliced shiitake mushroom caps (buy 2 ounces and remove the stems)

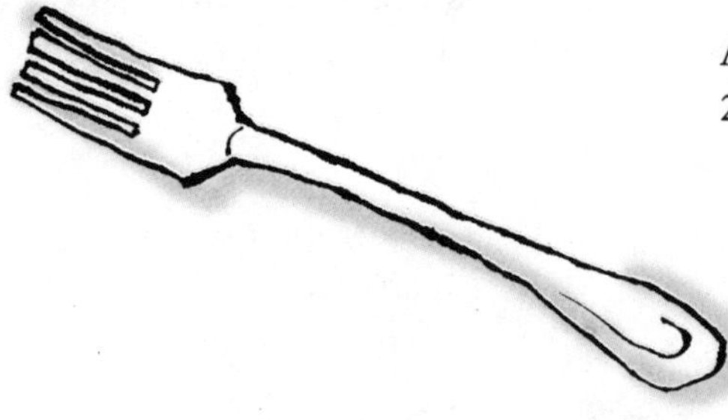

**FOR THE CAPELLINI:**

- ½ pound uncooked capellini
- 2 tablespoons sesame oil
- ¾ cup very thinly sliced scallions, white and green parts
- ½ teaspoon salt
- ½ teaspoon freshly ground black pepper
- 1 tablespoon peanut oil
- 1 tablespoon unsalted butter

**FOR THE CHICKEN BREASTS:**

- 1 tablespoon peanut oil
- 1 tablespoon unsalted butter
- Four 6- to 8-ounce boneless, skinless chicken breasts, trimmed of all fat and tendon
- ½ teaspoon salt
- ½ teaspoon freshly ground black pepper
- All-purpose flour
- 2 tablespoons chopped fresh Italian parsley

1. To prepare the sauce, mix the stock, oyster sauce, vinegar, chili paste, and sesame oil in a medium bowl and stir to combine well. Dissolve the cornstarch in this mixture. Set aside.

2. Heat a heavy-bottomed saucepan over medium-high heat. Add the peanut oil and heat until hot but not smoking. Add the ginger, garlic, lemongrass, onion, and mushrooms and cook for 2 minutes, stirring frequently.

3. Stir the chicken stock mixture and add it to the saucepan. Cook the mixture, stirring constantly, until it comes to a boil and thickens. Keep warm on the back of the stove or in a double boiler.

4. Cook the capellini in rapidly boiling water until it is al dente. Drain well. Toss with the sesame oil, scallions, salt, and pepper.

5. Heat the peanut oil and butter in a large nonstick skillet. When hot, quickly add the capellini. Press down on the pasta and level the top. Lower the heat to medium and press down on the pasta a couple of times to form it into a cohesive cake. Shake the pan often to prevent the pasta from sticking to the bottom.

6. After about 6 minutes, peeking all the while and noting how the bottom is browning, flip the cake over in the pan, using a single determined, confident, professional-chef jerk. If you are timid, there is another way. Cover the top of the pasta with a plate, pour the cooking oil into a metal container, and invert the pasta onto the plate. Return the oil to the skillet, then carefully slide the cake back into the skillet. Cook the cake for about 6 minutes more. It should have a crunchy crust on the top and bottom and a soft, moist center.

7. To prepare the chicken breasts, heat a heavy-bottomed sauté pan over medium heat. Add the peanut oil and butter and heat until hot but not smoking.

8. Meanwhile, sprinkle the chicken breasts with the salt and pepper and lightly coat them with flour. Pat gently to remove any excess. Sauté the chicken breasts for 3 to 4 minutes on each side or until golden brown and cooked through. Do not overcook.

9. Cut the capellini cake into 4 wedges and place on warm plates. Put a chicken breast on top of each wedge and spoon the sauce around the wedges. Sprinkle the parsley over the top of each serving and serve immediately.

# PANFRIED QUAIL WITH HUCKLEBERRY AND SAGE SAUCE

The sauce for the quail is sweet enough to act as a perfect foil, yet rich and substantial enough to have a presence of its own.

Serves 4 people.

- 8 semi-boneless quail
- 3 cups buttermilk
- ½ cup sugar
- 1 cup red wine vinegar
- 1 cup dry red wine with a little spice, such as a Syrah or zinfandel
- 4 cups rich brown game stock or beef stock (see page 4) or veal stock (see page 9)
- 16 fresh sage leaves or 2 teaspoons dried sage
- 2 sprigs fresh thyme
- 2 bay leaves
- 2 teaspoons black peppercorns
- 2 cups fresh huckleberries, gently washed and drained (other berries such as blueberries or blackberries can be substituted)
- Salt and freshly ground black pepper to taste
- Juice of 1 lemon
- 2 large egg yolks
- 2 cups all-purpose flour
- ½ teaspoon baking soda
- 1 teaspoon salt
- 2 teaspoons freshly ground black pepper, or to taste
- 1 cup peanut oil

1. Rinse the quail under cold running water. Pat dry. Put the quail and buttermilk in a large nonreactive bowl, cover, and marinate in the refrigerator for at least 4 hours or overnight, turning the quail occasionally.

2. To make the sauce, combine the sugar and vinegar in a heavy-bottomed nonreactive saucepan. Bring to a boil over high heat. Boil for 7 to 8 minutes or until caramelized and a rich mahogany brown.

3. Carefully stir in the wine and stock. Tie the sage, thyme, bay leaves, and peppercorns in cheesecloth to make a bouquet garni and add to the pan. Simmer the mixture over medium-high heat for 15 to 18 minutes or until it is reduced to ⅔ cup.

4. Add the berries and simmer for 10 minutes or until the sauce thickens slightly. Remove the bouquet garni and taste for salt and pepper. If the sauce is too sweet, you can adjust it by adding a few drops of lemon juice. Keep the sauce warm on the back of the stove or in a double boiler until ready to serve.

5. Remove the quail from the buttermilk and add the egg yolks to the buttermilk, whisking lightly to incorporate. Return the quail to the buttermilk and yolk mixture. This allows for a little heavier breading and also helps the crust to brown.

6. In a medium bowl, mix the flour, baking soda, teaspoon of salt, and 2 teaspoons of pepper. Remove the quail from the buttermilk and dredge lightly in the flour, shaking well to remove any excess.

7. Put the peanut oil in a cast-iron skillet. The exact amount will be determined by the size of your pan. You don't want the oil to cover the quail; you just want enough to come about halfway up the quail, so that turning them once will cook them. Heat the oil over medium-high heat to 300°F on a frying thermometer or until very hot but not smoking.

8. Add the quail breast side down, but no more than 4 at a time. Putting too many in the pan will bring the temperature of the oil down and will result in greasy quail. Panfry them for about 3 minutes, then turn them over and continue for 3 minutes more on the other side. Rotate them once 180° on each side. They should be nicely browned but still a little pink in the center. Drain on paper towels.

9. Place 2 quail each on 4 warm plates and top with the sauce. Serve immediately.

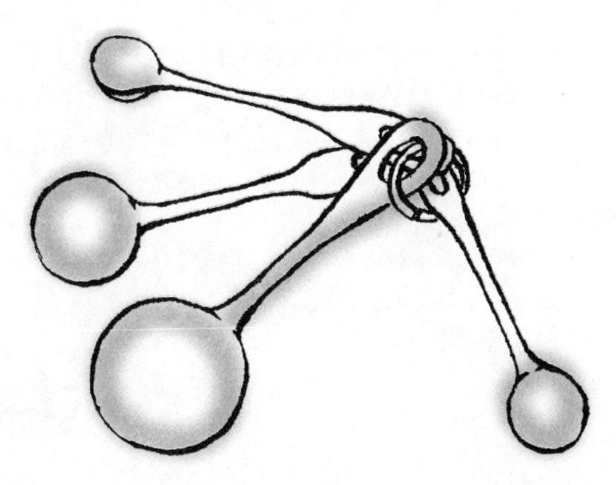

# BRAISED BLACK ANGUS SHORT RIBS CRUSTED WITH WADMALAW SWEETS

We first made this dish for a group of 400 people at the Celebration of Southern Chefs in 1998 and served it with our Salad of Watermelon, Watercress, and Scallions (see page 146). It was a great hit, illustrating the satisfying richness of braised meats. The preparation, including the period of marinating, is lengthy, but the final product certainly justifies your effort. (If you're in a hurry, you can skip the marinade.) The sweet flavor of the onion crust complements the rich beef, in the same way that a sweet sauterne wine plays off foie gras.

Serves 4 people.

**FOR THE MARINADE:**

- 4 to 6 pounds beef short ribs, cut into 3" serving pieces
- ¼ cup walnut oil
- 2 cups red wine
- 2 cups chopped yellow onions (about ½ pound)
- 4 carrots, peeled and roughly chopped
- 4 cloves garlic, peeled and chopped
- 2 bay leaves, crushed
- 3 sprigs fresh thyme, coarsely chopped

**FOR THE RIBS:**

- ¼ cup peanut oil
- Salt and freshly ground black pepper to taste
- 8 cups finely sliced sweet onions such as Wadmalaw Sweets, Vidalia, or Maui (about 2 pounds)
- 3 cups red wine
- 3 cups veal stock (see page 9) or beef stock (see page 4) or chicken stock (see page 5)
- 4 cloves garlic, peeled and minced
- 2 bay leaves
- 2 sprigs fresh thyme
- 2 large egg yolks

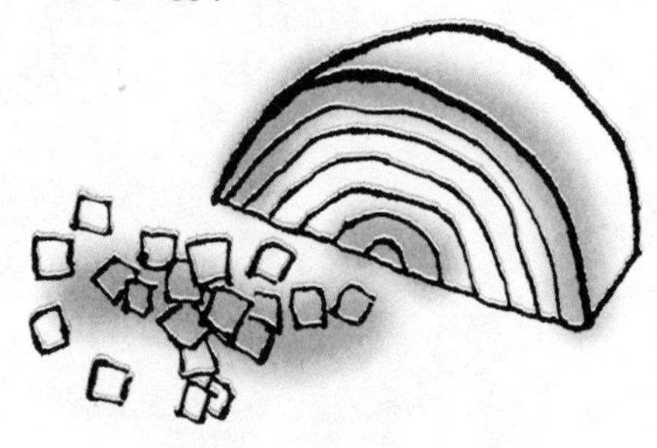

1. Place the short ribs in a large nonreactive pan. In a large bowl, combine the walnut oil, wine, onions, carrots, garlic, bay leaves, and thyme. Pour over the short ribs. Cover and refrigerate for 1 to 3 days, turning the meat 2 or 3 times.

2. When ready to cook the ribs, preheat the oven to 325°F.

3. Remove the short ribs from the marinade and pat dry. Strain the marinade and reserve the liquid.

4. Heat the peanut oil in a large ovenproof skillet with a cover over medium-high heat until nearly smoking. Add the ribs and brown on all sides. Remove to a platter and sprinkle liberally with salt and pepper.

5. Add the onions to the hot fat and cook over medium heat for 6 to 8 minutes or until they begin to brown, stirring well. Add the ribs, strained marinade, wine, and stock. Tie the garlic, bay leaves, and thyme in cheesecloth to make a bouquet garni and add to the skillet. Bring just to a simmer, cover, and transfer to the preheated oven. Cook for 2 to 2½ hours or until the meat is fork tender and just beginning to fall off the bone. Skim off any excess fat during the cooking. (The ribs may be simmered slowly on top of the stove over low heat instead of being cooked in the oven. In this case, they should be turned several times while cooking.)

6. Carefully remove the skillet from the oven. Remove the ribs and cool for about 15 minutes so that the crust will adhere properly. Increase the oven temperature to 350°F. Strain the onions from the cooking liquid and reserve both. Simmer the cooking liquid over medium-high heat for about 15 minutes or until it thickens to the consistency of heavy cream. Remove from the heat, strain, and keep warm until ready to serve.

7. Meanwhile, finely chop the drained onions in a food processor until close to, but not quite, a puree. The mixture should still have a little texture. Remove to a medium bowl, add the egg yolks, and mix well. Lightly season with salt and pepper.

8. Place the ribs on a baking sheet and spread the onion mixture thickly over them. Return to the preheated oven and bake until the ribs are heated through. Turn on the broiler and broil the ribs for 5 to 8 minutes or until the onion crust is crisp. Remove from the oven and drizzle with a little of the reduced cooking liquid. Serve immediately.

# HERBED CORN PANCAKES

Served often in the South, these are a pleasant change from normal pancakes. They are delicious slathered with fresh butter and maple syrup. For a real eye-opener, mix equal amounts of soft butter and sorghum together and apply generously.

Makes 60 silver dollar–size pancakes.

- 1½ cups yellow cornmeal
- 1½ cups all-purpose flour
- 1 tablespoon baking powder
- 1½ teaspoons baking soda
- 1½ teaspoons salt
- 3¼ cups buttermilk
- 1 cup amber beer
- 3 large eggs, lightly beaten
- 1 tablespoon sorghum
- 3½ tablespoons unsalted butter, melted
- 1 cup fresh corn kernels
- ¼ cup mix of chopped fresh chervil and chives
- Peanut oil for frying

1. In a medium bowl, combine the cornmeal, flour, baking powder, baking soda, and salt. Mix well.

2. In a large bowl, combine the buttermilk, beer, eggs, sorghum, and melted butter. Mix well.

3. Fold the dry ingredients into the wet ingredients. Fold in the corn kernels and herbs.

4. Heat ¼ cup of peanut oil in a heavy-bottomed frying pan until hot but not smoking, or brush some on a griddle. Pour the oil out of the frying pan and wipe the pan with a paper towel. Drop rounded tablespoons of the corn mixture into the pan or onto the griddle. Cook like pancakes—you should turn only once. You will have to periodically brush the pan or griddle with more oil so that the pancakes will not stick. You may keep the pancakes warm in a 200°F oven while you finish the batter.

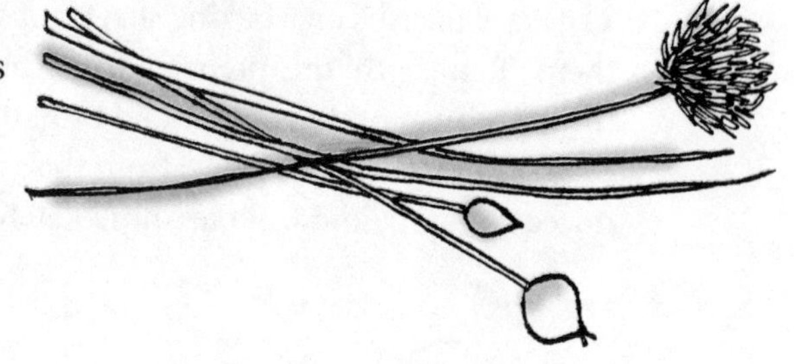

# CORN PUDDING WITH POBLANO CHILES

■ Sweet corn is available almost year-round, but this unusual flavor combination can make use of corn that is not quite "summer's best."

Serves 6 to 8 people.

6 cups fresh corn kernels
¾ cup pastry flour (cake flour may be substituted)
6 poblano chiles, cored, seeded, and finely chopped
11 large eggs, lightly beaten
2 tablespoons sugar (more to taste)
1 tablespoon salt
1 tablespoon freshly ground black pepper
¼ teaspoon pure vanilla extract
5 cups heavy cream

10" × 12" × 3" casserole dish, buttered
Baking pan deep enough to hold water around the casserole dish to just under its top

1. Preheat the oven to 350°F.

2. In a medium bowl, combine the corn kernels and flour. Toss to mix well. Add the chiles and toss to mix well.

3. In a large bowl, whisk together the eggs, sugar, salt, pepper, and vanilla. Whisk in the cream. Add the corn mixture and stir to combine well.

4. Pour the batter into the casserole dish. Place the dish in the baking pan and transfer to the preheated oven. Pour very hot water into the pan, filling it to just under the top of the casserole, being careful not to splash any water into the casserole. Bake the corn pudding for about 40 minutes or until a knife inserted in the center comes out clean. Remove from the oven and serve piping hot.

# SWEET CORN AND MOREL COMPOTE

This is an interesting side dish that combines exotic mushrooms with local produce.

Serves 4 people.

4 ears fresh corn
4 tablespoons unsalted butter
2 tablespoons minced shallots
2 tablespoons chopped fresh thyme or 2 teaspoons dried thyme
1 bay leaf
1 cup chicken stock (see page 5)
Salt and freshly ground black pepper to taste
2 cups washed, drained, and thinly sliced fresh morels (about 8 ounces whole)

1. Stand each ear of corn upright in a shallow bowl and remove the kernels with a sharp knife. Using the back of the knife, scrape the cobs down the sides to press out the "milk." Set aside.

2. In a large heavy-bottomed skillet over medium-high heat, combine 2 tablespoons of the butter with the shallots, thyme, bay leaf, ¼ cup of the stock, and salt and pepper to taste. Cover and simmer for 5 minutes. Add the morels and ½ cup more of the stock, cover, and simmer for 5 minutes.

3. Add the corn kernels with their milk and the remaining ¼ cup of stock. Cover the skillet and continue to simmer for about 5 minutes or until the morels and corn are tender. Cut the remaining 2 tablespoons of butter into 8 pieces and stir in until the butter is just melted. Add salt and pepper to taste and serve immediately.

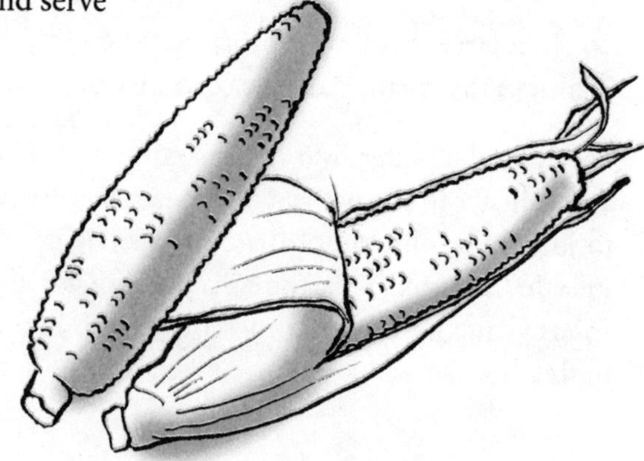

# GREEN BEANS WITH SWEET AND SOUR ONIONS

■ This delicious combination of beans and onions can also be served chilled.

Serves 6 to 8 people.

- 3 ounces streak o'lean or bacon
- ½ pound pole beans, washed and drained
- 4 tablespoons unsalted butter
- 4 cups julienned sweet onions such as Wadmalaw Sweets, Vidalia, or Maui (about 1 pound)
- 2 tablespoons sugar
- ¼ cup red wine vinegar
- ½ cup raisins
- Salt and freshly ground black pepper to taste

1. Slice the streak o'lean into ¼"-thick slices. Place in a small nonreactive saucepan, cover with water, bring to a boil, and simmer for 5 minutes. Drain the slices, refresh them by rinsing with cold water, and pat dry with paper towels.

2. Sauté the streak o'lean in a heavy-bottomed saucepan for 12 minutes or until it is crisp and the fat has melted.

3. Break the beans into 1" pieces. Add to the streak o'lean and just cover with water. Braise the beans, uncovered, for 30 minutes or until tender. Don't worry about the color. Remove from the heat and let the beans cool in their liquid.

4. Heat the butter in a nonreactive sauté pan over medium-high heat. Add the onions, reduce the heat to low, and cook, stirring occasionally, for 50 minutes or until they melt and then caramelize. As the liquid evaporates and the onions begin to caramelize, a thin glaze will begin to cling to the bottom of the pan. Add a tablespoon or 2 of water to deglaze the pan and, with a spoon or spatula, scrape up the glaze as it liquefies. The onions will absorb this liquid and its color. You may have to do this several times during the caramelization process. The onions should turn a medium dark brown, close to the color of peanut butter.

5. Add the sugar, stir well to combine, and cook for an additional 8 to 10 minutes. Deglaze the pan with the vinegar, scraping the bottom to loosen any browned bits. Cook, stirring occasionally, until the liquid has evaporated.

6. Add the raisins and stir to combine. Season with salt and pepper to taste.

7. Drain the beans and add to the onions. Toss to combine. Heat through and serve immediately.

NOTE: If you wish to substitute string beans for the pole beans, remove the stems and any strings. Bring a saucepan of salted water to a boil and drop in the beans. Cook the beans until they are tender but still bright green and slightly crunchy. Drain the beans and refresh them with cold water to avoid further cooking. Proceed with the recipe as directed.

# FRIED GREEN TOMATOES

Fried tomatoes are typically a stand-alone dish of vegetables. They are great to have with a spread of summer foods. At the restaurant, we sometimes use them the way Italians use toasts, making Southern "bruschettas" by topping them with panfried soft-shell crabs (see page 154).

Serves 8 people.

- 4 green tomatoes or firm red tomatoes if green aren't available
- 2 cups buttermilk
- 1 tablespoon Tabasco sauce
- 1 cup yellow cornmeal
- 1 cup all-purpose flour
- ½ teaspoon baking soda
- 1 teaspoon salt
- 1 teaspoon freshly ground black pepper
- ½ cup peanut oil
- 4 tablespoons unsalted butter

1. Core the top of each tomato. Slice the tomatoes into ½"-thick slices. Mix the buttermilk and Tabasco. Place the tomato slices in the mixture and marinate for 1 hour, turning occasionally.

2. In a shallow bowl, combine the cornmeal, flour, baking soda, salt, and pepper. Drain the tomato slices and carefully dredge them in the breading mixture. Place the slices on a baking sheet and refrigerate for 30 minutes to allow the breading to dry.

3. Heat the oil in a heavy 12" skillet over medium-high heat. Add the butter. When the oil and butter are hot, carefully place as many tomato slices in the skillet as will loosely fit in a single layer. If you overcrowd the skillet, the temperature of the fat will drop and you will end up with greasy tomatoes.

4. Panfry the tomatoes for 45 seconds to 1 minute on each side or until they are a nice golden brown. Remove to a plate lined with paper towels. You may hold the tomatoes in a 200°F oven while you finish frying the rest, but be sure to move quickly so they don't dry out.

NOTE: To serve the tomatoes with panfried soft-shell crabs, overlap 2 slices of tomato in the center of a plate. Place 1 crab on each side of the tomatoes and spoon the sauce from the crabs around the edges.

# CINDY'S SPICY COLESLAW

Cindy Clemmons came to us from Bardstown, Kentucky. She was a waiter for us and later became one of our managers at the Pawleys Island Inn. We soon realized that we had much in common and that we shared a fondness for Appalachian food. This Kentucky recipe became a favorite of ours and we still use it for picnics and barbecues.

Serves 10 to 12 people.

- 8 cups thinly julienned green cabbage (about 2 small heads)
- 4 cups thinly julienned Napa cabbage (1 small head)
- 2 cups thinly julienned red cabbage (1 small head)
- 2 cups cored, seeded, and julienned plum tomatoes (about 8)
- 2 cups thinly julienned red onions (about ½ pound)
- 2 cups peeled, seeded, and diced cucumber
- 1⅓ cups mayonnaise (I use Hellmann's)
- ⅓ cup sugar
- ⅓ cup plus 2 tablespoons apple cider vinegar
- 2 teaspoons Tabasco sauce, or to taste
- 2 teaspoons freshly ground black pepper, to taste

1. In a large bowl, combine the green, Napa, and red cabbages. Add the tomatoes, onions, and cucumber. Toss to mix well.

2. In a medium bowl, whisk together the mayonnaise, sugar, and vinegar. Add the Tabasco and pepper. Toss the vegetables with 1¼ cups of the dressing, adding more if you wish. Check the seasonings and serve. Any remaining dressing will keep, tightly covered, in the refrigerator for 2 weeks.

# PLANTATION SLAW

This slaw is a great mixture of vegetables, both raw and blanched, that's a refreshing change from the typical cabbage slaw.

Serves 8 people.

2 tablespoons plus ¼ teaspoon salt
2 quarts water
1 cup snow peas
1 cup baby asparagus or large asparagus cut in half lengthwise and then cut into quarter lengths
1 cup haricots verts or baby green beans
1 cup julienned zucchini
1 cup julienned yellow squash
1 cup peeled and julienned cucumber
1 cup julienned green bell pepper
1 cup julienned red bell pepper
1 cup julienned Napa cabbage
1 cup peeled, seeded, and julienned tomatoes
1 cup assorted chopped fresh herbs (tarragon and chervil are especially nice, but use whatever is available fresh, such as Italian parsley, chives, or sage)
1 large egg yolk
1 tablespoon Dijon mustard (I use Grey Poupon)
1½ teaspoons minced shallots
½ cup extra virgin olive oil
3 tablespoons red wine vinegar
1½ teaspoons fresh lemon juice
⅛ teaspoon freshly ground black pepper

1. Combine the 2 tablespoons of salt and the water and bring to a boil. First blanch the snow peas, then the asparagus, and finally the haricots verts. The approximate cooking times are: 1 minute for snow peas, 2 minutes for asparagus, and 4 minutes for haricots verts. After blanching, refresh each in an ice bath. Drain on paper towels. Julienne the snow peas. Wrap the vegetables in plastic wrap and refrigerate until ready to serve.

2. Combine the zucchini, squash, cucumber, bell peppers, cabbage, tomatoes, and herbs in a large bowl. Cover with plastic wrap and refrigerate.

3. Put the egg yolk, mustard, and shallots in a small nonreactive bowl, a blender, or a food processor. Whisk or process the ingredients until well combined.

4. Slowly whisk in ¼ cup of the olive oil or very slowly pour it into the blender or processor, teaspoon by teaspoon. Be careful not to add it too quickly or you will break the emulsion.

5. Slowly whisk or pour in half of the vinegar and half of the lemon juice. Slowly add the remaining ¼ cup of olive oil. Slowly whisk or pour in the rest of the vinegar and lemon juice. Add the remaining ¼ teaspoon of salt and the pepper.

6. Add the blanched vegetables to the large bowl of julienned vegetables. Toss with ¼ cup of the dressing, or to your taste. Check for seasonings and serve immediately.

**NOTE:** Any remaining dressing will keep, tightly covered, in the refrigerator for a week. If it separates, whisk to bring it back together.

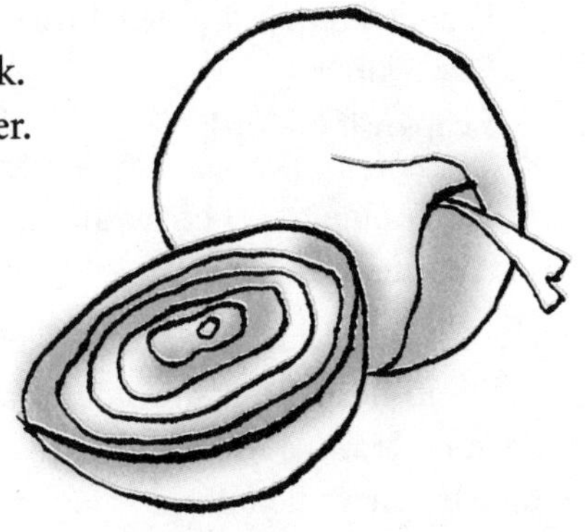

# PICKLED ONIONS

A piquant addition to sandwiches and a nice topping for grilled fish and meats, this is a very versatile condiment that couldn't be easier to make.

Makes about 6 cups.

- 1 pound red onions, peeled and sliced into thin rings
- 1 teaspoon salt
- ⅔ cup red wine vinegar
- ⅔ cup red wine
- ⅓ cup sugar
- 2 bay leaves
- 12 whole black peppercorns

1. In a large nonreactive bowl, toss the onions with the salt.

2. In a medium saucepan, combine the vinegar, wine, sugar, bay leaves, and peppercorns. Bring to a boil.

3. Pour the boiling liquid over the onions and marinate for at least 2 hours but not more than 4. Drain the onions, cover, and refrigerate until ready to use. Tightly covered, they will keep for a couple of weeks in the refrigerator.

# SOUR CHERRY ICE CREAM

If you love the combination of cherry and chocolate as much as I do, serve this with a topping of warm fudge sauce (see page 39).

Makes 2 quarts.

½ pound chopped, pitted dried sour cherries
½ cup kirsch
5 cups half-and-half
2 vanilla beans, split lengthwise
8 large egg yolks
1 cup sugar

1. Combine the cherries and kirsch in a small nonreactive bowl, cover, and refrigerate overnight.

2. The next day, put the half-and-half in a heavy-bottomed saucepan over medium heat. With the side of a spoon, scrape the seeds out of the vanilla bean pods and add both the seeds and the pods to the saucepan. Stir to combine the ingredients and bring to a low boil.

3. Meanwhile, put the egg yolks into the bowl of an electric mixer. With the whisk attachment, slowly beat the sugar into the yolks until the mixture lightens in color.

4. Prepare an ice bath by fitting an empty 3-quart bowl into a large bowl of ice.

5. Remove the half-and-half from the heat. Take 2 cups and slowly pour it into the bowl of the electric mixer, continuing to use the whisk attachment to combine it with the yolks and sugar. Slowly pour the mixture into the saucepan with the remaining half-and-half, now whisking by hand.

6. Return the saucepan to the stove. Stirring constantly with a wooden spoon or rubber spatula, gently cook the mixture over low heat for 5 to 10 minutes or until it is thick enough to coat the back of a spoon. You now have custard. Immediately strain the custard into the 3-quart bowl in the ice bath to avoid further cooking. Chill the custard overnight in a covered container. When ready to churn, pour the chilled custard into a prepared ice cream maker and proceed according to the manufacturer's instructions. Add the macerated cherries during the last minute of churning.

NOTE: For a variation, you may puree a quarter of the macerated cherries and fold the puree into the custard before you churn it. The remaining cherries should still be added during the last minute of churning.

# BUTTERMILK ICE CREAM

■ Originally the by-product of making butter at home, buttermilk was a staple of the South. Now it is cultured from either whole milk or no-fat milk. Its tangy taste accents many preparations. Sara Brewer, a longtime associate and friend, suggested this ice cream to me as part of a dinner I cooked at the James Beard House some years ago. Now we feature it on our dessert list often.

Makes 1½ quarts.

2 cups heavy cream
12 large egg yolks
¾ cup sugar
2 cups cold buttermilk
Pinch of salt
1 teaspoon white wine vinegar

1. Bring the cream to a low boil in a heavy-bottomed saucepan over medium heat.

2. Meanwhile, put the egg yolks into the bowl of an electric mixer. With the whisk attachment, slowly beat the sugar into the yolks until the mixture lightens in color.

3. Prepare an ice bath by fitting an empty 3-quart bowl into a large bowl of ice.

4. Remove the cream from the heat. Take 1 cup and slowly pour it into the bowl of the electric mixer, continuing to use the whisk attachment to combine it with the yolks and sugar. Slowly pour the mixture into the saucepan with the remaining cream, now whisking by hand.

5. Return the saucepan to the stove. Stirring constantly with a wooden spoon or rubber spatula, gently cook the mixture over low heat for 5 to 10 minutes or until it is thick enough to coat the back of a spoon. You now have custard.

6. Pour the cold buttermilk into the 3-quart bowl in the ice bath. Pour the custard into the buttermilk to avoid further cooking. Stir to combine. Stir in the salt and vinegar. Strain the custard into a refrigerator container, cover, and chill overnight. When ready to churn, pour the chilled custard into a prepared ice cream maker and proceed according to the manufacturer's instructions.

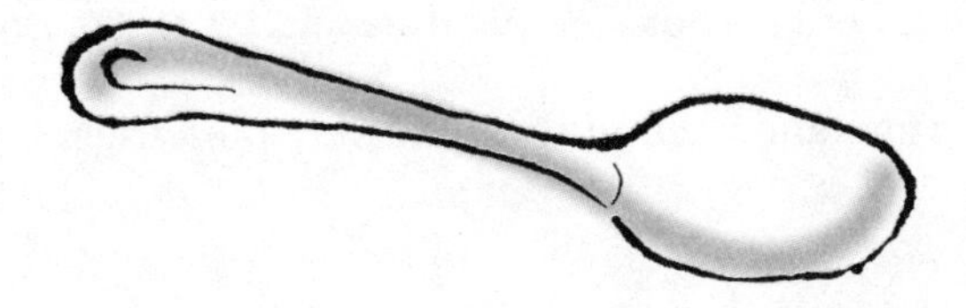

# BITTERSWEET CHOCOLATE SEMIFREDDO WITH HAZELNUT CREAM

■ Deanie Cooper, our pastry chef, came up with this dessert. Its sweetness and the flavor of the hazelnuts are just right for each other. It is fairly easy to make and can be prepared days before serving. We have learned that a small portion suffices, due to the richness of this confection.

Serves 10 to 12 people.

1 cup hazelnuts
10 ounces bittersweet chocolate, chopped into small pieces
6 tablespoons unsalted butter
1¾ cups heavy cream
3 tablespoons dark rum (I use Myers's)
¾ cup egg whites (about 12 large whites)
1 cup sugar
Pinch of salt
1 recipe Hazelnut Cream (recipe follows)
1 recipe Frangelico Strawberries (see page 97)

Candy thermometer

9" × 5" × 3" loaf pan lined with plastic wrap and kept chilled in the freezer

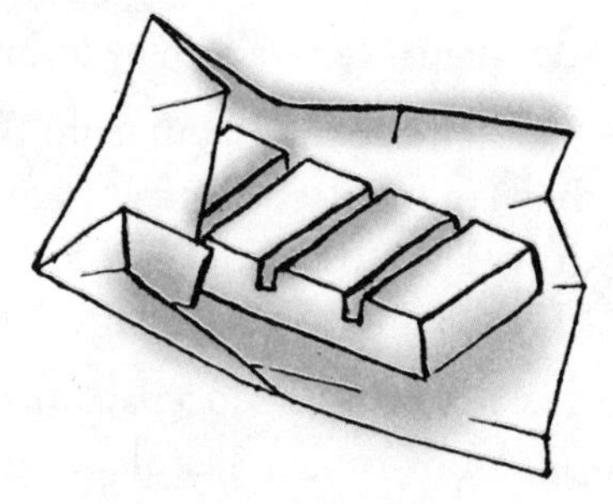

1. Preheat the oven to 325°F.

2. Place the hazelnuts on a baking sheet and toast in the preheated oven for about 6 minutes or until very lightly browned. Remove from the oven and cool to room temperature. Rub the hazelnuts in a clean terry cloth kitchen towel, working in batches if necessary, until the skin flakes off. Very tiny pieces of skin sometimes stick to the nuts, but you can ignore them. Crush the nuts and reserve.

3. Melt the chocolate and butter in the top of a double boiler over barely simmering water. Cool to room temperature and set aside.

4. Whip the cream and rum until stiff. Cover and refrigerate while beating the egg whites.

5. Clean the top of a double boiler and the bowl of an electric mixer well, making sure they have no traces of grease in them. Combine the egg whites, sugar, and salt in the top of the double boiler over simmering water and cook, whisking constantly, until the mixture registers 140°F on the candy thermometer. Pour the mixture into the bowl of the electric mixer. Using the whisk attachment, whip the mixture until it doubles in volume and cools to room temperature.

6. Moving quickly so that the egg whites do not break down, fold in the cooled chocolate. Fold in the rum cream and then the nuts. Spoon the mixture into the chilled loaf pan and smooth the top with a spatula. Freeze for at least 6 hours or until completely frozen, then cover the pan tightly with plastic wrap and return to the freezer until ready to serve. This can be done up to 5 days ahead of serving.

7. To serve, invert the loaf pan onto a cutting board and remove the plastic wrap from the sides and top. Cut the semifreddo into 10 to 12 slices with a knife dipped in hot water, wiping the knife after each slice. Drizzle hazelnut cream over the slices in a zigzag pattern and garnish the plates with the strawberries. Serve immediately.

## Hazelnut Cream

The addition of the hazelnut cream is what makes the semifreddo a truly special dessert. It's also nice as a topping for any poached fruit.

Makes 3 cups.

1 cup hazelnuts
2 cups heavy cream
1 cup Frangelico liqueur
1½ cups sugar

1. Toast and skin the hazelnuts according to steps 1 and 2 of the semifreddo recipe. Finely chop the nuts.

2. Combine the nuts and the remaining ingredients in a heavy-bottomed saucepan large enough to prevent boiling over. Whisk until all of the sugar is dissolved.

3. Simmer the mixture over medium heat, stirring occasionally, until it is reduced by a quarter and thick enough to coat the back of a spoon. Adjust the heat as necessary to prevent scorching or boiling. Cool to room temperature and refrigerate in a covered container until thoroughly chilled. The hazelnut cream can be made up to 3 days before using.

# PLANTATION COOKIES

■ These are great served warm from the oven with cinnamon ice cream, but you'll probably need to double the recipe—the cookies are that good.

Makes twenty-four 2" cookies.

- 1½ cups plus 2 tablespoons sugar
- 12 tablespoons unsalted butter, at room temperature
- 1 large egg
- 6 tablespoons sorghum or black molasses
- 1 cup chopped unsalted dry-roasted peanuts
- 2 cups all-purpose flour
- 2 teaspoons baking soda
- ¾ teaspoon ground ginger
- 1 teaspoon ground cinnamon
- ¾ teaspoon ground cloves
- ⅓ teaspoon ground nutmeg

1. Preheat the oven to 350°F. Line 2 heavy-duty baking sheets with aluminum foil or baking parchment paper.

2. Using the flat beater, beat 1 cup of the sugar and all of the butter in the bowl of an electric mixer until the mixture is light in color. Beat in the egg. Scrape down the sides of the bowl and beat in the sorghum or molasses. Beat in ½ cup of the peanuts.

3. In a medium bowl, sift together the flour, baking soda, ginger, cinnamon, cloves, and nutmeg. Add to the dough and mix well, scraping down the bowl at least once.

4. In a small bowl, mix the remaining ½ cup of peanuts with the remaining ½ cup plus 2 tablespoons of sugar. Scoop out the dough 2 tablespoons at a time. Form the dough into balls about the size of golf balls. Roll them in the peanut and sugar mixture and place on the lined baking sheets.

**5.** Bake the cookies in the preheated oven for 20 to 24 minutes. About halfway through the baking, switch the sheets from one rack to the other and reverse them back to front. This ensures more even baking. The cookies should be watched closely at the end of the cooking time. As soon as the edges are set, they are finished baking. They can overcook very quickly. Remove the cookies from the oven and place on wire baking racks to cool. Stored in an airtight container, they will keep for several days. They also freeze well.

# BERRY COBBLER

This is an easy and satisfying dessert for a crowd. Serve it with my vanilla ice cream (see page 37) for a special treat.

Serves 8 people.

- 7 tablespoons sugar
- 1 tablespoon all-purpose flour
- 6 cups juicy, ripe berries (we often use a mixture of blueberries, blackberries, and raspberries)
- 1 tablespoon freshly grated lemon zest
- 2 cups self-rising soft wheat flour, such as White Lily
- 9 tablespoons unsalted butter, cut into ½" pieces and chilled
- 1¼ cups heavy cream

9" baking dish at least 2" deep or 8 individual ovenproof bowls

**1.** To make the cobbler filling, mix 3 tablespoons of the sugar and the tablespoon of all-purpose flour in a large bowl. Add the berries and lemon zest and stir to combine. Let the berries macerate in this mixture for 1 hour at room temperature.

**2.** Preheat the oven to 350°F.

**3.** Place the self-rising flour and 2 tablespoons of the sugar in a large mixing bowl and combine well. Add 8 tablespoons of the chilled butter. Work the butter into the flour with a pastry cutter, a fork, or your fingertips until the butter pieces are a little larger than an English pea but not larger than a lima bean. If you are using your fingers, work quickly so that the heat of your hands won't melt the butter.

**4.** Pour in ¾ cup of the cream and, using light pressure, fold the mixture a few times with a plastic spatula until it just holds together. Do not overmix.

**5.** Turn the dough out onto a floured surface and quickly and gently knead it 6 to 10 times or until it just begins to be almost homogenized. There will be large pieces of butter throughout. Sprinkle a little flour under the dough to make sure it won't stick to the surface and lightly dust the top of the dough so it won't stick to the rolling pin. Roll the dough out to about a ⅝" thickness. The texture will resemble soft biscuit dough.

**6.** Pour the berries into the baking dish or divide it among the ovenproof bowls. Dot with 1 tablespoon of the chilled butter. Spoon 2 tablespoons of the cream over all.

**7.** If you are making a single large cobbler, cut the dough into 4" rounds and place the rounds next to each other on top of the cobbler filling. If you are making individual cobblers, cut the rounds slightly smaller than the bowls and put a round on top of the filling in each bowl. Use as much as needed of the remaining cream to brush the tops of the rounds. Sprinkle with the remaining 2 tablespoons of sugar.

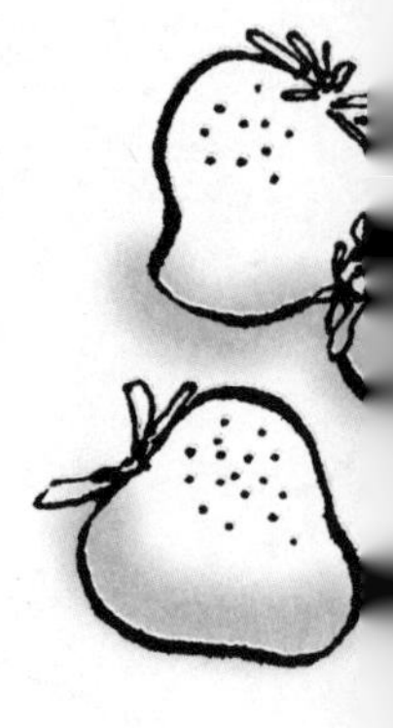

**8.** Bake the cobbler in the preheated oven for 40 to 50 minutes or until the rounds are cooked through and the filling is bubbly and thick. (Gently lift a part of the crust to make sure it is completely baked and not still wet.) Remove from the oven and serve warm.

# RUSTIC BERRY TARTS

These tarts are quick and easy and adaptable to almost all berries and fruit. Don't hesitate to use apples or pears—they're equally good.

Makes 8 individual tarts.

1 pint fresh blackberries
1 pint fresh blueberries
1 pint fresh strawberries
½ cup heavy cream
½ cup all-purpose flour
2 cups sugar

1 recipe Best Pie Dough (see page 28), unbaked
1 large egg and 2 tablespoons water, lightly beaten together
1 recipe Vanilla Ice Cream (see page 37)

1. Wash the berries, put them in a large bowl, and mix in the cream, flour, and 1½ cups of the sugar. Cover and refrigerate overnight.

2. The next day, preheat the oven to 400°F.

3. Divide the dough into 8 equal parts. Roll each part out on a lightly floured surface into a circle approximately 8" in diameter. Place ¾ cup of the berry mixture in the center of each circle. Fold the edges of the dough in toward the berries and gently press down to secure the edges. Brush each tart with the egg wash. Sprinkle the remaining ½ cup of sugar equally over each.

4. Place the tarts on greased baking sheets and bake in the preheated oven for 15 to 20 minutes or until the crust is golden brown. Serve warm, accompanied by a scoop of vanilla ice cream.

# SHORTCAKES WITH FRESH BERRIES AND VANILLA CREAM

■ The shortcakes for this recipe are a variation of the classic Southern biscuit. It's a quick and easy approach to a delicious dessert.

Makes four 4" shortcakes.

**FOR THE SHORTCAKES:**

2 cups self-rising soft wheat flour, such as White Lily
4 tablespoons sugar
8 tablespoons unsalted butter, cut into ½" pieces and chilled
¾ cup plus 2 tablespoons heavy cream

**FOR THE FILLING:**

4 cups washed and sliced fresh strawberries
⅔ cup sugar
⅔ cup fresh orange juice
¼ cup Grand Marnier liqueur (optional)

**FOR THE VANILLA CREAM:**

1½ cups heavy cream
⅓ cup sugar
1 tablespoon pure vanilla extract
Pinch of salt

**TO ASSEMBLE:**

2 cups best-quality strawberry preserves
⅔ cup confectioners' sugar
4 sprigs fresh mint

1. To make the shortcakes, preheat the oven to 425°F.

2. Place the flour and 2 tablespoons of the sugar in a medium bowl and combine well. Add the chilled butter. Work the butter into the flour with a pastry cutter, a fork, or your fingertips until the butter pieces are a little larger than an English pea but not larger than a lima bean. If you are using your fingers, work quickly so the heat of your hands won't melt the butter.

3. Pour in ¾ cup of the cream and, using light pressure, fold the mixture a few times with a plastic spatula until it just holds together. Do not overmix.

4. Turn the dough out onto a floured surface and quickly and gently knead it 6 to 10 times or until it just begins to be almost homogenized. There will be large pieces of butter throughout. Sprinkle a little flour under the dough to make sure it won't stick to the surface and lightly dust the top of the dough so it won't stick to the rolling pin. Roll the dough out to about a 1" thickness.

5. Cut the dough into 4" rounds. Use as much as needed of the remaining cream to brush the rounds. Sprinkle with the remaining 2 tablespoons of sugar. Place the rounds on an ungreased baking sheet and bake in the preheated oven for about 18 minutes or until they are crispy and brown on the top and bottom but not dry in the middle. Remove from the oven and cool on a rack.

6. To make the filling, toss the strawberries with the sugar, orange juice, and Grand Marnier in a large bowl. Reserve.

7. To make the vanilla ice cream, combine all the ingredients in the bowl of an electric mixer. Using the whisk attachment, whip the mixture until it forms soft peaks. Cover and refrigerate until ready to use.

8. To assemble, split the shortcakes in half, making a top and a bottom.

9. Spoon 1 tablespoon of the strawberry preserves onto each of the shortcake bottoms. Spoon half of the vanilla cream over the preserves. Divide the strawberries among the shortcakes, spooning them over the cream. Drizzle the strawberries with the remaining preserves and spoon the remaining vanilla cream on top. Crown with the top halves of the shortcakes, dust with the confectioners' sugar, and garnish each with a sprig of fresh mint. Serve immediately.

# FRIED PEACH PIES

For many years now, the Varsity Drive-In restaurant in Atlanta has pleased thousands of people with its excellent fast food served with unique Southern hospitality. When looking for a new dessert for early summer, our pastry chef, Deanie Cooper, inspired by my fond reminiscences of the Varsity's peach pie, came up with this version of an old Southern favorite.

Makes 6 individual pies.

- 4 medium peaches
- 2 cups sugar
- 2 tablespoons ground cinnamon
- 1 recipe Best Pie Dough (see page 28), unbaked
- 4 cups peanut oil
- Cinnamon sugar: 2 tablespoons ground cinnamon and ½ cup sugar, well combined
- 1 recipe Butter Pecan Ice Cream (see page 85)

1. Peel and slice the peaches, toss them in the 2 cups of sugar and 2 tablespoons of cinnamon, cover, and refrigerate overnight.

2. The next day, drain the peaches and put the juice in a heavy-bottomed nonreactive saucepan. Cook over medium-high heat until the juices have reduced by a quarter and are a syrupy consistency. Reserve.

3. Divide the dough into 6 equal parts. Roll each piece on a lightly floured surface into circles approximately ⅛" thick and 6" in diameter. Place ½ cup of the peaches on half of each circle. Fold the other half over the peaches to make a half-moon. Seal the edges of the dough with the tines of a fork. At this point, the pies can be covered in plastic wrap and refrigerated for up to 1 day.

4. Heat the oil in a medium heavy-bottomed skillet to 350°F on a frying thermometer. Fry the pies in the hot oil for 2 minutes on each side or until golden brown. Do not add too many to the skillet at a time or the temperature of the oil will drop and the pies will be greasy. Remove the pies with a slotted spoon, pat off any excess oil, and sprinkle with the cinnamon sugar.

5. Place each pie on a plate, place 2 scoops of butter pecan ice cream next to each pie, and spoon the reserved peach syrup around all. Serve immediately.

# TOASTED CORN CAKE WITH BRANDIED FIGS

I served this with great success at the James Beard House in New York in 1996. The audience was a little skeptical when they first saw it on the menu, though I couldn't help but notice that they all cleaned their plates.

Serves 8 people.

6 tablespoons unsalted butter, at room temperature
⅓ cup packed light brown sugar
3 large eggs plus 2 large egg yolks
¼ teaspoon pure vanilla extract
¾ cup stone-ground yellow cornmeal
½ cup all-purpose flour
1¼ teaspoons baking powder
¼ teaspoon five-spices powder
4 tablespoons unsalted butter for brushing cake slices before toasting, at room temperature
1 recipe Buttermilk Ice Cream (see page 219)
1 recipe Brandied Figs (recipe follows)

9" × 5" × 3" loaf pan, buttered

1. Preheat the oven to 350°F.

2. Put the butter and brown sugar in the bowl of an electric mixer and beat with the flat beater until the mixture is fluffy and light in color. Add the eggs and the additional yolks 1 at a time, scraping down the bowl after every 2 eggs. Add the vanilla and beat until the mixture is light and well mixed.

3. In a medium bowl, sift together the cornmeal, flour, baking powder, and five-spices powder.

4. Mixing now by hand, gently add the dry ingredients to the butter mixture. Combine thoroughly.

5. Spoon the batter into the loaf pan and bake in the preheated oven for about 45 minutes or until a toothpick inserted in the middle comes out clean. Be careful not to overcook the cake. Invert the cake onto a wire rack and cool to room temperature. Keep wrapped in plastic wrap until ready to serve.

6. Cut the cake into ½" slices, slather generously with the softened butter, and place under the broiler until the butter and the cake begin to brown. Top each slice with buttermilk ice cream and brandied figs. Serve immediately.

## Brandied Figs

We make these year-round, using fat, fresh figs in the summer and good dried figs at other times of the year. We are especially fond of black mission figs.

Makes 3 cups.

4 cups sugar
2 cups water
1 cup brandy
1 vanilla bean, split lengthwise
1 stick cinnamon
1 whole clove
1 pound figs (fresh or dried)

1. Mix the sugar, water, and brandy in a medium saucepan and bring to a simmer. With the side of a spoon, scrape the seeds out of the vanilla bean pod. Add both the seeds and the pod to the saucepan. Add the cinnamon and clove and stir well. Simmer for 45 minutes or until the mixture has reduced by half. Remove and discard the vanilla bean pod, cinnamon stick, and clove.

2. Stir in the figs, remove the saucepan from the heat, and let sit for 10 minutes before using, or cool to room temperature. Tightly covered, the figs will keep for a week in the refrigerator.

# Two Suggested Menus from the Grill

Charleston Chile-Pickled Shrimp /194

The Osteen Family's Sunday Grilled Chicken /251

Grilled Vegetable Salad /261

Cornbread /25

Sour Cherry Ice Cream with Plantation Cookies /218, 222

Grilled Lamb Ribs with Shallot-Pepper Butter /242

Tuna Burgers with Ginger-Mustard Glaze /250

Pickled Onions /217

Cindy's Spicy Coleslaw /215

Shortcakes with Fresh Berries and Vanilla Cream /225

# The Art of the Grill

Grilling, especially when done outdoors, has became an icon of everything we love about the nineties: low fat, casual, accessible, brightly flavored, and quick. But grilling is also associated with camaraderie. I have found that friendships are frequently forged around a grill as the food cooks and sizzles, and everyone joins in for basting and turning.

What grilling is *not,* however, is synonymous with barbecue. In the South, barbecue is a serious subject. Considered one of the glories of Southern food, true barbecue adheres to a strict procedure: long, slow cooking over indirect heat. In the Lowcountry, barbecue is confined exclusively to pork, and large cuts are used (whole pigs, up to two hundred pounds, are not uncommon). Here and throughout the South, the traditional method for cooking barbecue is in a pit. Lacking a pit, a grill with the ability to control heat placement is the perfect alternative. The lengthy process can take up to fourteen hours, which is why barbecue is what you get only after a long, hot day in the sun—preferably with a couple of cool brews on hand. Anything else is simply grilling—no less wonderful, but not barbecue. This chapter contains advice on both subjects—how to grill and how to barbecue.

That the history of Southern cooking in general, and Lowcountry cooking in particular, is intertwined with the outdoors is something I have long known. That my own personal history is so connected to cooking outside is something I realized only when I sat down to write this chapter. You see, a good part of my story can be revealed by telling about two unique culinary events that occurred annually in Pawleys Island. The first, a pig pickin', happened at the conclusion of every summer; the second, an oyster roast, took place each January around the time of the Ducks Unlimited banquet.

## A Lowcountry Pig Pickin'

In the eighties, my wife, Marlene, and I had a restaurant in Pawleys Island, South Carolina, appropriately named the Pawleys Island Inn. Each June, as soon as the final school bell tolled, throngs would descend on our little barrier island about seventy-five miles north of Charleston. The population of Waccamaw Neck, usually no more than a couple of thousand, swelled to well over ten thousand every summer. For twelve frantic weeks, Marlene and I, and about seventy-five hardworking employees and managers, tried frantically to keep up with the pace. Although the hours seemed endless, the work excruciating, the demands extraordinary, somehow we all survived (and perhaps became even better friends for having endured it together). And so, by September, when just about everyone had gone home, we were all certainly ready for, and deserving of, a party. Marlene and the staff used my birthday, September 17, as an excuse to throw a big one. I still think it was more of an end-of-summer celebration than a birthday party, but I never failed to be grateful. Naturally, my birthday party always took place outside, either in someone's backyard or by the swimming pool of the Litchfield Inn, and grilling and barbecue were what it was really all about.

Marlene and the Susans (then our managers, now owners of the wonderful Rice Paddy restaurant in Georgetown, South Carolina) would descend on our food and beverage suppliers to obtain the provisions for our feast. Big Fish George always showed up with a fifty-pound (or larger) grouper. One year he brought lobsters, which he kept in the kiddie pool at the Litchfield Inn until dinnertime. Other vendors provided ducks, chickens, quails, and vegetables. And there was no end in sight of beer and wine, all chilling in huge tubs of ice. But the highlights were always the upside-down margaritas and the pig.

As for the upside-down margaritas—that tradition really started on the island before we ever bought the inn. Marlene has always said that she never felt rightfully established there until her rite of passage with the upside-down margarita. That happened one evening soon after we bought the inn, when a Murrells Inlet restaurateur came by, picked Marlene up, placed her horizontally across the top of the bar, and poured a shot of tequila down her throat. Quickly lifting her head to keep her from choking, he then stuffed a lime in her mouth. That was generally how it was done, and done more than a few times at the bar at the Pawleys Island Inn. This method, however, isn't really practical outdoors. No bar, you see. So the Susans and Penny, our longtime friend and bartender, filled a small keg with tequila and hung it from a pole. Victims were seated on a chair under the keg and opened their mouths to receive the tequila poured down their gullets when the spout was released.

While it may sound extreme to non–South Carolinians, it was actually quite pleasurable—and not nearly as toxic as one might presume.

Now about the pig pickin'. It normally took about a 150-pound pig and a large PDQ cooker, a type of cooker that is legendary in the Lowcountry. Invented by Mr. Rast, owner of the famous Rast Barbecue on Johns Island, South Carolina, this barbecue cooker is distinct from a grill because it uses only indirect heat and is made entirely of stainless steel. A PDQ cooker will last forever (thankfully, as they're hugely expensive) and is a badge of honor among barbecue aficionados.

The first thing to know if you're going to have a pig pickin' is that you have to start *real* early in the day (if not the night before), have lots of cold beer nearby, and be absolutely certain that there is a fine stereo system with a good stack of bluegrass music on hand. It's just no fun otherwise.

## RECIPE FOR A PIG PICKIN'

Take a hog that has been split in half and eviscerated and massage the insides with a barbecue rub (see pages 262–73). Barbecuing means low heat and slow cooking, so begin by setting a fire in your cooker using slow-burning coals. When the fire has reached the appropriate low heat, you can spread the split pig, skin side down, over the grill. Although some people turn the pig halfway through cooking, I have found that you can eliminate this difficult step by keeping the heat low enough throughout the entire process.

You should have lots of vinegar shake (see page 262) on hand to flavor the pig, a squirt bottle filled with water to subdue the flames from pig drippings, and a clean rag that has been tied to the end of a four-foot-long stick for the barbecue mop. The rag is for dipping into the shake, and the long stick enables you to reach all sides of the pig without getting burned. That dipping-and-basting action is what we call "doing the barbecue mop dance."

Eight to twelve hours later, or when the internal temperature registers 155° to 160°F on a meat thermometer, your pig will be ready. Ready, that is, to have its meat picked from its bones and dunked into more of the shake or your favorite barbecue sauce (see pages 262–73). I guarantee you that the first time you put this meat into your mouth, chewing it slowly, savoring the succulent meat and the smoky, vinegary flavors, you will finally understand that food doesn't get better than this. My friend John Egerton described that moment perfectly in *Southern Food:*

> And finally, in the golden light of a Southern dawn, there comes an exhilarating moment of truth when every message of the senses is saying in

unison, "It's ready," and the first charred, crusty, tender, smoke-and-sauce-anointed taste of the meat confirms it. Truly, there is nothing quite so fine as genuine barbecue at the instant of its readiness. Clear to the bone, barbecue is a savory slice of Southern history, a pulled chunk of the region itself, at its ever-loving best.

And know this to be as true: There are only two things to serve with this pig—coleslaw and cornbread.

## A Lowcountry Oyster Roast

Every winter, when the waters surrounding Pawleys Island had reached cold enough temperatures to produce oysters with the right amount of salinity, there were oyster roasts. The best was usually in January at the fund-raiser for Ducks Unlimited—an organization dedicated to the preservation of the Lowcountry wetlands and the survival of the ducks that live there. The banquet was normally held at a nearby plantation and it was a big social gathering. Everyone in town came—it didn't really matter whether you cared about the ducks or the wetlands. It was enough that your friends were all there and that there were oysters roasting.

We would gather around huge charcoal-fueled grills trying to stay warm in the glow of the fire, helped by a little bourbon. Heaped on the grills were our local cluster oysters. Throughout the saltwater marshes and waterways of the Waccamaw Neck, oysters grow in huge clusters—as many as eight stuck together in a clump. They are a pretty muddy and messy affair, but the fun seems to be in the dirt.

The term "oyster roast" is somewhat of a misnomer, as the oysters are actually steam grilled rather than roasted. But that's probably just nit-picking. What happens is this: The raw oysters are literally shoveled onto large grill grates, which are set over a medium-hot charcoal fire, and allowed to cook on the grill for three to four minutes or until they pop open. They are then removed from the grill with shovels and spread onto tables that are set with rolls of paper towels, saltine crackers, lemons, and various sauces. Each guest, wearing a glove (more to prevent burns than avoid dirt) and armed with an oyster knife, digs in, removing the warm, shiny bivalves from their shells, flinging the shells into waiting trash cans, dipping the oysters into sauce, sliding them onto crackers, and popping them into their mouths. It's wonderful fun, great theater, and the oysters taste sublime! And you don't need to live in South Carolina to do it.

## GRILLING GUIDELINES AND TIMETABLES

These guidelines and timetables provide a rule of thumb for cooking fish, poultry, meat, and vegetables, but remember that the most accurate predictor of any food's doneness is a peek into its interior. Don't be afraid to pick up the food, touch it, and even cut into it if necessary.

# Seafood

For the most part, seafood grilling requires a lower heat because a heavy crust is not desired. The end result should be a piece of fish that is just stiffened on the outside. In general, the sturdier the fish, the better it will do on the grill. Delicate fish like flounder or cod will fall apart on the grill. Likewise, very bony fish, like shad and catfish, are not as good for grilling as are fish fillets.

The key to keeping fish from sticking to the grill is a clean and very hot grate. To get the grate hot enough while maintaining a lower heat, keep the rack on top of the fire throughout the grilling process. Coat the fish *very lightly* with oil before grilling and for its first 2 or 3 minutes on the grill, don't move the fish. Thicker fish—salmon, tuna, and shark—should be cooked until they show a uniform opacity, while thinner fish and shrimp and lobster should have a trace of translucency. Fish steaks should normally be turned once during the cooking process, while thinner fillets often cook through without turning. Shellfish like shrimp and scallops will cook best on a skewer. Finally, the key to successful seafood grilling is to obtain the freshest possible fish.

### SHELLFISH

**Shrimp and Sea Scallops:** 2 to 3 minutes per side over a medium-hot fire.

**Lobster:** (2 to 2½ pounds, split in half lengthwise, claws and legs removed): All pieces about 5 to 7 minutes per side over a medium-low fire.

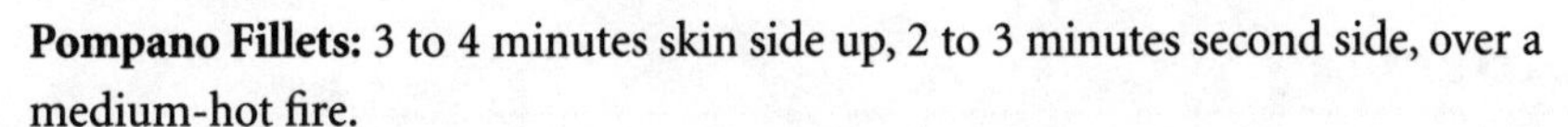

### FISH FILLETS AND FISH STEAKS

*All instructions assume 8-ounce portions*

**Pompano Fillets:** 3 to 4 minutes skin side up, 2 to 3 minutes second side, over a medium-hot fire.

**Salmon Fillets** (skin on, ¾" to 1" thick): 5 to 6 minutes skin side down, 3 to 3½ minutes second side, over a medium-hot fire.

**Salmon Steaks** (1" to 1½" thick): 5 to 6 minutes per side over a medium-hot fire.

**Mahimahi Fillets** (about 1" thick): 5 to 6 minutes per side over a medium-hot fire.

**Bluefish Fillets** (1½" to 2" thick): 5 minutes on first side, 5 to 8 minutes on second side, over a medium-low fire.

**Swordfish Steaks** (about 1½" thick): 5 to 7 minutes per side over a medium-hot fire.

**Tuna Steaks** (about 2" to 3" thick): 4 to 5 minutes per side over a medium-hot fire.

**Halibut Steaks** (about 1½" thick): 5 to 6 minutes per side over a medium-hot fire.

**Monkfish fillets:** 6 to 8 minutes per side over a medium-hot fire.

**Mackerel Steaks:** 3 to 4 minutes per side over a medium-hot fire.

**Red Snapper Fillets:** 5 minutes per side over a medium fire.

**Grouper Fillets:** 5 to 7 minutes per side over a medium-hot fire.

**Sea Bass Fillets:** 5 to 7 minutes per side over a medium-hot fire.

### WHOLE FISH

**Red Snapper, Trout, Ocean Perch, Bluefish, Mackerel, and Striped Bass** (with bones, 1½ pounds): Grill 4 to 5 minutes without moving over a medium-hot fire. Gently move fish to another spot on the grill, but don't turn. Continue to cook 2 to 3 minutes. *Roll* the fish over and continue to cook another 10 minutes. The fish should be opaque throughout when done.

**Rainbow Trout** (boned, 10 to 12 ounces): 4 to 5 minutes per side over a medium-hot fire.

### OTHER CUTS OF FISH

**Skate Wings** (12 ounces each): 6 to 8 minutes per side over a medium-hot fire.

**Shad Roe:** (6 to 8 ounces each): 3 to 4 minutes per side over a medium fire.

## Poultry

The flavorless supermarket chickens we buy in stores today can be greatly improved simply by brining; you will discover a marked improvement both in the flavor and juiciness of the bird. Make a brine by adding ¾ cup of kosher salt (or 6 tablespoons of table salt) and ¾ cup of sugar to 1 quart of water.

Submerge the chicken in the brine and refrigerate for at least 1½ hours. When ready to cook, remove the chicken from the brine, pat dry, and season with a rub or salt and pepper before grilling.

Poultry is cooked when the meat is completely white with no sign of translucence. You can also check for doneness with a meat thermometer inserted into the thickest part of the bird; the internal temperature should read 160°F. When grilling duck and fattier birds, keep the bird on the perimeter of the fire so that the fat doesn't drip into the flames.

For some recipes, I have noted that the bird should be butterflied. To butterfly a bird, remove the backbone with a knife and, using the heel of your palm, press down on the breast, gently flattening the bird until the breastbone cracks.

**Chicken Leg-and-Thigh Quarters:** 12 to 15 minutes per side over a medium-hot fire.

**Chicken Legs Only:** 8 minutes per side over a medium-hot fire.

**Chicken Thighs Only** (bone in): 8 to 10 minutes skin side down, 4 to 6 minutes second side, over a medium-hot fire.

**Chicken Wings:** 5 minutes per side over a medium-hot fire.

**Boneless Chicken Breasts, Skin On** (10 to 12 ounces): 8 to 10 minutes skin side down, 5 to 6 minutes second side, over a medium-hot fire.

**Boneless Chicken Breasts, Skinned** (6 to 8 ounces): 4 minutes per side over a medium-hot fire.

**Chicken Breasts, Bone In and Skin On** (10 to 12 ounces): 8 to 10 minutes per side over a medium-hot fire.

**Rock Cornish Game Hens** (butterflied): 15 minutes per side over a medium-low fire.

**Turkey Fillets** (½" thick, about 10 ounces): 4 to 5 minutes per side over a medium-hot fire.

**Duck Breasts** (10 to 12 ounces): 6 minutes skin side down, 5 to 7 minutes second side, over a medium fire.

**Duck Leg Quarters:** 15 to 18 minutes per side over a medium fire.

**Quail** (whole, butterflied): 6 to 8 minutes per side over a medium-hot fire.

**Squab** (whole, butterflied): 10 minutes skin side up, 5 minutes second side, over a medium fire.

## Meat

When grilling fatty cuts of meat like rack of lamb, place the meat around the edges of the fire, fat side up, in order to prevent flare-ups. When cooking dense meats like steak, you should remove the meat from the grill just prior to reaching the required degree of doneness, as it will continue to cook for several minutes once removed from the heat.

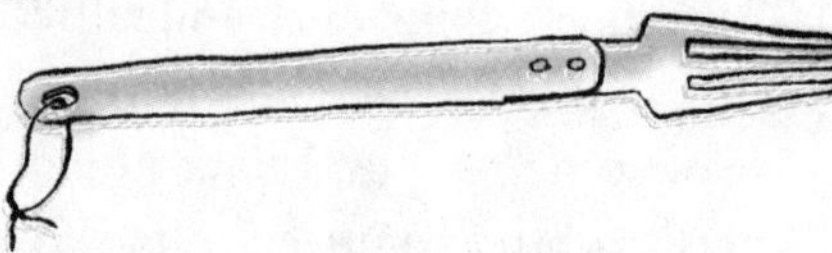

**Leg of Lamb** (boneless, butterflied, 4 to 5 pounds): 4 to 5 minutes per side over a hot fire, then move to a place on the grill where there are no coals, cover, and cook for another 15 to 20 minutes. The lamb should rest for 5 to 10 minutes before slicing and serving.

**Lamb Chops** (1½" thick, 10 to 12 ounces): 6 to 7 minutes per side over a medium fire.

**Rack of Lamb** (frenched): 15 minutes per side or until well browned over a medium to medium-hot fire (an instant-read thermometer will register 125°F for rare to medium rare).

**Veal Chops** (bone in, 12 to 14 ounces): 8 to 10 minutes per side over a medium fire.

**Flank Steaks** (16 ounces): 5 to 7 minutes per side over a hot fire for medium rare.

**New York Strip Steaks** (1½" thick, 12 to 16 ounces): 5 to 7 minutes per side over a hot fire for medium rare.

**Whole Beef Tenderloin** (3 to 4 pounds): Over a medium-hot fire, grill 7 minutes on first side, 7 minutes on second side, then 3 to 4 minutes on each of the last 2 sides. The total cooking time should be about 20 to 25 minutes.

**Filet Mignon** (2" to 3" thick, 8 to 10 ounces): 6 to 8 minutes per side over a hot fire for medium rare.

**Rib Eye Steaks** (12 to 16 ounces): 5 to 7 minutes per side over a hot fire for rare.

**Top Round** (cut into 2"-thick slices): 5 minutes per side over a hot fire.

**Thin-Cut Pork Chops** (4 to 5 ounces): 3 minutes per side over a hot fire.

**Pork Porterhouse Chops** (double-thick chops, 14 to 16 ounces): Over a hot fire, 3 to 4 minutes per side or until nicely seared, then move to a side of the grill with no fire and cook 10 more minutes per side or until the inside is cooked through and slightly pink.

**Pork Tenderloin** (12 to 14 ounces): Sear on both sides for a total of 5 minutes over a hot fire, then move to the side of the grill to a low heat and cook for 10 to 12 minutes, turning occasionally. The inside should be a light pink.

**Rabbit** (whole, 4 pounds): 15 to 20 minutes per side over a low fire in a covered grill.

**Venison Loin** (2¼-pound loin, cut into 2 pieces): Sear 5 to 6 minutes per side over a medium-hot fire. Remove from the grill and let rest for 5 minutes before slicing and serving.

## Vegetables

Because of their high water and low fat content, vegetables must have a coating of oil before grilling so you don't end up with cardboard and ash.

**Shiitake Mushrooms** (wiped clean, stems removed): 3 to 5 minutes per side over a hot fire.

**Button Mushrooms** (stemmed and cleaned): 3 to 5 minutes over a hot fire.

**Portobello Mushrooms** (6" to 8" each): 3 to 4 minutes per side over a medium-hot fire.

**Asparagus** (stalks trimmed ¼"): 3 to 4 minutes over a medium-hot fire.

**Zucchini and Yellow Squash** (cut lengthwise in ½"-thick slices): Over a medium-hot fire, 3 minutes per side or until well browned.

**Eggplant** (cut lengthwise into 1"-thick slices): 4 to 5 minutes per side over a medium-hot fire.

**Peppers** (quartered and seeded): 3 to 5 minutes per side over a medium-hot fire.

**Corn on the Cob** (husked, silk removed, and blanched in boiling water for 2 minutes): 3 to 4 minutes per side over a medium-hot fire.

**Tomatoes** (medium, halved): 3 to 5 minutes per side over a medium fire.

**Red and Yellow Onions** (large, peeled and quartered): 8 to 12 minutes per side over a medium fire.

**Leeks** (trimmed and cleaned): 30 minutes total, turning occasionally, over a medium fire.

# GRILLED LAMB RIBS WITH SHALLOT-PEPPER BUTTER

In 1994, these lamb ribs were awarded the prestigious Golden Dish Award, presented by *GQ* magazine to the 10 best dishes of the year from around the world. They have been on the menu at my restaurant for a number of years, giving nod to the notion that eating with your hands is a singular pleasure. Alan Richman, the food and wine critic at *GQ*, is a great fan of these ribs. He wrote that he was having lamb at the legendary restaurant of Paul Bocuse when a strange feeling came over him: he realized that he'd rather be at Louis's chewing on some lamb ribs. You'll like them, too.

Serves 4 people.

**FOR THE LAMB:**

4 racks lamb ribs
¼ cup extra virgin olive oil
2 tablespoons chopped garlic
4 sprigs fresh thyme
1 sprig fresh rosemary
2 sprigs fresh Italian parsley
1 tablespoon freshly ground black pepper

**FOR THE SHALLOT-PEPPER BUTTER:**

¼ cup white wine
¼ cup champagne vinegar
⅓ cup finely diced shallots
¼ cup coarsely ground black pepper
½ teaspoon salt
12 tablespoons unsalted butter, cut into 8 pieces
Salt to taste

1. Place the lamb ribs in a shallow nonreactive dish. Sprinkle with the olive oil, garlic, thyme, rosemary, parsley, and pepper. Cover and refrigerate overnight.

2. When ready to cook, prepare a medium-hot grill.

3. While the grill is heating, prepare the sauce. Combine the wine, vinegar, shallots, pepper, and ½ teaspoon of salt in a small heavy-bottomed saucepan. Bring the mixture to a boil over medium-high heat. Maintain a vigorous boil and let the mixture reduce until it thickens and the bubbles start to enlarge. Reduce the heat until the mixture drops to a low boil.

4. Remove the saucepan from the heat. Using a wire whisk, quickly beat in the butter, a piece at a time. Add salt to taste. Keep the sauce warm on the back of the stove until ready to use.

5. Slowly grill the ribs over the medium-hot fire. Medium-rare ribs should take about 6 minutes on each side, for a total of 12 minutes per rack. Sprinkle the ribs with a little salt while they grill. When they are done, place on a carving board and let rest for 10 minutes before slicing.

6. Since lamb ribs are rather small, they do not have an abundance of meat and they require a rather tricky slicing technique. Slice the first rib bone off the rack, cutting as close to the bone as possible and leaving as much meat as possible attached to the second rib. Discard the first bone. Slice the second rib off the rack by cutting as close as possible to the third rib bone. This gives the second rib lots of meat on both sides of the bone. Discard the third bone. Continue to cut the ribs in this manner, discarding every other bone.

7. To serve, arrange the ribs on a platter and drizzle them with some of the sauce. Pass any extra sauce separately. For individual servings, stack 4 of the ribs "tent style" on each plate and drizzle the sauce over the top. Serve immediately.

# BARBECUED SHRIMP ON BISCUITS

Charleston has a couple of net-shrimp seasons that are mostly for the take-home shrimper. There is a great smelly local shrimp bait that is used to get the new shrimp into the net. As the shrimp are still in the estuary during these seasons, they tend to be small. When we get some, we use this procedure—a variation on a New Orleans recipe—and cook up the batch, heads and all, and pass them out at the bar. They're messy as can be, but really succulent and delicious. For this dressed-up version, we use larger shrimp, and they are grilled instead of cooked in the sauce. You'll find that the taste is uniquely different.

Before you get started on this recipe, take a look at your grill. If the rods are too far apart, the shrimp could fall through. You can purchase a grid at specialty cookware shops to place on top of the rods when grilling shrimp, scallops, vegetables, or other small items.

Serves 4 people.

**FOR THE SAUCE:**

12 tablespoons unsalted butter
½ cup Worcestershire sauce (I use Lea & Perrins)
⅔ cup ketchup
8 tablespoons guava paste (see note)
8 ounces beer (light or dark)
2 teaspoons salt
6 tablespoons freshly ground black pepper

**FOR THE BISCUITS:**

½ recipe Buttermilk Biscuits (see page 27)
4 tablespoons unsalted butter, at room temperature

**FOR THE SHRIMP:**

1 pound large fresh shrimp, shelled but with the tail left on
Salt and freshly ground black pepper to taste

1. To prepare the sauce, combine the butter, Worcestershire sauce, ketchup, guava paste, beer, salt, and pepper in a nonreactive saucepan. Simmer over medium heat, whisking continuously, until the butter has melted and the ingredients begin to come together. Continue to simmer for about 10 minutes or until thickened. Set aside.

2. Prepare the biscuits. After they are baked and are cool enough to handle, split them and butter the halves on both sides with the soft butter.

3. Prepare a hot grill. Butterfly the shrimp by making a lengthwise slit down the backs. Salt and pepper the shrimp. Grill for 2 minutes on each side or until pink, turning only once. Remove to a bowl and cover loosely with aluminum foil to keep warm.

4. Place the buttered biscuit halves on the grill and cook for about 1 minute on each side or until nicely browned and crisp on both sides. Place 4 grilled biscuit halves on each of 4 plates. Spoon a tablespoon of the sauce on each biscuit half and top with a shrimp. Serve immediately.

NOTE: Guava paste is available at Latin grocery markets. You may substitute guava preserves, but you must use twice as much to achieve the same flavor.

# PINK GAZPACHO WITH GRILLED SHRIMP

■ Faison Cushman, one of our sous-chefs, brought back this recipe from her extensive travels. It immediately became a summer standard.

Serves 6 people.

1 cup large croutons (see steps 3–5 on page 61), soaked in cold water for 10 minutes
2 cucumbers, peeled, seeded, and cut into 1" pieces
2½ pounds ripe tomatoes, peeled, seeded, and chopped
½ cup chopped yellow onion
2 red bell peppers, seeded and chopped
3 cloves garlic, peeled
1 cup cold water
Juice of 2 lemons
⅓ cup red wine vinegar
1 tablespoon balsamic vinegar
1 tablespoon paprika
4 teaspoons salt
½ cup mayonnaise (I use Hellmann's)
Salt and freshly ground black pepper to taste
1 pound large fresh shrimp, shelled and cleaned

1. Using a food processor, puree the croutons, cucumbers, tomatoes, onion, peppers, garlic, and water. You will probably have to do this in several small batches, using some of the water in each; if you fill the food processor too full, it will leak.

2. Combine the mixture in a large bowl with the lemon juice, vinegars, paprika, and 4 teaspoons of salt. Whisk in the mayonnaise until well combined. Add salt and pepper to taste. Refrigerate, covered, for at least 2 hours or overnight.

3. When ready to cook the shrimp, prepare a hot grill. While the grill is heating, place the shrimp on skewers. Grill the shrimp for 2½ minutes on each side or until pink but still juicy and succulent. Remove from the grill and let cool to room temperature.

4. When ready to serve, check the chilled soup for seasonings. Ladle into 6 soup bowls and top each with several grilled shrimp. Serve immediately.

# WARM BEAN SALAD WITH GRILLED SHRIMP

■ This is a terrific prelude to a special dinner and equally satisfying with a bowl of soup as a light lunch.

Serves 4 people.

1 tablespoon minced garlic
2 tablespoons minced fresh rosemary
4 tablespoons extra virgin olive oil
¼ teaspoon kosher salt
½ teaspoon freshly ground black pepper
1 pound large fresh shrimp, shelled and cleaned
½ pound dried Great Northern beans
¼ cup finely diced streak o'lean, rind removed
2 cups sliced yellow onions (about ½ pound)
4 sprigs fresh thyme
2 small bay leaves
½ teaspoon salt
3 cups chicken stock (see page 5)
1 large tomato, cored, seeded, and diced
1 tablespoon fresh lemon juice
Salt and freshly ground black pepper to taste
2 cups arugula or other assertive greens, gently washed and dried
4 sprigs fresh rosemary

1. Combine 1½ teaspoons of the garlic, 1 tablespoon of the minced rosemary, 2 tablespoons of the olive oil, the kosher salt, and ¼ teaspoon of the pepper in a nonreactive bowl. Add the shrimp and toss to coat well. Cover and refrigerate for at least 3 hours or overnight, turning occasionally.

2. Pick through the beans for stones and imperfections. Wash well in cold water. Cover with water and soak overnight.

3. The next day, drain the beans and rinse with cold water. Heat the streak o'lean in a heavy-bottomed pot over medium-high heat. When the fat starts to melt, reduce the heat to medium-low so that the meat doesn't brown before all of the fat is rendered. Cook for 1 to 2 minutes, raise the heat to medium-high, add the onions, and sauté, stirring occasionally, for about 5 minutes or until lightly browned.

4. Add the thyme, bay leaves, remaining ¼ teaspoon of pepper, ½ teaspoon of salt, chicken stock, and beans and bring to a simmer. Reduce the heat to low and cook the beans, maintaining just a bare simmer, for about 1 hour or until they are tender but not mushy. Drain the beans, remove the thyme sprigs and bay leaves, and set the beans aside to cool to room temperature.

5. Prepare a hot grill. Remove the shrimp from the marinade and place them on skewers. Discard the marinade. Grill the shrimp for 2½ minutes on each side or until pink but still juicy and succulent. Remove from the grill and let cool to room temperature.

6. Heat the remaining 2 tablespoons of olive oil in a heavy-bottomed sauté pan. Add the remaining 1½ teaspoons of garlic and tablespoon of minced rosemary and heat, stirring, for 2 to 3 minutes or until fragrant. Add the beans and cook over medium heat for 5 minutes or until heated through. Remove the pan from the heat and add half of the diced tomato, the lemon juice, and salt and pepper to taste.

7. Place ½ cup of the arugula on each plate and top each with ½ cup of the beans and 5 or 6 grilled shrimp. Sprinkle with the remaining diced tomato and garnish with the rosemary sprigs. Serve immediately.

# GRILLED RAINBOW TROUT WITH BACON BUTTER

■ Rainbow trout is not a Lowcountry fish, but we are able to get it from the North Carolina Blue Ridge Mountains. Our clientele has become very attached to this great fish.

Serves 4 people.

- 2 slices lean bacon, finely chopped
- ¾ cup finely minced shallots
- ½ cup seeded and finely chopped tomato
- ¾ teaspoon finely chopped fresh thyme or ¼ teaspoon crumbled dried thyme
- ⅓ cup dry white wine
- ⅓ cup apple cider vinegar
- Salt and freshly ground black pepper to taste
- 16 tablespoons unsalted butter, cut into 4 pieces and at room temperature
- ¼ cup chopped fresh parsley
- Four 10-ounce trout, boned but with heads and tails left on

1. Cook the bacon in a skillet until it is crisp. Transfer to paper towels to drain, leaving the rendered fat in the skillet. Add the shallots to the skillet, cover, and cook over moderately low heat, stirring occasionally, for 10 minutes or until softened.

2. Stir in the tomato, thyme, wine, and vinegar. Add salt and pepper to taste. Bring the liquid to a boil and cook over medium heat, stirring occasionally, for 5 minutes or until thickened. Swirl in the butter, 1 piece at a time, until melted and creamy. Add the reserved bacon and the parsley and remove from the heat. Keep the sauce warm on the back of the stove until ready to serve.

3. Prepare a medium-hot grill. Cut the small fins off the trout with kitchen shears. Grill the trout for 4 to 5 minutes per side, being careful to gently *roll* the fish over when turning. When cooked, they should be opaque in the center and just firm to the touch.

4. Carefully remove the trout to a warm serving platter, spoon the warm bacon butter over the fish, and serve immediately.

# GRILLED TUNA STEAKS WITH MELTED ONION AND MINT SAUCE

■ Because it is so dense, tuna is a good fish for the grill. Try to have your fishmonger cut steaks that are at least 1" thick. The thicker cuts are much easier to grill and tend to stay a little moist, which is important.

This recipe is a variation on an old Sicilian preparation that uses fried fish served cold. I think the sauce is actually much better on hot grilled fish.

Serves 4 people.

- 8 tablespoons extra virgin olive oil
- 5 tablespoons sherry wine vinegar
- 1 tablespoon honey
- 1 cup water
- 8 cups julienned Wadmalaw Sweets or other sweet onions such as Vidalia or Maui (about 2 pounds)
- 1 cup chicken stock (see page 5)
- Four 8- to 10-ounce tuna steaks (about 1" thick)
- 4 tablespoons peanut oil
- Salt and freshly ground white or black pepper to taste
- 2 tablespoons chopped fresh mint

1. Combine 4 tablespoons of the olive oil with the vinegar, honey, and water in a small heavy-bottomed saucepan over medium heat. Bring to a boil and cook for 15 minutes or until the mixture is reduced to ¾ cup.

2. Meanwhile, combine the remaining 4 tablespoons of olive oil with the onions and stock in a heavy-bottomed saucepan over medium-high heat and cook, stirring occasionally, for 25 minutes or until the liquid has almost evaporated and the onions have begun to caramelize. As this happens, a thin glaze will begin to cling to the bottom of the pan. Add a tablespoon or 2 of water and, with a spoon or spatula, scrape up the glaze as it liquefies. The onions will absorb this liquid and its color. You may have to do this several times during the caramelization process. Cook the onions until very light golden brown, about the color of a good chicken stock.

3. Combine the vinegar and honey mixture with the onion mixture in a bowl and mix well. Cover lightly with aluminum foil and keep warm while grilling the tuna steaks.

4. Prepare a medium-hot grill. Lightly rub the tuna steaks with the peanut oil and season with salt and pepper. Place the steaks over the coals and grill for 4 to 5 minutes per side, being careful not to overcook the steaks. You may check for doneness by gently bending the steak and looking into its middle. The steaks should be opaque in the center and just firm to the touch.

5. While the tuna steaks are grilling, add the fresh mint to the onion sauce. Remove the steaks from the grill to warm serving plates and top with the sauce. Serve immediately.

# TUNA BURGERS WITH GINGER-MUSTARD GLAZE

This is another bar favorite. We serve the burgers on potato bread rolls with a heaping serving of Plantation Slaw (see page 216). The glaze is also good with other dark fish, such as salmon, marlin, or mackerel.

Makes four 8-ounce burgers.

- 2 pounds fresh tuna
- 3 teaspoons minced garlic
- 2 tablespoons plus 2 teaspoons Dijon mustard (I use Grey Poupon)
- ⅔ teaspoon cayenne pepper
- ½ teaspoon salt
- 4 large pinches freshly ground black pepper
- 1 cup teriyaki sauce
- 1 cup veal stock (see page 9) or chicken stock (see page 5)
- 3 teaspoons peeled and minced fresh ginger
- 4 tablespoons honey
- 4 tablespoons champagne vinegar
- 4 tablespoons peanut oil
- 4 cups thinly sliced yellow onions (about 1 pound)
- 2 teaspoons soy sauce

1. Thinly slice the tuna, then chop it by hand until it is the consistency of ground beef. In a small bowl, combine 2 teaspoons of the garlic and 2 teaspoons of the mustard with the cayenne pepper, salt, and pepper. Add this to the tuna and lightly mix together. Form 4 patties. Cover and refrigerate until ready to grill.

2. Combine the teriyaki sauce, stock, ginger, honey, vinegar, and remaining teaspoon of garlic and 2 tablespoons of mustard in a heavy-bottomed nonre-

active saucepan. Stir well. Cook over medium-high heat, stirring occasionally, for about 15 minutes or until thick enough to coat the back of a spoon. Cool to room temperature.

3. Heat the peanut oil in a medium saucepan over medium-high heat until it is hot but not smoking. Add the onions and cook, stirring frequently, for about 15 minutes or until well browned. Remove from the heat. Stir in the soy sauce. Keep warm while the burgers are being grilled.

4. Prepare a hot grill. Grill the burgers for 1 minute over high heat, give them a quarter turn to make grill marks, and grill for 4 minutes. Turn the burgers over, brush them with the cooled glaze, and grill for 1 minute. Give them a quarter turn to make grill marks and grill for an additional 3 minutes. Turn the burgers over once more, brush them with the glaze, and grill for 1 more minute to allow the glaze to cook. Remove the burgers from the grill, top with the caramelized onions, and serve on warm, soft rolls.

# THE OSTEEN FAMILY'S SUNDAY GRILLED CHICKEN

My family presents more than its fair share of considerations when it's time to make a menu for a full gathering. Most won't eat meat because they live in fear of fat, and some don't like the taste of fish, but all of them love flavor. This chicken is what we make, more times than not. It's not too complicated for a Sunday afternoon; it can be prepared and then kept at room temperature for a little while (don't refrigerate it or it will lose its flavor). This is a good dish to accompany with a hot skillet of cornbread.

Serves 4 to 6 people.

- 2 tablespoons Dijon mustard (I use Grey Poupon)
- 2 tablespoons dark German mustard
- 2 tablespoons mustardy tomato–habanero hot pepper sauce (I use Inner Beauty hot sauce)
- ½ cup fresh lemon juice
- 1 tablespoon freshly ground black pepper
- 3 tablespoons extra virgin olive oil
- ¼ cup chopped fresh herbs of your choice (I use Italian parsley, thyme, and rosemary)
- One 3-pound chicken, cut into serving pieces
- Salt to taste

1. In a small bowl, combine the Dijon mustard, German mustard, hot sauce, lemon juice, pepper, olive oil, and herbs to make a marinade.

2. Place the chicken pieces in a nonreactive bowl, pour the marinade over them, cover, and refrigerate for at least 2 hours but not more than 4.

3. Prepare a medium-hot grill. Remove the chicken pieces from the marinade and grill until just cooked through, basting with the marinade. The wings will need about 5 minutes per side; the legs, 8 minutes per side; the breasts, 10 minutes per side; and the thighs, 12 minutes per side. Sprinkle the chicken with salt and serve. Discard any leftover marinade.

# GRILLED QUAIL WITH A BOURBON AND GREEN PEPPERCORN GLAZE

■ This is a quick and delicious way to prepare quail. All of the prep work can be done in advance and the cooking takes only about 10 minutes from start to table. Declare it okay for everyone to pick up the bony pieces with their fingers to get all of the quails' juicy goodness.

Serves 4 people.

**FOR THE MARINADE:**

½ cup bourbon
½ cup honey
8 semi-boneless quail

**FOR THE GLAZE:**

¼ cup Dijon mustard (I use Grey Poupon)
1½ teaspoons Tabasco sauce
1 large egg yolk
½ cup peanut, olive, or walnut oil
One 4-ounce jar green peppercorns, drained and slightly crushed
3 tablespoons bourbon
¼ cup minced shallots

1. To make the marinade, combine the bourbon and honey. Toss the quail in it. Place them in a single layer in a nonreactive dish, cover loosely with plastic wrap, and refrigerate for at least 8 hours or overnight, turning occasionally.

2. The next day, prepare a hot grill.

3. To make the glaze, whisk together the mustard, Tabasco, and egg yolk in a small bowl. Whisking constantly, slowly add the oil a tablespoon at a time until well incorporated. The glaze should be thick. Add the green peppercorns, bourbon, and shallots.

4. Remove the quail from the marinade and pat dry. Discard the marinade. Brush liberally with the glaze and put on the grill. If your grill has a top, don't close it; the quail should be done on an open grill to keep them crisp. Grill the quail quickly, 2 to 3 minutes per side, maintaining a high heat so that they end up with a crispy outside and a juicy, medium-rare inside. Serve immediately. Discard any remaining glaze.

# BERRY-MARINATED GRILLED DUCKLING

This preparation results in a very delicious duck that is tender but not fatty. It produces glistening, almost lacquered, mahogany pieces of duck that always seem to impress guests, yet it's not difficult to do.

Serves 4 people.

- 2 ducks (4½ to 5 pounds each), cut in half lengthwise
- ¼ cup brandy
- ½ cup cassis
- 4 cups dry red wine
- 1 cup sliced onion
- ½ cup peeled and sliced carrots
- 2 sprigs fresh thyme
- ¼ cup black peppercorns
- 3 cups duck stock (see page 6) or chicken stock (see page 5)

1. Place the ducks in a large nonreactive pan. In a large bowl, combine the brandy, cassis, wine, onion, carrots, thyme, and peppercorns. Pour over the ducks. Cover and refrigerate overnight, turning at least twice.

2. The next day, preheat the oven to 450°F.

3. Remove the ducks from the marinade. Strain the marinade, reserving the liquid and discarding the solids. Place the ducks skin side up on a rack in a roasting pan. Roast in the preheated oven for 25 minutes or until they are a rich, dark mahogany color.

4. Remove the ducks from the oven and let cool to room temperature. Remove the breasts from the carcass by scraping the breast meat away from the breastbone with a small, sharp knife. Cut the leg joints free as well. This can be done the day before grilling if the duck pieces are then tightly wrapped in plastic wrap and refrigerated.

5. When you are ready to serve the dish, prepare a hot grill.

6. Meanwhile, put the reserved marinade in a heavy-bottomed saucepan and vigorously boil it over high heat for about 12 minutes or until thick enough to coat a spoon. Do the same in a separate saucepan with the stock. Combine the reduced marinade and stock and simmer for 5 minutes over low heat to let the flavors meld. Divide the mixture in half. You will use half to baste the ducks. Reserve the other half and keep it warm to pass separately at the table.

7. Put the leg quarters over the edge of the coals so that they will grill slowly. Basting frequently, cook for about 30 minutes. They should be tender and succulent.

8. Put the breasts over the hot part of the grill for the last 10 minutes of the legs' cooking time to crisp the skin. Baste them 2 or 3 times; be careful not to dry them out.

9. Place the grilled duck on a platter or individual plates and pass the reserved sauce separately. Discard any leftover basting sauce.

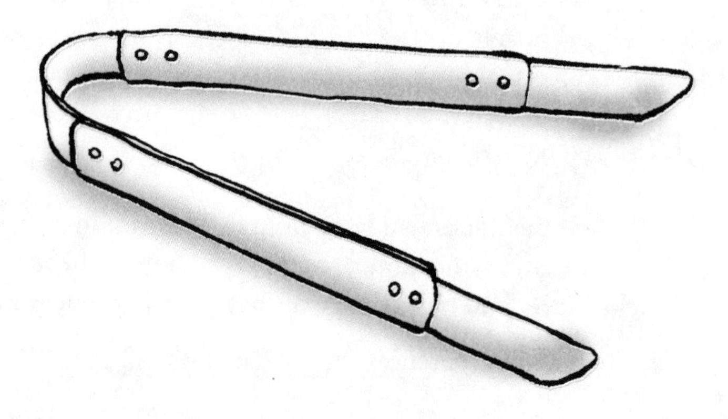

# GRILLED LEG OF LAMB

This recipe includes a marinade for the lamb, but you could substitute a green chile rub (see page 263). Either way, plan ahead, as you will want to age the lamb in the rub or marinade for 24 hours before grilling.

Serves 8 people.

One 7- to 8-pound leg of lamb, trimmed of excess fat, boned, and butterflied by the butcher (4 to 4¾ pounds boneless)
2 large yellow onions, peeled and chopped
6 large cloves garlic, peeled and chopped
1 tablespoon chopped fresh thyme
½ teaspoon red pepper flakes
¾ cup red wine vinegar
½ cup honey
⅓ cup Worcestershire sauce (I use Lea & Perrins)
½ tablespoon salt
1½ teaspoons freshly ground black pepper

1. Place the lamb in a large nonreactive pan. Using a food processor, puree the remaining ingredients until smooth. Pour over the lamb. Cover and refrigerate for at least 8 hours or overnight, turning at least twice.

2. Using a covered grill, prepare a medium-hot fire on 1 side.

3. Discard the marinade and pat the lamb dry. Place the meat on the grill and sear both sides directly over the glowing coals, then grill for 4 to 5 minutes per side or until well browned. Move the lamb to the side of the grill where there are no coals, cover, and cook for 15 to 20 minutes for medium rare or until done to taste. (You can check the meat by notching a side.)

4. Transfer the lamb to a cutting board and let rest for 10 minutes. Slice the lamb thinly across the grain. Serve with your choice of Louis's Guava-Peanut Barbecue Sauce (see page 269), Spicy Mole Sauce (see page 271), or Wadmalaw Sweets BBQ Sauce (see page 272).

# MARINATED AND GRILLED FLANK STEAK

A staple of the grill, flank steak is very flavorful and tender, but only if properly marinated, so be sure not to take shortcuts.

Serves 4 to 6 people.

½ cup plus 2 tablespoons extra virgin olive oil
1 tablespoon red wine vinegar
¼ cup soy sauce
1 teaspoon minced garlic
1 teaspoon Colman's English mustard or a spicy Dijon mustard
1 teaspoon Worcestershire sauce (I use Lea & Perrins)
½ teaspoon Tabasco sauce
½ teaspoon freshly ground black pepper
One 1½-pound flank steak, trimmed of all fat and gristle

1. In a medium bowl, whisk together ½ cup of the olive oil with the vinegar, soy sauce, garlic, mustard, Worcestershire sauce, Tabasco, and pepper to make a marinade. Place the steak in a nonreactive pan, pour the marinade over it, cover, and refrigerate for at least 3 hours or overnight, turning occasionally.

2. Prepare a hot grill. Remove the steak from the marinade, reserving the marinade to baste the steak while grilling. Thoroughly wipe the steak dry. Rub the steak with the remaining 2 tablespoons of olive oil and grill for about 7 minutes on each side for rare, or 8 minutes on each side for medium rare, basting frequently. Discard any unused marinade.

3. Remove the steak to a cutting board and let it "repose" for 5 minutes to allow the juices to settle before slicing.

# GRILLED BEEF TENDERLOIN WITH GREEN CHILE RUB

■ We originally used this rub for lamb, but soon found it was great for beef. With either meat, make sure you don't let the rub overcook and burn or it will get a bitter flavor.

Serves 4 people.

¼ cup minced garlic
¼ cup chopped fresh cilantro
¼ cup chopped fresh Italian parsley
¼ cup chile powder (preferably freshly ground from dried chiles)
¼ cup crushed coriander seed
¼ cup minced green chiles, such as poblano, serrano, jalapeño, or a combination (seeded or not, depending on your proclivity for heat)
2 tablespoons black peppercorns
Four 5- to 6-ounce tenderloin steaks (about 1" thick)

1. Combine the first 7 ingredients in a food processor fitted with a metal blade and pulse until the mixture is the consistency of rough paste. Rub the meat with the paste, place it in a nonreactive pan, cover, and refrigerate overnight.

2. The next day, prepare a hot grill. Grill the steaks for 3 minutes on each side for rare and 5 minutes per side for medium rare. The outside of the steaks should be dark brown and crusty. Remove from the grill and let rest for 5 minutes before serving.

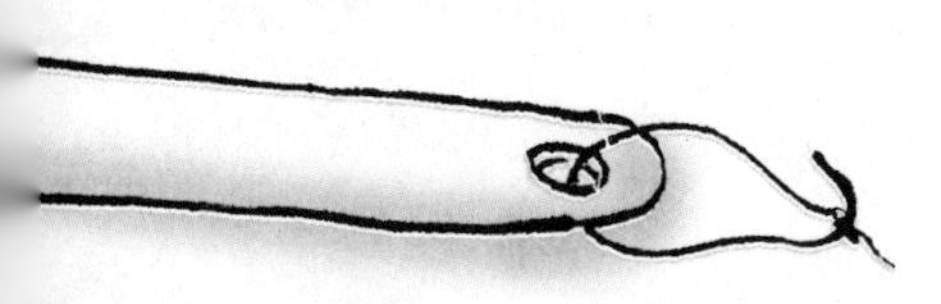

# GRILLED PORK PORTERHOUSE

Grilled Pork Porterhouse was on the menu the day that Louis's opened and has been a great hit from then on. I believe that we coined the term. I wanted to serve a pork chop in the fashion of a great porterhouse steak, thought by many to be the best cut of beef. In the beginning, we encountered some resistance to cooking pork medium with a little pink showing in the center, but it's perfectly safe and ensures a much more tender and juicy chop.

Serves 4 people.

- 1 tablespoon minced garlic
- 16 juniper berries, crushed
- 1 tablespoon finely minced fresh sage or 1 teaspoon dried sage
- 2 tablespoons kosher salt
- 1 tablespoon freshly ground black pepper
- 2 teaspoons Preserving Spices (see page 2)
- 4 center-cut, closely trimmed pork loin chops, each weighing 12 to 14 ounces

1. In a medium bowl, mix the garlic, juniper berries, sage, salt, pepper, and preserving spices. Rub the mixture over the chops. Place the chops in a single layer in a nonreactive pan, cover loosely with plastic wrap, and refrigerate for 12 to 24 hours, but no longer, or they will become too salty.

2. When you are ready to grill the chops, rub the excess marinade off them with a damp paper towel. Prepare a medium-hot grill. Grill the chops approximately 8 minutes per side for medium rare or 10 minutes per side for medium. (Grilling them any longer will dry them out.) Serve immediately.

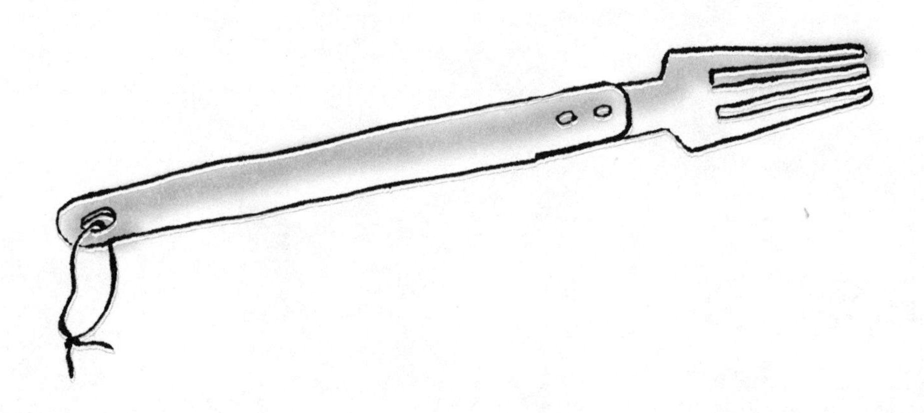

# GRILLED SHIITAKE MUSHROOMS

This side dish was on Louis's opening menu. It's quick and easy for a grilled dinner and you can substitute other mushroom varieties with equal success.

Serves 6 people.

6 tablespoons extra virgin olive oil
3 tablespoons minced garlic
½ cup minced shallots
2 sprigs fresh thyme
¼ teaspoon salt
¼ teaspoon freshly ground black pepper
18 shiitake mushrooms, about 1½" in diameter, stems removed
12 peeled whole shallots
6 skewers (if wooden, soak in water for 30 minutes before using on the grill)

1. In a small bowl, combine 2 tablespoons of the olive oil with the garlic, shallots, thyme, salt, and pepper to make a marinade. Place the mushrooms in a nonreactive pan, pour the marinade over them, and let them sit at room temperature for 30 minutes.

2. Preheat the oven to 350°F.

3. In a small bowl, combine the shallots with a tablespoon of the olive oil and toss. Place on a baking sheet and roast in the preheated oven for about 15 minutes or until tender. Remove from the oven and set aside.

4. Prepare a medium-hot grill with a cover. Remove the mushrooms from the marinade. Strain the marinade, reserving the liquid and discarding the solids.

5. Skewer 3 shiitakes, going through the front of the caps on a slight bias. Skewer 2 roasted shallots. Repeat with each of the remaining skewers.

6. Whisk the remaining 3 tablespoons of olive oil into the reserved marinade. Brush over the shiitakes and shallots. Place the skewers on the grill, mushroom cap side down. Close the top of the grill and cook for about 5 minutes. Turn the skewers, baste, and grill for about another 2 minutes. The grilling time will vary depending on the size of the mushrooms, the grill, and the temperature of the air. You want the mushrooms to be just tender but not mushy. Discard any leftover marinade and serve the mushrooms immediately.

# GRILLED PORTOBELLO MUSHROOMS

■ These big, beefy mushroom caps grill in about the same time as a small steak. They can be grilled without being marinated if you're in a hurry, but they benefit greatly from the flavor that marinating adds.

Serves 4 people.

- 8 ounces portobello mushrooms
- 3 tablespoons extra virgin olive oil
- 2 large cloves garlic, peeled and finely chopped
- 1 tablespoon chopped fresh Italian parsley
- Pinch of dried marjoram
- Salt and freshly ground black pepper to taste

1. Wipe the mushrooms clean with a damp paper towel. Trim off the stems.

2. In a small bowl, combine the oil, garlic, parsley, and marjoram. Add salt and pepper to taste. Place the mushrooms in a large nonreactive bowl, pour the marinade over them, and refrigerate for 30 minutes to 1 hour.

3. Prepare a hot grill. Remove the mushrooms from the marinade and place on the grill with the rounded side down. Grill for 2 minutes. Turn the mushrooms over and brush with the marinade. Grill for 2 to 3 minutes more or until tender and lightly browned. Discard any leftover marinade and serve the mushrooms immediately.

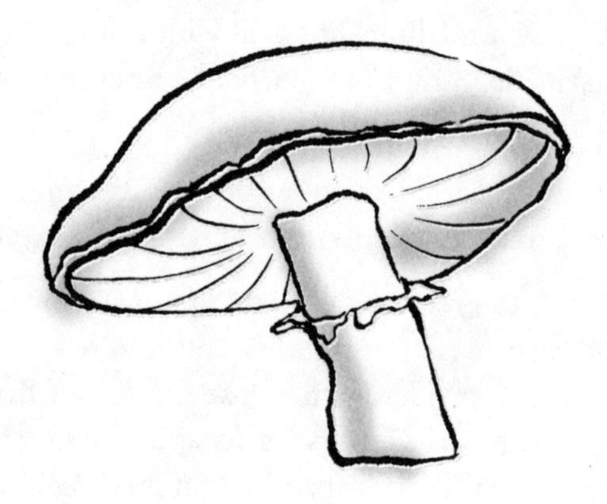

# GRILLED VEGETABLE SALAD

At the restaurant, this salad is a bed for our grilled salmon. It can also stand alone as a salad, or combine it with some cooked penne for a great pasta salad.

Serves 6 people.

- 1 large eggplant, peeled and cut into ⅓"-thick rounds
- 2 zucchini, cut lengthwise into ⅓"-thick slices
- 2 yellow squash, cut lengthwise into ⅓"-thick slices
- 2 medium red onions, peeled and cut into ⅓"-thick slices
- 2 medium jícama, peeled and cut into ⅓"-thick slices
- 4 tablespoons extra virgin olive oil
- ½ teaspoon salt
- ½ teaspoon freshly ground black pepper
- 1 red bell pepper, cored, seeded, and diced
- 1 poblano pepper, cored, seeded, and diced
- ½ cup Toasted Cumin Vinaigrette (see page 14)
- Salt and freshly ground black pepper to taste

1. Prepare a hot grill.

2. Toss the eggplant, zucchini, yellow squash, onions, and jícama in the olive oil. Add the ½ teaspoon of salt and ½ teaspoon of pepper and toss. Grill the eggplant, zucchini, and yellow squash for 3 minutes on each side or until just tender. Remove from the grill. Grill the onions and jícama for 12 minutes on each side and remove from the grill.

3. When cool enough to handle, dice the grilled vegetables evenly into medium pieces. Toss with the diced peppers. Add the vinaigrette, mix well, and salt and pepper to taste. Serve immediately.

# Grill Rubs, Marinades, Shakes, Glazes, and Sauces

The key to grilling is what you do before, during, and after, with rubs, marinades, shakes, glazes, and sauces. Here's an overview of your choices.

**Rubs and Marinades.** These kinds of preparations make it wonderfully easy to infuse meat, fish, and poultry with flavor. Rubs and marinades are typically left on the food for some time before cooking begins, often up to 24 hours. You will need about 1 to 2 teaspoons of dry rub for each serving, and about 1 cup of marinade for every 2 to 3 pounds of meat, fish, or poultry.

**Shakes and Glazes.** Basting with a shake or a glaze as the food grills can add wonderful taste nuances while keeping the food juicy and moist.

**Sauces.** The perfect sauce can bring out the flavor of even the most ordinary piece of meat or fish. The amount of sauce you serve will depend on its potency. Consistency is also relevant—you will need less of a thicker sauce than a thinner one. Use about 2 to 3 tablespoons of an intensely flavored sauce per serving; for lighter-flavored sauces, count on ⅓ cup per serving.

Many sauces can also be used for basting, but be sure not to pass any of the basting sauce at the table. Always pass sauce that has been reserved separately.

## VINEGAR SHAKE

■ This shake is used continually during the slow cooking of pork, either on the grill or in a pit. It is also called a mopping sauce—dip a clean cloth in the sauce and shake it over the meat.

Makes 1 quart.

- 2 cups white distilled vinegar
- 2 cups apple cider vinegar
- 2 tablespoons sugar
- 2 tablespoons red pepper flakes
- 2 tablespoons Tabasco sauce

**OPTIONAL ADDITIONS:**

- Sliced onions
- Sliced jalapeño, poblano, or serrano peppers, seeds in
- Crushed garlic cloves

Combine the vinegars, sugar, red pepper flakes, and Tabasco in a large jar with a lid and shake. Let stand overnight for the flavors to develop. Tightly covered, the shake will keep in the refrigerator for a month.

If using any of the optional additions, mix them in and put the shake in the refrigerator for a week to develop maximum flavor.

# BARBECUE RUB FOR PORK

This is a spicy dry rub that is rubbed on pork and left on overnight. While the pork is cooking, it can be mopped with either Debbie Marlowe's BBQ Sauce (see page 268) and/or our vinegar shake (see page 262). Pork butts, ribs, chops, and roasts all have an affinity for this rub.

Makes 1 cup.

- 1 tablespoon salt
- 1 tablespoon sugar
- 1 tablespoon light brown sugar
- 1 tablespoon ground cumin
- 1 tablespoon chile powder (preferably freshly ground from dried chiles)
- 1 tablespoon freshly ground black pepper
- 1½ teaspoons cayenne pepper
- 2 tablespoons spicy Hungarian paprika

1. In a small bowl, combine all of the ingredients and mix well.
2. Rub the meat with the mixture, place the meat in a nonreactive pan, cover, and refrigerate overnight.

# GREEN CHILE RUB

This is a very thick and spicy rub. Use it on almost any kind of meat—lamb, pork, chicken, rabbit, veal, or beef.

Makes 1 cup.

- ¼ cup minced garlic
- ¼ cup chopped fresh cilantro
- ¼ cup chopped fresh Italian parsley
- ¼ cup chile powder (preferably freshly ground from dried chiles)
- ¼ cup crushed coriander seeds
- ¼ cup minced green chiles, such as poblano, serrano, jalapeño, or a combination (with the seeds if you like heat)
- 2 tablespoons black peppercorns

1. Combine the ingredients in a food processor fitted with a metal blade and pulse until the mixture is the consistency of rough paste.
2. Rub the meat with the paste, place the meat in a nonreactive pan, cover, and refrigerate overnight.

# SORGHUM GLAZE FOR PORK

Sorghum, a sweet syrup made from the sorghum plant, is very similar to molasses. Many Southerners consider it to be superior to molasses, owing to its delicacy as a sweetener.

This glaze should be thin and have a tangy, spicy flavor. It's best used with the lighter meats and poultry, such as pork, chicken, and rabbit. A strong, assertive fish, such as mackerel or salmon, could also do well with this glaze. At our restaurant, we use it on big, juicy pork porterhouse chops.

Makes 1½ cups.

- 2 tablespoons peanut oil
- ¼ cup minced shallots
- 2 tablespoons minced poblano chiles
- 2 tablespoons minced garlic
- 1 tablespoon peeled and minced fresh ginger
- 1 tablespoon minced jalapeño chiles
- 1 tablespoon red pepper flakes
- 1 tablespoon plus 1 teaspoon ground cumin
- 2 tablespoons chile powder (preferably freshly ground from dried chiles)
- 1 cup chicken stock (see page 5)
- 1 cup veal stock (see page 9) or beef stock (see page 4)
- 2 tablespoons honey
- ½ cup sorghum
- 1 tablespoon tomato paste
- 1 tablespoon plus 1 teaspoon red wine vinegar

1. Heat the peanut oil in a small heavy-bottomed saucepan over medium heat. When hot, add the shallots, poblano chiles, garlic, ginger, jalapeño chiles, red pepper flakes, cumin, and chile powder. Stir to combine well. Cover the saucepan and sweat the ingredients for 7 to 8 minutes, stirring 3 or 4 times.

2. Add the chicken stock and veal or beef stock. Stir to combine well. Increase the heat to medium-high and bring the mixture to a boil. Add the honey, sorghum, tomato paste, and vinegar. Bring to a brisk simmer. Reduce the heat to medium and simmer, stirring occasionally, for 20 minutes or until the mixture is reduced by a third.

3. Use immediately or cool to room temperature, cover, and refrigerate. Tightly covered, the glaze will keep in the refrigerator for 2 or 3 days.

# CHAD'S HOMEMADE BBQ SAUCE

This is intended to be a fairly thin sauce to brush on chops and chicken when you grill them; it will thicken as the meat cooks on the grill. The amount I use for Barbecued Pork Rillettes (see page 51) is relatively small and the sauce's thinness allows it to be absorbed by the pork, rather than coating the pork as would a thick sauce. If you want a thicker sauce for some other dish, don't strain out the vegetables—just puree the sauce in a food processor. And if you like a spicy barbecue sauce, try using jalapeño chile powder, but eliminate the regular chile powder.

Makes 8 cups.

- 2 tablespoons extra virgin olive oil
- 1 cup peeled, seeded, and chopped plum tomatoes
- 1 cup minced garlic
- 1½ cups chopped poblano peppers
- ½ cup chopped red bell pepper
- ¼ cup plus 1 tablespoon chopped fresh cilantro
- 2 tablespoons spicy Hungarian paprika
- 1 tablespoon plus 1½ teaspoons chile powder (preferably freshly ground from dried chiles)
- 1½ teaspoons ground cumin
- 4 cups veal stock (see page 9) or beef stock (see page 4) or chicken stock (see page 5)
- ⅓ cup Worcestershire sauce (I use Lea & Perrins)
- ¼ cup Dijon mustard (I use Grey Poupon)
- ¾ cup ketchup
- ½ cup packed dark brown sugar
- Salt and freshly ground black pepper to taste

1. In a heavy-bottomed nonreactive saucepan, heat the olive oil over medium-high heat until hot but not smoking. Add the tomatoes, garlic, poblano peppers, bell pepper, and cilantro and sauté for 5 minutes, stirring occasionally. Add the paprika, chile powder, and cumin and cook for 4 minutes.

2. Add the stock, Worcestershire sauce, mustard, ketchup, and brown sugar. Stir well and bring the sauce to a boil. Adjust the heat so that the sauce cooks at a slow boil for 20 minutes. Stir occasionally to prevent the sauce from scorching and skim off any impurities that rise to the top.

3. Add salt and pepper to taste. Strain through a coarse sieve, gently pressing the solids to release their liquids. Reheat the sauce and use immediately or cool to room temperature, cover, and refrigerate. Tightly covered, the sauce will keep in the refrigerator for 1 week.

# BACON BUTTER SAUCE

There are many uses for bacon in Southern cooking. As I write this, we are serving the season's last soft-shell crabs. This butter is the perfect accompaniment for those delicious crustaceans. It's also terrific with any grilled fish, but especially good with trout and on spring's shad roe. And once, by some kitchen happenstance, we had some leftover bacon butter and used it as a gravy for creamy grits, where it was judged a winner by the kitchen staff.

Makes 1¾ cups.

- 2 slices lean bacon, finely chopped
- 1 leek (about 1 pound), halved lengthwise, thinly sliced crosswise, and washed well
- ½ cup finely chopped seeded tomato
- ¾ teaspoon finely chopped fresh tarragon or ¼ teaspoon crumbled dried tarragon
- ⅓ cup half-and-half
- ⅓ cup chicken stock (see page 5)
- Salt and freshly ground black pepper to taste

1. In a medium skillet, cook the bacon over medium-high heat until crisp. Transfer to paper towels to drain.

2. In the fat remaining in the skillet, cook the leek, covered, over moderately low heat, stirring occasionally, for 10 minutes or until softened. Stir in the tomato, tarragon, half-and-half, stock, and salt and pepper to taste. Bring the sauce to a boil, reduce the heat to medium, and cook, stirring occasionally, for 5 minutes or until the sauce is thickened. Stir in the bacon. Keep warm until ready to use.

# COGNAC BARBECUE SAUCE

As barbecue is one of my favorite things in the world, we have experimented with all sorts. We have found that this sauce, being lighter and a little more sophisticated than most, is really good on a big grilled veal chop. If you want to use it on pork, substitute bourbon for the cognac.

Makes 4 cups.

¼ cup extra virgin olive oil
¼ cup peanut oil
2 cups sliced yellow onions (about ½ pound)
½ cup peeled and sliced carrots
6 large cloves garlic, peeled
1 tablespoon peeled and chopped fresh ginger
2 bay leaves
5 pounds fresh tomatoes, peeled, seeded, and quartered
¼ cup red wine vinegar
¼ cup packed light brown sugar
¼ teaspoon Tabasco sauce
1 teaspoon Worcestershire sauce (I use Lea & Perrins)
½ teaspoon Colman's English mustard or spicy Dijon mustard
1 teaspoon cayenne pepper
½ cup cognac
Salt to taste

1. Heat the oils in a heavy-bottomed saucepan over medium-high heat until almost smoking. Add the onions and carrots and cook for about 8 minutes or until softened and just beginning to brown. Add the garlic, ginger, and bay leaves and cook for 5 minutes, stirring frequently to prevent scorching.

2. Add the tomatoes, vinegar, and brown sugar. Reduce the heat to medium, cover, and cook for 10 minutes, stirring occasionally. Uncover and cook for about 20 minutes or until most of the liquid is gone, stirring occasionally to prevent scorching.

3. Remove the bay leaves from the mixture. Puree the mixture, using a food mill or food processor, and return it to the saucepan. Add the Tabasco, Worcestershire sauce, mustard, cayenne pepper, and cognac and mix well. Stir in salt to taste. Simmer for 5 minutes or longer, depending on how thick you like your barbecue sauce. Use immediately or cool to room temperature, cover, and refrigerate. Tightly covered, the sauce will keep in the refrigerator for 1 week.

# DEBBIE MARLOWE'S BBQ SAUCE AND MARINADE

This is another mopping sauce used for basting pork as it is grilling or cooking in a pit. It is good on pork that has been rubbed with our Barbecue Rub for Pork (see page 263). It can also be served as a condiment alongside the cooked pork (but don't save any that you used for basting; reserve some separately). Debbie's sauce is different from most barbecue sauces because of the addition of butter.

Makes ¾ cup.

- ½ cup melted butter
- 2½ cups apple cider vinegar
- 3 tablespoons red pepper flakes
- 1 tablespoon fresh lemon juice
- ⅛ teaspoon salt
- ⅛ teaspoon freshly ground black pepper

1. Combine all of the ingredients in a heavy-bottomed nonreactive saucepan and mix well. Place the pan over medium heat and bring the sauce to a simmer.
2. Simmer, stirring occasionally, for 1 hour or until the sauce reduces to approximately ¾ cup. Use immediately or cool to room temperature, cover, and refrigerate. Tightly covered, the sauce will keep in the refrigerator for a month.

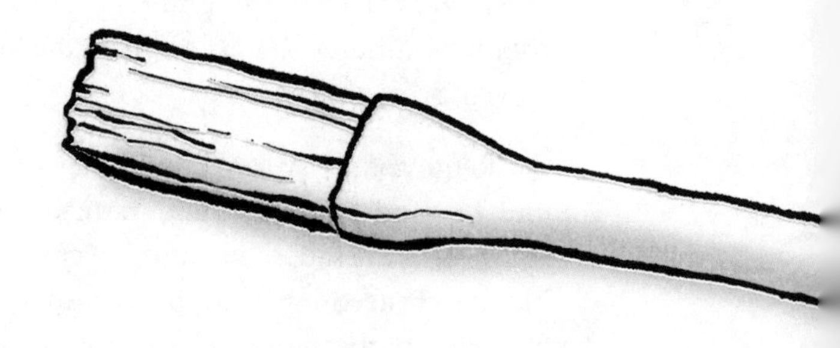

# LOUIS'S GUAVA-PEANUT BARBECUE SAUCE

■ This is a thick, rich sauce of dipping consistency that's good with grilled shrimp, scallops, fish, chicken, and squab. It can be used for basting if you're careful not to let it scorch.

Makes 2 cups.

12 ounces dark beer (I use Beck's)
½ cup molasses
¼ cup fresh lemon juice
¼ cup Worcestershire sauce (I use Lea & Perrins)
¼ cup peanut oil
2 teaspoons apple cider vinegar
1½ teaspoons chile powder (preferably freshly ground from dried chiles)
1 teaspoon minced garlic
1 teaspoon dry mustard (I use Colman's English mustard)
1 teaspoon kosher salt
½ teaspoon dried oregano
½ teaspoon dried thyme
⅓ teaspoon cayenne pepper
Generous ½ cup creamy peanut butter
3 tablespoons guava jam

1. Combine all of the ingredients in a large heavy-bottomed nonreactive saucepan over medium heat. Stir to mix well. Bring the sauce to a simmer and cook for about 35 minutes or until it has reduced by half.

2. Remove the pan from the heat and allow the sauce to cool slightly. Use immediately or cool to room temperature, cover, and refrigerate. Tightly covered, the sauce will keep in the refrigerator for 1 week.

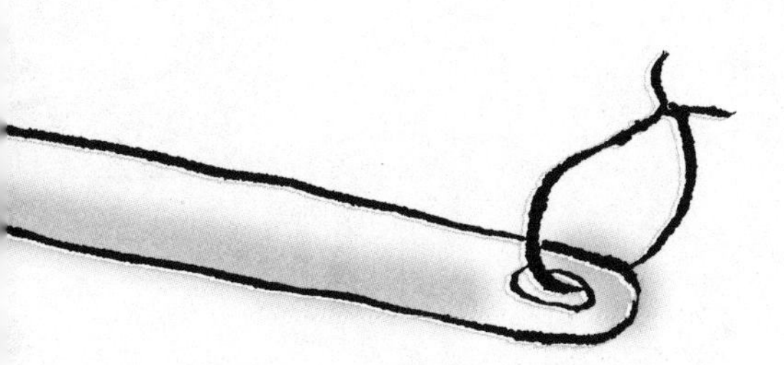

# SMOKED ONION AND BOURBON BUTTER

This is an assertive sauce that can be served with steaks, pork chops, venison, or almost any kind of red meat.

Makes 1 cup.

1 cup red onions, peeled and sliced into ¼"-thick rings
3 tablespoons bourbon
2 tablespoons veal demi-glace (see page 10) or beef demi-glace (see note)
¼ teaspoon salt
⅛ teaspoon freshly ground black pepper
2 tablespoons unsalted butter

Mesquite chips

1. Fire your grill to the highest temperature or prepare the hottest coals. Wrap about 1 cup of mesquite chips in foil, punch holes in the foil, and place on the fire to provide seasoned smoke. Place the onions around the edges of the grill, close the top, and smoke the onions, turning once, for 15 minutes or until well cooked and slightly browned.

2. Combine the onions, 2 tablespoons of the bourbon, and the demi-glace in a sauté pan over medium-high heat. Heat thoroughly. You can add up to 2 tablespoons of water to thin the mixture if it is too thick.

3. Add the salt, pepper, and butter and heat until the butter melts. Add the remaining tablespoon of bourbon, stir to combine, and heat through. Serve immediately.

NOTE: Beef demi-glace can be made by the same procedure as veal demi-glace (see page 10).

# SPICY MOLE SAUCE

This is a good all-purpose sauce to serve with grilled meats such as chicken, veal, steak, pork, or rabbit. It's not a basting sauce, but should go on top of the grilled meat or under it, or it can be passed separately.

Makes 6½ cups.

¼ cup sliced almonds
¼ cup sesame seeds
2 tablespoons pine nuts
2 tablespoons extra virgin olive oil
½ cup peeled, seeded, and diced plum tomatoes
¼ cup finely diced red bell pepper, white inner ribs removed
2½ teaspoons seeded and chopped poblano pepper
2 tablespoons chopped fresh cilantro
2½ teaspoons spicy Hungarian paprika
1½ teaspoons chile powder (preferably freshly ground from dried chiles)
¾ teaspoon cayenne pepper
1½ teaspoons ground coriander
1½ teaspoons ground cumin
½ cup raisins
3 cups veal stock (see page 9) or beef stock (see page 4) or chicken stock (see page 5)
2 tablespoons unsweetened cocoa powder
2 tablespoons honey
Salt and freshly ground black pepper to taste

1. Preheat the oven to 350°F.

2. Place the almonds, sesame seeds, and pine nuts on a baking sheet with sides and bake in the preheated oven for 5 minutes. Remove them from the oven, stir, and return them to the oven for 5 minutes more or until they are toasted. Transfer to a cool baking sheet so that they will not continue to brown.

3. Heat the olive oil in a heavy-bottomed nonreactive pan over medium-high heat until hot but not smoking. Add the tomatoes, bell pepper, poblano pepper, and cilantro. Stir to combine and sauté for 5 minutes, stirring occasionally.

4. Slowly add the paprika, chile powder, cayenne pepper, coriander, and cumin, stirring constantly. Sauté the mixture for 4 minutes, stirring frequently. Add the toasted almonds, sesame seeds, and pine nuts and the raisins, stir to combine, and sauté for 4 minutes, stirring regularly and reducing the heat as necessary to prevent scorching.

5. Add the stock and stir. Bring the mixture to a simmer and cook for 20 minutes, stirring occasionally. Add the cocoa powder and honey and stir to combine. Season to taste with salt and pepper. Remove the pan from the heat.

6. When cool enough to handle, puree the sauce. Reheat the sauce and use immediately or cool to room temperature, cover, and refrigerate. Tightly covered, the sauce will keep in the refrigerator for 2 or 3 days.

# WADMALAW SWEETS BBQ SAUCE

Our Wadmalaw Sweets produce a terrific savory condiment that is delicious with any kind of grilled steak, pork, chicken, or Italian sausage.

Makes 6 cups.

- 1 medium red bell pepper, cored, halved, and seeded
- 1 medium poblano pepper, cored, halved, and seeded
- 1 large Wadmalaw Sweet or other sweet onion such as Vidalia or Maui, peeled and quartered
- 2 tablespoons peanut oil
- 4 tablespoons unsalted butter
- 4 cups very thinly sliced Wadmalaw Sweets or other sweet onions such as Vidalia or Maui (about 1 pound)
- 3 cups chicken stock (see page 5)
- 1 jalapeño pepper, cored, halved, and seeded
- 3 tablespoons raisins
- 3 tablespoons toasted pine nuts
- ¼ cup ketchup
- 2 tablespoons Dijon mustard (I use Grey Poupon)
- 3 large cloves garlic, peeled and crushed
- 12 ounces dark beer (I use Beck's)
- 2 tablespoons honey
- 1 teaspoon ground cumin
- 1 teaspoon ground coriander
- 1 teaspoon chile powder (preferably freshly ground from dried chiles)
- ¼ cup plus 2 tablespoons unsweetened cocoa powder

1. Preheat the oven to 450°F.

2. In a medium bowl, toss the bell pepper, poblano pepper, and quartered onion with the peanut oil. Roast on a baking sheet in the preheated oven for 20 to 30 minutes or until the vegetables just begin to char. (Because it is

smaller, the poblano pepper will be ready to remove before the bell pepper or the onion.) When roasted, immediately place the peppers in a bowl and cover tightly with plastic wrap. Let them steam for a few minutes, then peel them.

3. Heat the butter in a heavy-bottomed pan over medium heat. Add the sliced onions and cook slowly, stirring occasionally, for about 15 minutes or until they are very soft and beginning to color. Remove from the heat and reserve.

4. Put the roasted peppers and quartered onion in a heavy-bottomed pot with the stock, jalapeño pepper, raisins, pine nuts, ketchup, mustard, garlic, beer, honey, cumin, coriander, chile powder, and cocoa powder. Stir to combine well. Bring the mixture to a simmer over medium heat. Simmer gently for 15 minutes, stirring occasionally.

5. Remove the mixture from the stove and let cool. Process in a food processor until the mixture is a coarse consistency. Work in batches if necessary; if the processor is too full, the liquid will leak out.

6. Combine the mixture with the reserved sliced onions and stir to mix well. You may keep the sauce warm for up to 2 hours or cool to room temperature, cover, and refrigerate for up to 3 days.

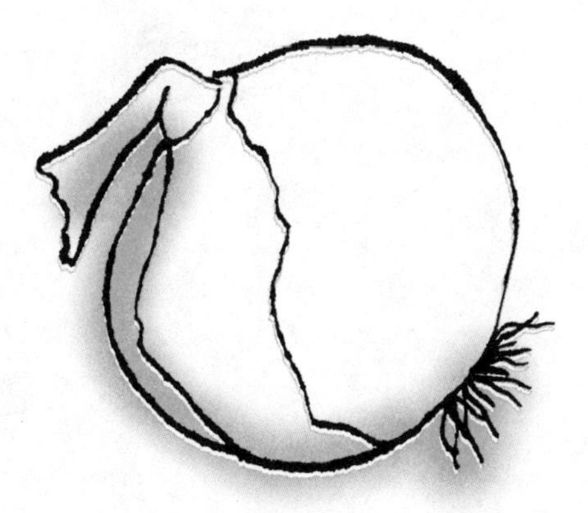

# Index